Justo Pérez de Urbel

A Saint Under Moslem Rule

Translated from the Spanish
By
A Benedictine of Stanbrook Abbey
Worcester, England

Adapted by the Editor

Catholic Authors Press
www.CatholicAuthors.com

Nihil obstat: DOM JUSTIN MACCANN, O.S.B.
Imprimatur: W. E. KELLY, Ab. Pres.
Nihil obstat: H. B. RIES, Censor librorum
Imprimatur: ✠ SAMUEL A. STRITCH, Archiepiscopus Milwaukiensis
July 17, 1937

First published 1937
Reprinted 2007 Catholic Authors Press

ISBN: 978-0-9782985-7-9

Catholic Authors Press

www.CatholicAuthors.org

PREFACE BY THE GENERAL EDITOR

DOM JUSTO PÉREZ DE URBEL, O.S.B., has written a book of unusual power, scholarship, and interest. Though restricted in point of time to the ninth-century period of Moorish domination in Cordova, it is in reality a typical picture of the conquering Moslem civilisation in Europe, painted on a vast canvas and filled with soul-stirring episodes. The reader finds himself close to the beginning of the vast epic conflict between Islamism and Christianity, one of the most portentous events in the whole course of history.

Although confined to the results of purely historical research, yet the book, with its dramatic central theme, its wealth of local colour, its numerous heroes and heroines portrayed to the life, its violent soul struggles, and the tremendous issues at stake, has all the fascination of romance. The action at first moves leisurely, except for the sudden and convulsive storm of a gigantic revolution which is suppressed with equal suddenness. Two antagonistic and incompatible cultures are unrolled before us. The narrative then quickly culminates in the final chapters and proceeds to its climax with breathless rapidity.

But what renders the book of absorbing interest in our age is that it assists us in an astonishing way to understand the Spain of our day. From the Moslem rule of the ninth century to the Communist occupation in the twentieth is an easy transition.

The interval of more than a thousand years can make but little difference as we study the temper of the Spanish people.

In both periods we behold them capable of the most notable sanctity in their own lives and the most heroic sacrifices for Christ and His Church. But then as now, we witness also the proneness of many to relinquish the creed of their fathers and the splendid traditions of their race. For the promise of a broth of pottage, which they were likely never to receive, they passed over blindly to a destructive foreign foe — Moslem in the one case, Bolshevist in the other; anti-Christian as were the followers of Mohammed, or essentially anti-God and opposed to all religions as is the Moscow International. Thus the events of the ninth century find their distant but authentic echo in the twentieth. The same sinister power invisibly urges on the forces under the red flag, with its sickle and hammer, that once stirred up the hordes which swarmed like locusts in the wake of the crescent.

Among the worst persecutors of Christianity, the most crafty plotters for its destruction, the most ruthless destroyers of convents and churches in the days of the Moslem were renegade Catholics whom a Christian mother had suckled at her breasts. It is all but another exemplification of the age-old adage that the best in its decline becomes the worst. Spain, unfortunately, is not an isolated example among the nations of the earth.

Great Christian leaders stand forth in the period under consideration in this book. Some, with powerful and striking qualities, tower like gnarled oaks that have for centuries wrestled with the storms upon their mountain promontories. Others, no less shaken by the bitter winds of adversity, still bear themselves aloft, graceful and erect, like cedars upon Lebanon. Among these must be counted Eulogius, the central figure of this history, who even in the midst of conflicts could preserve unharmed his fair serenity of soul.

But heroes and heroines we here meet with in goodly numbers. The latter in particular deserve our deepest admiration for their strength of character, their charm and delicacy of sentiment, and their courage worthy of an Esther, ready to die for her people. Freely and rejoicingly they lay down their lives, keeping their tryst of blood with Christ. Among the glorious women martyrs who followed the direction of Eulogius stand out particularly the marvellous virgins Flora, Columba, and others whom St. Theresa of Avila may well have had in mind when, as a child, she set forth to seek for martyrdom at the hands of the Moslem. But that was not the victory God had in store for her.

But not least of all, we are privileged to follow, through the pages of this volume, the beginning, growth, and wonderful consummation of one of the world's finest and most enduring friendships. Before it all the bright examples of classical antiquity pale by comparison. It is a union like that which knit together into one the souls of David and of Jonathan, but which continued undiminished through a lifetime of studies, labours, perils, conflicts, and imprisonments. Nor could it be ended by the bloody steel of the executioner. It was the friendship, intensely human yet at the same time profoundly spiritual, which existed between Eulogius and Alvaro, both in the Church's calendar of saints — the one wise, discreet, enthusiastically zealous; the other fiery, often erratic, but eternally faithful. Eulogius not seldom needed the prodding, and always the encouragement of his friend to urge him into action, but once in the foremost of the fray he nobly bore the brunt of the entire battle. Alvaro outlived him to pray at his tomb and erect to him that poet's monument which has endured for a thousand years and bids fair to outlast still many another millennium. He expected no less of it, but it was all for his Eulogius, his other self, the man who in life and in death remained one soul with him. We shall look far through history to find another friendship like to this, so great, so good, so noble, so perfectly unselfish, so undyingly significant.

But these were two only of the brave warriors who, like

Esperaindeo and Sansón, fought no less valiantly with pen and word than others of their blood with spear and sword in future years, until victory came at last. Chance of victory there was none for Cordova at this bleak hour. There was question only of instilling hope and heroism into the failing hearts of Christians by showing them that men and women would never be wanting them to carry on the conflict until the victory should be won.

But there are still quite other features that go to make up the value of this book. And these, too, are of signal importance in our day.

In the first place it leads us through a glorious renaissance of letters — classical, patristic, Hispano-Roman — such as men did not faintly dream could have existed in far-off and forgotten Cordova of the ninth century, cut off as it was from all communication with the Christian world. In Eulogius the author sees the last of the great Hispano-Romans, with their brilliant line of writers and of saints.

In the second place, the book presents us with a picture, minutely faithful, of the Moslem splendour of the time, its wealth and luxury, its army of black recruits picked and purchased in the market place, its open sensuousness in morals that might make the Christian shudder at the thought of it. Cordova was ranked after Constantinople as the second largest city in the Europe of that day. Its incomparable mosque has been described as the vision of a dream. The Caliph's own private library is said to have contained 400,000 manuscripts. But by way of contrast let us mention only a single instance. In the western part of the city stood the ancient church of San Acislo y Santa Victoria, scorched by fire and battered by time. It was known to the Moors as "The Church of the Burnt." Here four hundred Christian warriors, after fighting valiantly for days, took their refuge and chose rather to perish in the flames set to it than surrender to the Moor. So we behold the two antagonistic civilisations crowded into that single city — but to the conqueror belonged the spoils.

Finally, and most interesting in our day of liturgical revival, we come here into intimate contact with the old Mozarabic rite of the Catholic Church, as it was practised by the Cordovan Christians. It is rich with all the song and poetry and the delicate aroma of the East. We listen to chants and prayers, attend a baptism, wedding, and ordination, each performed in this ancient and most beautiful Oriental liturgy. And lastly, under the starry stillness of the night, we witness the solemn and triumphant services performed over the martyred body of the leader of the Mozarabic Christians. Reverently we bow our heads while our souls are stirred to their very depths.

Properly to adapt this book for an English-reading public considerable rearrangements, eliminations, and changes were at times imperative. For these the General Editor assumes the responsibility. Nothing new, however, has been introduced, and nothing of consequence to the reader has been omitted. The original title, *San Eulogio de Cordoba*, while significant to the Spaniard, would have conveyed no recollections to English and American readers, no hint of the tremendous life-and-death struggle, the religious and cultural conflict between two civilisations, portrayed here. A special prize offered by the Madrid *Voluntad*, in 1927, for the best life of a Spanish saint was unanimously accorded the author by a distinguished jury representing various religious orders, as well as the Real Academia de la Historia and the Real Academia Española. But this added approval is hardly needed for the book.

JOSEPH HUSSLEIN, S.J., PH.D.
General Editor, Science and Culture Series

St. Louis University,
January 12, 1937.

CONTENTS

Preface by the General Editor . . . . . .

Chapter
- I. Under the Heel of the Moslem . .
- II. Education in Ninth-Century Cordova
- III. A New Dawn of Christian Learning .
- IV. Eulogius and Alvaro: A Friendship for Life . . . .
- V. A Marriage and an Ordination . .
- VI. Glowing Ideals of Priestly Life . .
- VII. Mozarabic Monasticism: A Romance of Sanctity . . . .
- VIII. Ardent Searchers After Truth . . .
- IX. The Endless Struggle with Heresies
- X. The Journey That Took a Year . .
- XI. A Ninth-Century Classic Renaissance
- XII. Moslem Splendours and the Christian Yoke . . . .
- XIII. The Religious Conflict Deepens . .
- XIV. Beginnings of Martyrdom — Perfectus and Juan . . . .
- XV. A Fearless Band of Martyrs . . . .

Chapter		Page
XVI.	The Ardent Champion of the Martyrs	133
XVII.	Prosody and Prison Walls	143
XVIII.	The Virgin Martyr Flora	148
XIX.	Aurelius and Natalia, Félix and Liliosa	162
XX.	A Dramatic Climax and a Panic	172
XXI.	A Reign of Greed and Desolation	183
XXII.	More Martyrs and Their Enemies	191
XXIII.	A Lull in the Deadly Storm	202
XXIV.	A Triumphant Martyrdom. The Apologético	208
XXV.	The Twofold Vindication of Eulogius	218
XXVI.	Lucretia. Eulogius Receives His Crown	223
XXVII.	Epilogue: The Aftermath	231
Appendix: The Manuscript Library of Eulogius		242

A SAINT UNDER MOSLEM RULE

A Narrative of Moslem Rule in the Days of
St. Eulogius of Cordova

CHAPTER I

UNDER THE HEEL OF THE *MOSLEM*

OUR NARRATIVE opens at about the year 811 of the Christian era. Scarcely a century had passed since the fateful day when Cordova succumbed to the Moor. Conqueror and conquered still dwelt within the same walls, but under vastly different conditions.

The conquest was hardly completed when the beautiful hills about the city, the fertile fields and olive orchards passed from the control of the old Spanish nobility to become the possession of Arab soldiery and immigrants from Barbary. Barefoot and in rags they had entered Spain, but quickly they made themselves masters of the soil and lorded it in the princely residences where they now lived surrounded by all the refinements of luxury.

Invariably the same fate was accorded each Spanish town as it fell under Moorish dominion. The conquerors lost no time in possessing themselves of the strongest and the finest quarters of the cities, driving back the Christians into the least desirable sections. As a matter of military tactics this served also to render futile any possible uprising on the part of the conquered people desiring to regain their independence. Besides, there was the explicit warning of the Koran that: "The temptation of idolatry is worse than the carnage of war." Christians must be shunned and despised.

All this had taken place at Cordova. The Moorish upper classes there occupied the splendid mansions situated in the Axarquía. They dwelt in the princely suburb of Muniat-Almoguira, which extended to the east along the river bank to Medina; in Azahira de Almanzor and the ward of Balath-Moguits, where Moguits, the conqueror of Cordova, had met with the strongest resistance. The emir's own fortress stood in the middle of the Arab quarter, near an ancient Roman bridge. But the original inhabitants were herded together in the despised Almedina.

Here, in what was known as the Tiraceros section, lived the noble family that for centuries had held an honoured place among the citizens of Cordova, under the distinguished name of Eulogius. Its members once acted as judges in this patrician city, and here its ancestors, before the days of the fatal conquest, had occupied a magnificent palace that rose in grandeur on the banks of the Guadalquivir, near the cathedral of San Vincente. So they believed that they should uphold their dignity as members of the senatorial rank, an honour retained by them ever since the days of the old Roman rule. But now their descendants could do no more than remember with regret the former splendours of their ancient House, whose power had passed away forever.

Old Eulogius, the present head of the household, bore the shocks of fortune with the worthy courage then still to be found in the impoverished nobles of the mountain places of Santander. He looked upon the intruders not only as infidels, but as fierce barbarians, uprooters of a civilisation that had been the pride of his ancestors. His family were of the same opinion. None of them had made any compact with the unbelievers. Better to be despoiled of all, of power, of influence, of possessions, than to apostatise! Lax Christians had found a very simple formula by which to keep their riches. They had but to repeat the profession of the Moslem faith: "Allah is Allah and Mohammed is his prophet." There were numberless apostasies in those days, and the old senator Eulogius saw with shame that even some members of his own race had betrayed the Faith.

But in his household the spiritual treasure of the past was

kept intact, while the material riches passed to the Moors. His dwelling must have been one of the small houses of old Cordova. The narrow street admitted of no sunshine, but through the vestibule and open doorway might be seen the *patio,* surrounded by columns and shaded from the sun by an awning stretched from one gallery to the other. A fountain played in the midst, surrounded by pots of flowers. There, too, may have been a niche with a picture, like those that Saint Isidore had in his library, or such as are still to be seen in old Cordovan patios. Around the fountain worked the women, and sometimes the slaves as well, for the patio was both garden and workroom. Doña Isabel superintended the women's work; some little boys played together in a corner, and old Eulogius bent his weary body over the illuminated Bible, the family heirloom, which brought him forgetfulness of the evils of the times.

Suddenly the peaceful family gathering was disturbed by a stentorian cry. It was the ritual proclamation from the minaret of the neighbouring mosque, calling the Moslems to pray, with faces turned to the mihrab and the forefinger of their right hand touching the right ear. First came a deafening shout: "Allah is great!" Then a faint reply: "Truly there is no God but Allah!" Gradually the voice gathered strength and declared: "I testify that Mohammed is the messenger of Allah." Another pause, and in answer to the subdued response, came the sonorous cry: "Come to worship; Allah is great, there is no God but Allah."

From the streets, the fields, the ramparts, the houses, devout Moslems responded to the muezzin and murmured the sacred words of their liturgy: "There is no power nor strength save in Allah, great and exalted."

But the response from the ward of the Bordadores to the blasphemous words that came from the minarets was of a very different kind. The moment he heard the cry, the old grandsire looked up from his book and made the sign of the cross on his forehead. His action was followed by the rest of the household. Then Eulogius tearfully recited the words of the psalmist:

"O God, who shall be like to Thee? Hold not Thy peace, neither be Thou still, O God! For lo; Thine enemies have made a noise: and they that hate Thee have lifted up the head."

Five times a day the crier mounted the minaret to proclaim officially the hour of prayer; five times — at dawn, at noon, in the afternoon, at sunset, and at night — the terrible old veteran repeated his impetration with trembling voice, while scalding tears ran down his wrinkled cheeks and a fierce light flashed in his eyes. It was no surprise if the perfect mildness taught by the Gospels was at such a time not reflected in one who had witnessed the destruction of the glorious past, and looked on the misfortunes of the day.

Born at the beginning of the Moorish invasion, he had spent his youth amid the turmoil of the conquest and civil war, and had watched the politic mildness of the victors develop by degrees into open tyranny. If at first he had nursed hopes of restoration, he was forced to confess that the loss was now irreparable. All that remained for him was to preserve his household from the infidelity around them and accept with resignation the yoke that became daily more unbearable.

Men have talked of the toleration shown by the Moors in Spain. That is utterly false. It is true that as a rule the emirs did not have recourse to sanguinary measures, but their whole legislation and administrative organisation was in itself a malevolent persecution, so that it required heroism to profess the Christian religion. It is true, too, that Christians might govern themselves by their own laws — the statute law they had inherited from the Visigoths — and that they had magistrates elected by them to administer justice. Thus the Count of Andalusia resided in Cordova and held authority over all the Spaniards who had been faithful to their religion. Under his rule were a large number of civil, administrative, economical, and judicial officers, besides judges, almoxarifes charged with receiving taxes, clerks of the market appointed to inspect weights and measures, architects, surveyors, and constables.

Although the Christians appeared to enjoy so many privileges, yet hatred and contempt characterised all the Moslems' relations with them. The two races lived in separate districts of the cities and looked upon one another as unclean. "Ask neither for light nor fire from the polytheists," Mohammed wrote in the Koran: "Do not make friends with the Christians or you will become like them." "God" an *alfaquí*[1] commented, "has disgraced the polytheists and their sectaries: He has humbled and denounced them; has driven them from Him, deprived them of help, and ruined them after branding them with contempt and infamy." "Let not the believer," says the Koran, "love infidels, rebels against God and His prophet, even if among them should be his father, son, brother, or ally."

Pride of race, swollen by a century of conquests, coloured the daily intercourse of the conquerors and the conquered in its smallest details. "God has blessed His people," proudly declared an alfaquí: "He has allotted the power to them and has cursed the other nations, against whom all vengeance is lawful."

Many a time did old Eulogius, the illustrious representative of the Spanish Visigothic aristocracy in Cordova, feel his blood boil at the insults offered him to mark his inferiority. If he met a Mohammedan in the street, it was he who had to make a low bow. If he was sitting at the door of his house, he must rise and offer the Moslem his seat. On the paths, in the squares, the worst place was for him. He must not appear

---

[1] An expounder of Mohammedan law or the Koran, a member of the Moslem sacerdotal caste.

in rich or showy clothing before the Moslem, nor ride on horseback, nor wear a sword, nor make or keep one in his house. At this price alone could he purchase the right to live and practise his religion, and even then, with many restrictions.

What the conquest had begun to effect was now being completed by an arbitrary legislation regarding property. This, combined with an impossible scheme of taxes, was bound in the end to bring about the final expropriation of the *dimmies*, or conquered race. Besides other taxes, every Christian was obliged to pay to the Moslem treasury, as yearly impost on the land, the *jarach*. He was further burdened with the *chizia* or poll tax, which all who were not Mohammedans were bound to pay in return for the condescension of the Moors in allowing them to dwell in the land of the prophet. The *jarach* was rarely less than 20 per cent of the products, and sometimes amounted to half. The *chizia* had to be paid before the new moon, and regarding it the Moorish law read: "Every man who has come of age among enfranchised subjects must render as tribute four golden doblas" — an exorbitant sum for those days that would be equal to 500 pesetas in modern Spain.

But the insulting manner in which the money was collected was the worst trial. At times the aged Eulogius looked more gloomy than usual. He gazed into space, forgetful of his book. Yet if the voice of the muezzin reached his ears he gave forth the words of the psalm with greater confidence than ever: "O God! Thine enemies have made a noise: and they that hate Thee have lifted up the head." Then his heart was wrung with terrible anguish. Sometimes the eldest of the little boys playing in the patio would run up to him, moved by his tears, and console him, saying:

"What is the matter, Grandfather? Why are you so sad? Have the infidels hurt you?"

"Nothing, little one, nothing. Let us trust in God."

Though the old man answered thus, he had suffered much on such days. Leaving his room with the money in his hand, he had found in the court a Moslem, seated in an official capacity, smiling on him sarcastically. Taking by the throat the venerable old man, he shouted:

"*Dimmí*, enemy of God, pay the poll tax."

The other Moslems followed this example. They insulted the Christian, showered him with blows, pushed and mocked him, and spat on his grey hair. So, at last, Eulogius would leave the court with crimson face and tears in his eyes. Like treatment was systematically accorded him every month.

So unendurable in fact did this become that many Christians condemned themselves to perpetual seclusion, in order that their existence might remain unknown to the Moors. Others feigned illness, or entered the mosque reciting the Moslem formula, thinking that it would suffice if they remained Christian at heart. The greater number apostatised both in body and soul. A Mussulman jurisconsul has written: "There is need for the *dimmíes* to undergo this abasement, for it may make them end by believing in Allah and his prophet, and not till then will they be freed from this shameful yoke."

Far from apostatising, Eulogius clung more closely to the creed of his ancestors, in which he found strength to bear such taunts and injustices. There were many souls in Cordova with like valour, who formed a fervent and numerous body, in spite of the apostasies. Within their houses they dragged the chain of servitude in silence, as they described it; in the churches they cried with tears to God imploring Him to deliver them from this frightful yoke, to bring back the liberty of the past, and permit them to serve Him in peace. These are the favours asked for in the hymns, the prayers, and almost all the liturgical formulas recited by the poor persecuted Christians of those days.

At that time, the observance of the Feast of St. Clement was introduced. In his Mass the priest prays:

> Deign, O Lord, to deliver by Thy peace the remnant of afflicted Christians, so that we who endure the most cruel and depraved yoke that is imposed on us by other nations, may, while peacefully proclaiming the true peace, finally enter Paradise. . . . Grant that we may not be perverted from our holy purpose by the heathen and unregenerate. Break their keen arrows: confound the wicked plots they lay against us, so that those who in this world suffer their many insults and unspeakable gibes for the name of Thy Son, may receive remission of their sins in the next on account of the faith they profess, for which they are condemned to beggary and death.

This was the cry of the poor Mozarabic Church on the eve of the most sanguinary persecution. Bitter times were coming. But the man whom God destined to uphold them was already born. He was the boy who played in the patio of the Tiraceros quarter, in whose soul the old Eulogius had implanted a character and ardent faith such as his own. Already the time had come when an event would take place that should remain indelibly impressed upon his memory.

The caliph Omar had cruelly declared: "We ought to live at daggers drawn with the Christians, as should also our descendants so long as Islam lasts." The conquerors of the Peninsula followed this advice to the letter, but they were dealing with a people who shrank from no acts of heroism. Even renegades suffered from this policy, which was worthy of the Bedouins. Their position was as unbearable as that of the Christians. They were excluded from all share in the higher offices of the state, treated with disdain and insolence by the Arabs, and relegated to servile work, so that their apostasy had only freed them from the humiliating payment of the poll tax. Many former slaves were now freedmen of Allah, but in reality they were as downtrodden as the rest. They still bore the brand of slavery on their forehead and at every step were liable to hear themselves insulted as slaves, and sons of slaves, a term which the Moors never used for Christians.

Having become Mohammedans out of policy, many of these renegades were still Christian at heart, but they lacked the strength given by religious practices to bear their subjection and social inferiority. As we have seen, the Christians wished only to live peacefully, proclaiming the true peace, but the renegades understood not their language. The time had come in which, with their strong muster roll, they meant to call to account the privileged class, composed of foreign soldiers who aimed at monopolising all power and property. The struggle was inevitable.

The renegades were joined by the alfaquíes, the sacerdotal cast, who also had reason to be discontented. This party began their work by defaming the ruling emir, Alháquem I (796-822), a man cold-blooded, hard, energetic, and above all very jealous of his authority, wherein he differed greatly from his father who had ruled before him. Intent on centralising in his hands all political power, he had naturally wounded their pride. While certainly not an irreligious man, he was naturally jovial and expansive, and the irresistible charm of the Andalusian vintage made it impossible for him to keep the Mohammedan laws regarding wine. In fact, men spoke openly in the mosques of his irreligion and dissipation. They insulted him in the streets, called him rude names, and went so far as to threaten him to his face in the principal mosque. "Come and pray, drunkard," cried the people when the muezzin announced the hour of prayer from the minaret. The alfaquíes, on their part, were led by the religious fanatic Jahya, who held it a sin to listen even to a musical concert.

Meanwhile, Alháquem strengthened the fortifications of his palace and its environs, had the moats dug deeper, and ceaselessly reinforced the famous guard of mamelukes, called by the populace the *mudos* (mutes). By the gate of the fortress he set a regiment of cavalry, composed of 1,000 picked Berber cavalry, that they might always be at hand to defend him.

In 814, the public anger at last broke out, in the month of Ramadhán, when men's minds, roused to religious frenzy by the fast, were more ready to listen to cries for vengeance. It was in the suburb of Mediodía, the ancient Roman city of Secunda, separated from Cordova by the river. This had now become one of the richest, most populous quarters, and contained the fertile land cultivated by the hard-working landowners. In this section stood the Mussulman schools. About four thousand students heard in them lectures given by the alfaquíes, the Sultan's enemies. Hundreds of copyists, men and women, transcribed the books that came from Damascus, Basora, Medina, and Bagdad.

It so happened at this time that a mameluke went to an armourer and asked him to polish his sword. The man refused under the pretext that he had other work to do. Angry words ensued, followed by a quarrel that resulted in the death of the armourer.

The news of this tragic event spread like wildfire and aroused violent indignation. The dwellers in the suburb of Mediodía believed that the hour of vengeance had come. Seizing the first arms they could lay their hands upon, they hurled threats against the emir. In a few moments the revolutionary excitement had spread throughout the whole city. From all quarters streamed forth a ceaseless crowd of revolutionists seeking liberty or death.

Looking out from the height of his terrace, Alháquem saw them advance, "like dense, black clouds," says an Arab writer. He thought at first that a charge of cavalry would suffice to disperse them; but the cavalry were repulsed and the revolutionaries, having taken the bridge, prepared to assail the fortress.

The emir asked his Christian page, Jacinto, to bring him a flask of civet, leisurely perfumed his beard and hair, and with perfect self-possession presented himself to his household. He spoke a few words to his nephew Obaidalá, his most valiant officer, and restored confidence to the soldiers. His swarthy face, his proud and haughty bearing, controlled and encouraged them.

Accompanied by a few brave men-at-arms, Obaidalá opened the door of the palace, ventured to pass through the amazed crowd, and turning into the Calle Mayor, or "chief street," which was bordered on the one side by the embankments of the Guadalquivir and on the other by the splendid palaces of the Arab nobles, reached a ford that crossed the river a little farther down. By this he arrived at the suburb of Mediodía.

Meanwhile the emir followed, facing the insurgents, who soon found themselves driven into a morass. Their villages were on fire. Alháquem had acted as other tyrants had done in similar cases. His plan was to engage the rebels, while Obaidalá set fire to the suburb. When the men saw their houses burning they gave up fighting, but caught between two fires, they perished helplessly.

This plan completely dispersed the combatants. The rabble rushed back to save their wives and children and the combat became a frightful slaughter. The *mudos,* Negroes from Africa, and the *rubios* from the shores of the Baltic, who could not understand the cries for pity, slaughtered without mercy, so that the squares and streets and suburbs ran with blood. Many, however, found safety in flight. Three hundred heads of the principal victims were impaled in front of the palace and their bodies, hung up on the banks of the river, made a ghastly line from the Almasura to the Prado de los Marjales.

After this terrible vengeance, Alháquem assembled his viziers and consulted them as to how the conquered should be treated. Opinions differed. The emir, followed by the moderate party, decided upon granting them a pardon. But it was a characteristic Moslem pardon. The district of Mediodía, the principal seat of the insurrection, was to be pillaged, burnt, and levelled to the ground. The inhabitants, taking with them whatever they could carry conveniently, must leave Andalusia in three days, under pain of being crucified. Many of the proscribed took refuge in Toledo, which at that time had rebelled against the government of Cordova. A band of the exiles, consisting of 8,000 families, found a new home in the city of Fez, which Prince Edris had just finished building as the capital of his kingdom. For many centuries it contained a quarter called that of the Andalusians. The greater number of the exiles, led by an adventurer who was a native of Pedroche, went to sea. For several months their white flags brought terror to the cities on the shores of the Mediterranean. Finally they took possession of Alexandria, and disembarking on the Island of Crete, founded there an independent state which lasted for more than a century.

Meanwhile the alfaquíes, who had stirred up the tumult, received free pardon, and the sultan, not fully satisfied with the vengeance he had taken, spent his leisure time in writing verses against the unhappy exiles.

> As the mender of old clothes uses his needle to patch together the pieces of cloth, so, with my sword, did I join my provinces in one.
> I bade that the skulls of my rebel subjects should be divided into two parts like the gourd, to lie on the ground and shine in the rays of the sun.
> They will tell you whether I wearied or not in wounding them.
> Overcome with terror, they fled to escape death; but I, remaining in my palace, despised them.
> The fray being over, I forced them to drink my deadly poison.

Probably old Eulogius was no longer alive at this time, but he left his name, and with it his zeal, to one of the boys who had been playing in the patio. Having been educated in a fundamentally Christian home, the child inherited an unalterable love for his religion and a profound hatred for Mohammedanism. From the moment he first opened his eyes, all that he saw around him gave him an aversion for the invaders. As the victim of their rapacious natures, as a Spaniard, and as a Christian, he knew them to be his irreconcilable enemies. No doubt the slaughter at Mediodía made an indelible impression on his soul. It accounts for the patriotic and religious enthusiasm of the younger generation. His own father, the son of old Eulogius, may have been involved in it. We know nothing of his name or life, but it is certain that he died young and that his whole family history would have inclined him to join in the revolt, in the hope that it might restore his rights to him.

One thing is certain: hardly were the years of infancy over when Eulogius became a little champion of the conquered people against the impositions of their conquerors. When he heard the cry of the muezzin from the minaret, calling the city to prayer, he made the sign of the cross on his forehead and recited the verse of the Psalm:

"Let them all be confounded that adore graven things, and that glory in their idols" (Ps. 96:7).

This formula is more expressive than that his grandfather had used. Eulogius well knew the seduction exercised on the Christians by the power of Islam, which increased daily. He saw that apostasies were more frequent and feared lest the Faith should wane. Full of indignation he prayed that its enemies might be confounded. Five times a day he made this invocation: at sunrise, at midday, in the afternoon, at sunset, and again at night.

CHAPTER II

EDUCATION IN NINTH-CENTURY *CORDOVA*

THE CHURCH in the quarter of the Tiraceros was dedicated to the blessed martyr, St. Zoilus. It was a second home for Eulogius. Thither the newly born infant had been brought to receive the saving waters of baptism. When this had been conferred the godfather, perhaps his own grandfather, Eulogius, lifted the shivering little body of the boy from the baptismal font, and presented him to the priest to be confirmed with the sacred chrism. He was next given the Bread of Life, steeped in the Wine of Salvation. It was the practice of Infant Communion that had been familiar in the early Christian Church.

Following these rites the priest pronounced the liturgical words that were marvellously to be realised in the child's future life: "Eulogius, I sign thee with the cross. Fear God and hope in the Lord whose light will illuminate thee, whose power will uphold thee, whose sign I imprint on thy forehead."[1] From that time Eulogius often entered the church of the blessed martyr.

There were many churches in Cordova for the boy to visit as he grew up, but he loved the church of San Zoilo best. It was his own. It reminded him of the glorious times whereof his grandfather had told him, the times when, as he himself was later to say, "the splendid cult of the Christian Faith shone forth, the dignity of the venerable priesthood was

---

[1] Dom Ferotin, *Liber Ordinum*, pp. 24–36.

revered, and art worked wonders in the construction of the basilicas."

The church of San Zoilo had been erected just two centuries earlier, in the year 613, by Agapius, a Bishop of Cordova.[2] It was indeed one of the marvels worked by art in Spain during the reign of the Gothic kings. The saint himself, in whose honour it was built, had been one of a band of twenty Christians put to death in the early fourth-century persecutions, probably under the Emperor Diocletian. When these martyrdoms took place neither the Arabs nor the Goths had as yet come to Spain. The Romans then held sway along the shores of the Betis. The churches and mosques of later times were thus preceded by the grand circus, the theatre, the forum, the senate house, and the temples, in which worship was paid to the gods — to the Manes, Bacchus, Apollo, Janus, and Augustus.

St. Zoilus held all these gods as vain idols.

"Why do you lose the best part of your youth and disgrace your noble blood by professing the Christian religion?" the proconsul asked him.

But Zoilus set little value on his youth or noble birth or life. He willingly resigned them all that in him might be realised the words: "To him that overcometh, I will give to eat of the tree of life, which is in the paradise of My God" (Apoc. 2:7). Protected by his faith, he stood firm.

The proconsul, therefore, ordered him to be beheaded, and in order to withdraw his body from the veneration of the faithful, had it buried in the pagan cemetery. But some three hundred years later, Bishop Agapius discovered it and in honour of the martyr raised the splendid church in which his relics were now exposed for the veneration of the faithful. To little Eulogius the life of St. Zoilus was always to remain an inspiration and, we might almost say, a prophecy.

---

[2] For the history of Agapius and the acts of St. Zoilus, see *España Sagrada*, Vol. X, pp. 221–226 and pp. 491–507.

One day, when Eulogius was seven years old, his mother led him to kneel before the shrine of the blessed martyr that he might be enrolled as a pupil in the school attached to it. A priest came forward and recited the customary prayer, duly inserting the child's own name:

> O Lord Jesus Christ, who didst open the mouth of the dumb and perfect Thy praise by the lips of children, open the mouth of this Thy servant Eulogius that, receiving the gift of wisdom and profiting by the instruction henceforth to be given him, he may praise Thee for all eternity.

This was followed by the blessing, which heaven was to fructify marvellously:

> May holy Church, thy true Mother, receive increase by thy means and benefit beyond reckoning.

"Amen," answered all the pupils of the church of San Zoilo, receiving into their ranks this new companion. Eulogius thus began his career as a student.

But his mother wished him to study in order that he might consecrate himself to God and become a priest in this church of the holy martyr. Since the Mozarabic liturgy, which is so beautiful and maternal, has a blessing and prayer for every event in life, the ceremony was now prolonged still further.

Eulogius knelt in the middle of the choir. The priest clothed him with a tunic, over which he put an alb, the lower part of which was open on both sides. He then cut the boy's locks, leaving only a ring of hair round his head. Meanwhile the choir sang: "Suffer the little children to come unto Me, for of such is the kingdom of God."

The ceremony ended with the act of signing the cross on the boy's tonsure, accompanied by a prayer and blessing.

Eulogius was now offered to God and had become a little cleric. Henceforth it would be his business to study and serve in the church of the blessed St. Zoilus. As a sign of his clerical rank and an emblem of his spotless life, he would wear the *enebladium,* a white linen garment resembling part of the modern collegiate gown, which his mother had woven for him with loving care. Another child, named Leovigildo, who entered at the same time as a student in the church of San Cipriano, also at Cordova, was later on to tell us how the *enebladium* is the resplendent emblem of the cleric: "It covers his throat and breast to remind him that he should always strive to bring forth good things out of the good treasure of his heart."[3]

Adjoining the church of San Zoilo was a spacious building that had formerly been the home of a hundred monks consecrated to the service of God and the honour of His martyr. It was now a college of priests who had in their care a hundred students, forming the school or seminary of the church. The fourth council of Toledo, inspired by St. Isidore of Seville, whose powerful intellect vitalised the Middle Ages, wrote the following canon:

> From the years of adolescence, every age is inclined to evil, but no period is more dangerous than that of adolescence; therefore, boys who wish to be admitted to the priesthood must dwell together in a house near the church under the direction of an ancient who shall instruct their mind and examine their life.

This rigorous vigilance was not exercised over Eulogius. In all the colleges of Cordova of that time there seem to have been day boarders and extern pupils at the classes. Eulogius appears to have been of their number. Probably he returned home for the night, and it is certain that he could go outside the college without exciting attention.

But the discipline must none the less have been rigorous. We may understand it better if we remember the customs of the time. Thus Alcuin, one of the great authorities of his age on this subject, said:

---

[3] *De Habitu Clericorum,* Chapter VI, edited by the Most Reverend Dom Luciano Serrano.

> Spare yourself no trouble in watching over and instructing the young scholars in holy discipline and Catholic learning. Teach the lads purity of heart and body, encourage frequent confession and assiduity in manual and mental work, so that they may practise the former without murmuring and the latter without vainglory.

The constitutions of Bec, the college in which Lanfranc and St. Anselm were trained, decree:

> When a boy wants to speak to one of his schoolfellows, he must ask permission and speak aloud. During the *siesta*, it is forbidden to speak, to read, or write.

The most profound respect for the children's souls, the most perfect carrying out of the classic aphorism: *maxima debetur puero reverentia*, "the greatest reverence is due to youth," inspired these preventive rules of education, which were eminently characteristic of the grandeur and refinement of the Middle Ages.

At Bec, the scholars each had a log of wood to sit on, and in other schools, a truss of straw. But in the college of San Zoilo, in Cordova, they probably sat on the ground. Eulogius and his young schoolfellows took the same position as the little Moors who went to the mosque to be taught by the alfaquíes. No one but the master had a chair. We can still see the stool painted in the old miniatures. By the master's side was the terrible *ferula*, the *palmatoria*. "I too have felt its sting on my palms," wrote St. Braulius, the Bishop of Saragossa, to his friend Tajón.

The first task set Eulogius in the parish school was to "calculate," *calcular*, as St. Isidore calls it. This meant learning the alphabet. The teacher was called the *calculator*. We have here the survival of an ancient custom. The poet said: *Ponatur calculo, adsint cum tabula pueri.*

The master held up a tablet or smooth stone on which was written a letter and gave its name to his scholars, who had to copy it. Eulogius took up his bone punch, his *estaquiello* (peg) as Berceo calls it, set his wax tablets on his knee, and traced the lines with a firm hand. Then the *calculos* were passed round to the pupils who had to name the letters written on them, until they knew how to join them together, first into syllables, and then into sentences. This is how Eulogius learnt to read and write. But he had still to learn how to pronounce the famous line in which the grammarians included the whole alphabet: *Adnexique globum zephırique Kanna secabant.*

All the psalms and hymns were learnt by heart. As the boys could not read, and it would have been impossible to give each one a psalter, the master had to say every verse repeatedly until, one by one, the hundred and fifty psalms, with the vast quantity of hymns in the Mozarabic liturgy, had taken their place in the little heads of the schoolboys. It was a hard task, but indispensable, in order that the youthful clerics might take part in the Divine Office.

Meanwhile the precentor undertook a like task in regard to the Antiphonal. A century later, Sancho el Major of Navarre, describing what a cleric ought to be, said that he must speak well, sing well, chant the psalms well, and know the liturgy thoroughly. Much of this was derived from the Antiphonal. A copyist of the time thus sings its praises:[4]

> O great and sacred Antiphonal,
>   how sweet are thy melodies!
> Thou dost court men's senses
>   and soften hard hearts with thy
>   peaceful influence.
> Thou art the prince of all delights.
> Thou dost chant of all things,
>   great and little, in sounds that

---

[4] These verses are from the first part of the Antiphonal of León, a magnificent example of Mozarabic literature written in the tenth century over another manuscript of the time of King Wamba. See the edition brought out by the monks of Silos.

> seem stolen from the angels in
> heaven, filling with melody the
> temple day and night.

This music, composed in happier times by the great Visigoth bishops, was transmitted from one generation and church to another. The neumatic notation, that of our old liturgical books, had neither key nor line, and only indicated the ascending and descending movements. In order to read it a knowledge of the traditional chants was required, since it rendered them only approximately. The art of the precentor consisted in repeating the melody until the children could sing it correctly. The Spanish music masters also taught their pupils some verses written by St. Eugenius which we find in a copy made in Cordova at the time. Ridiculing the bad singers it says: "A harsh voice is like an ass braying, a pig grunting, or the husky neighing of a mule. . . . I beg you not to tire yourself if you are to sing in this manner. Let your lips rest, do not strain your throat nor injure your lungs. God cannot like what men dislike."[5]

After spending the first two or three years of his school days learning these rudiments, Eulogius began to study the *trivium* and *quadrivium*. During the Middle Ages all colleges taught some part of each of the seven sciences, giving the preference to the one the professor liked best. Eulogius gave special attention to grammar, which opened the secrets of Latin to him. Latin was then not only the language of the Church but also the literary idiom of the conquered Spaniards. In his home the Romance dialect was used which was the common language of all Spaniards, understood also by the Arabs. It still held its own valiantly against that of the

---

[5] The manuscript mentioned in the text is that called the *Samuélico* codex, from the name of the principal copyist, a Mozarabic of Cordova named Samuel. It is also to be found in the cathedral archives of León and we owe to it many interesting particulars about the culture of the Christians of Cordova during the time of St. Eulogius.

EDUCATION IN NINTH-CENTURY CORDOVA 21

invaders. This vitality was due to the continual addition of Catalan, Navarrese, and Castilian elements. Ecclesiastical Latin, which differed very slightly from it, had lost the elegance and correctness that distinguished it two centuries before, since there were few means of studying it. In St. Isidore's time — the seventh century — the Latin written in Spain surpassed that of any country in Western Europe, but by the ninth century little remained of the splendid culture created by the great Archbishop of Seville and Doctor of the Church.

Education in the classics had almost entirely disappeared. It is enough to say that in the schools of Cordova the *Aeneid*, the favourite book of medieval grammarians, was unknown.

For this, St. Isidore was partly to blame. He who had such love for antiquity, and the most intimate knowledge of classic literature, who studded all his writings with quotations from the pagan authors, severely condemned the reading of their books. In the *Regula* he forbade it altogether to monks, and his third book of "Sentences" contains such phrases as:

> "It is forbidden to read the fictions of the poets, for the allurement of their empty fables gives rise to voluptuous desires. Men sacrifice to devils not only by burning incense to them but by delighting in their words. . . . Besides, what effect has love of human knowledge save to make men vain?"

True, the great Doctor of the Church refuted these reasons by declaring that profane science might be useful when utilised for higher ends, but the following generation took notice solely of his condemnation. The invasion of the Moors and their barbarian policy did the rest.

In the class attended by Eulogius, however, the grammar of Elius Donatus was used. The authority of this author was universally respected because he had taught St. Jerome. The *Donatus Minor*, as his book was called, had as a companion volume a collection of moral maxims inspired by Christianity, known as *Cato, the Censor*. Like all the schoolboys of the Middle Ages, St. Eulogius learnt it by heart. There are traces of its affected, decadent style in his writings, and in one place he quotes two lines from it. Besides the Psalms, he read the verses of Juvencus and of St. Eugenius of Toledo.[6] The latter, from the seventh to the twelfth century, was the model and source of inspiration for all Spaniards who attempted to write epitaphs and epigrams.

It was from these authors that Eulogius learnt to exercise his memory, to construe, analyse, and translate until he was able to talk in Latin with his schoolfellows at recreation and to fathom the hidden sense of the Scriptures. The last-named purpose was indeed the chief aim of those who learnt that ancient tongue.

These studies comprised all his classical education, so that later on he could say, with a spice of bitterness: "I make no claim of knowing the liberal arts, for my masters gave me no instruction on the subject." He learnt, however, the Greek alphabet, which was found in the principal Spanish writings of the day. At Silos, Cardeña, and Ripoll, as in Cordova and Toledo, the copyists made a display of their knowledge by writing Latin names in Greek characters. He studied rhetoric and logic, mastered the general plan of the second volume of St. Isidore's *Etymology*, and may perhaps have been taught the very rudimentary philosophy known by the learned men of Cordova at that time.

Through its study of astronomy the *quadrivium* taught Eulogius to note the position of the principal constellations, as also the length of the shadow cast by the human body in the different hours of the day and seasons of the year. These sciences were necessary to regulate the liturgical Offices of the day and night.

Probably no musical instruction was added to the practical

---

[6] St. Eugenius, Bishop of Toledo, A.D. 647 to 657. He took part in several councils. Some of his writings are still extant.

exercises taken under the direction of the precentor, notwithstanding St. Isidore's rather strange assertion that "there could be no perfect instruction without music."

Besides all this, Eulogius would certainly not omit copying on his wax tablet the map of the earth from the *Apocolipsis* of Beatus. This would be the chief thing taught in what was then called Geometry. He had further to study arithmetic, which taught him the division of time by the Greeks and Romans, the laws of the solar cycle, the laws of embolism, the epact, the golden number, the dominical letter, and other matters of the kind required by clerics for the special knowledge of the calendar. These complicated theories were varied by curious problems given in the form of riddles to arouse the children's imagination and curiosity.

"A snail was invited to dinner by a swallow that lived a league away," said the teacher, "but the poor snail could only travel ten feet a day."

The children, wide-eyed, smiled at the proposition. The master asked: "How long did it take the snail to reach the swallow's house?'

Before venturing on these intellectual gymnastics, however, Eulogius had learnt to write numbers in Roman letters, and perhaps to translate them into Moorish numerals, for the manuscripts of the time give us the first known Arabic figures. He also knew how to reckon with the fingers. Each movement of the fingers signified a number in the schools of that age. The master bent the little finger of his left hand until it touched the palm, and the scholars all cried "one." But if he bent the little finger of the right hand in the same way, he meant not one, but a thousand.

Yet the science of numbers held a higher application in those times than that of a mere solution of problems. Men saw in numbers something sacred and esoteric. Some presaged misfortune; others were of good omen. St. Isidore wrote: "Do not despise the study of numerals for they shed rays of light that illuminate many of the mysteries of Holy Scripture. Deprive things of their number, and they will all perish." Eulogius, too, believed in this secret power, and speaks in one of his works of the mysteries enclosed in the number six; a number perfect in all its parts, that indicates the perfection of the world. So, indeed, he had been instructed by the great encyclopedia of the etymologists.

Arithmetic thus acted as a bridge between liberal and ecclesiastical studies. These, in turn, were combined with canonical learning, the principal subject of training for the priesthood.

Eulogius, eager for knowledge, concentrated all the efforts of his soul on his studies. His master read and explained to him the "Sentences" of St. Isidore, which were the earliest essay toward a theological *Summa* in medieval times. Here was revealed for the first time the marvellous harmony of Christian doctrine which the Archbishop of Seville made to revolve around three principal ideas: God, man, and the world. But beyond all this, Eulogius sought the very founts of Holy Scripture and tradition. His biographer tells us that he had a deep knowledge of the Bible and never tired of investigating the "Sentences." His one pleasure was to study the law of the Lord both day and night.

CHAPTER III

A NEW DAWN OF *CHRISTIAN LEARNING*

FROM THE first, Eulogius was regarded by his schoolfellows as a prodigy of learning. Among them shone several who later were to become valiant defenders of the Faith. It may be that at his very side, in the Cordovan schoolroom sat a clever, eager-minded boy, for whom were destined in the future many enemies, many struggles, and an illustrious name. It was Sansón, a few years younger than Eulogius, who was to be his successor in the church of San Zoilo and who later continued his struggles in defence of the Church.

Eulogius had now reached the threshold of youth. Because of his precocious talent and goodness he was known among the Christians of the city as "the master of the teachers." No longer finding in his school anything to satisfy his thirst for learning, he undertook a pilgrimage of knowledge, visiting all the churches and monasteries of Cordova in search of new instructors, no matter how far distant they might be. Nor could he be deterred by any fear of insults and ill treatment from the Moors.

Large numbers of the youth of Cordova were possessed of the same love of knowledge. The city was on its way to becoming once more the prolific mother of learning, the *Cordoba fecunda* of Martial, the city *praepotens alumnis* whereof Sidonius Apollinaris wrote in the fifth century.

On their side the Moslems were as eager for knowledge as the Christians. The mosques were filled with youths who crowded to hear the various notable alfaquíes, the disciples of Málic ben Anas and other famous teachers of the East.

The Mediodían quarter had now risen from its ashes and, according to a Moorish historian, swarmed with a turbulent crowd of five thousand students. Some grouped themselves around Jahya ben Jahya, the great authority on the malequí law; others listened to the celebrated teacher Abdelmelic ben Habib, the inexhaustible source of picturesque traditions, who spoke with genuine Andalusian charm. Still others, more fond of novelties, were eager to hear the last doctrinal vagaries of the East, and gathered around the pulpit of Bequí ben Majlad, renowned for his independent opinions which often betrayed him into absurdities.

The teaching of these learned contemporaries of Eulogius was, like that of the Christian instructors, almost exclusively theological and canonical, with this obvious difference: that the Christian teaching was based on the Holy Scriptures while the Moorish relied on the Koran. Moslem learning in Spain at the time was a faithful reproduction of that of the East, without the slightest admixture of traditional Spanish culture. Seneca and Osius, St. Isidore and Tajón did not exist for the haughty alfaquíes who taught in the mosque of Abu-Otmán, in the great Assembly, and in the other Mohammedan schools of Cordova. Said of Toledan, the historian of Arab philosophy, could state with the greatest sincerity — so far as his knowledge went — that Spain had no learned men until the Moslems conquered it. "There is only a remembrance," he adds, "of ancient talismans, the work of the Christian kings, that are believed to have existed in certain regions."

The Christians, on their side, had a poor opinion of Moslem teaching. Living side by side with the Moors, elbowing them from day to day, they knew nothing of their religion and despised their culture. Their own learning, unfortunately, was but a very small and deteriorated residue of that which in former times had enriched the famous schools of Seville. The Moslems assiduously collected the writings of the Visigoth authors, but ignored the many other Christian classics. St. Augustine's *City of God* was rare and almost impossible to find in Andalusia. After the invasion no writings but those of Beatus could be procured for the libraries of Seville and Cordova. The Mozarabic knew nothing of the Carlovingian renaissance. The brilliant dawn of Moorish learning in Cordova no doubt dispersed the embers that remained of St. Isidore's influence.

But the hum of students' voices round the schools of Islam roused a thirst for learning among the youths who were faithful to the Christian religion. Many Christians had no objection to becoming pupils of the Moorish teachers. This in turn brought about as a protest against the ever growing absorption of Islam, a more solid and strict organisation of the Christian schools in the porticoes of the churches. From these schools were to come forth the great champions of the Faith in the struggles then under way against heresy and unbelief. From these schools, too, burst forth that sudden blaze of light, resplendent as the glory of the ancient Hispano-Roman learning of Seneca and St. Isidore that in former years illumined the countryside and cities of Andalusia.

Naturally, one of these schools was that belonging to the cathedral — not the old cathedral of San Vicente, which the Moors had taken to make of it their chief mosque, but the church of the *Tres Santos*. It stood in the eastern quarter of Cordova, near the river. Another school was attached to the church of San Cipriano. But for a time the most famous of all seems to have been that of San Acisclo, the renowned church of the *Encarcelados* (Imprisoned) and *Quemados* (Burnt) Christians, *Canisat alasra,* which stood near Balad-Moguits, the eastern district, already referred to whose name recalls the Moorish warrior who slaughtered four hundred heroes at his entrance into Cordova. The church of San Acisclo gloried in these martyrs of their fatherland, and the loyal descendants of ancient Spain found comfort and strength within its precincts.

Besides the parish schools within the city, those of the monasteries were scattered around the outskirts of Cordova or hidden among the rocks of the mountains, whither resorted the students from all parts of the emir's domains. Among them, also, were slaves and freedmen from Asturias and the south of France who, when once they entered Cordova, felt the urge of learning. Nor were all preparing for the priesthood. "Priest" was not a synonym for a learned man in Cordova. Not merely were there secular grammarians but also theologians who were artisans, businessmen, and mamelukes, all of whom frequented the courts of the churches and monasteries for the pleasure of listening to distinguished lecturers or of keeping in contact with the literary and religious traditions of the past. Some feeling of the kind made Eulogius wander through the narrow streets of the city and the still narrower passes of the mountain ridges. No obstacle deterred him when there was a chance of finding a grain of truth. Out of regard for the feelings of his teachers at San Zoilo he took care that his escapades should not come to their ears for the time. But his absences became daily longer and more frequent. In each school he found a master who taught him something new, who spoke to him of some ancient book or interpreted some text of Holy Writ that before had baffled him.

Thus for the first time, too, he came into contact with men who later would shed lustre on the Church in Cordova. Among his teachers was the devout Vicente, "the most learned doctor of theology of our age," as a contemporary called him. Among his fellow students no doubt were Cyprian, the future panegyrist of nobles and martyrs, the ingenuous poet of illuminated Bibles and ladies' fans; Leovigildo, who in years to come would write in an involved style of the mystic meaning of priestly vestments; and Saul, his own intimate friend in the struggles and persecutions of the future. As St. Basil met Julian, the future Apostate, at Athens, so Eulogius may have met Servando, for a long time the malicious villain who would let loose a host of evils on the Church of Cordova, but who then was still a penniless boy, a servant in the church, whose work it was to cleanse the altars, sweep the steps, or act as beadle in the parish schools.

One day Eulogius returned home in better spirits than ever. He would no longer henceforth wander from school to school, seeking new light from constantly different masters. He had found the wise and holy one for whom his heart had longed.

This was Esperaindeo, an abbot of the city, to whose teaching he submitted himself with devotion and enthusiasm. In him he found all the experience of age and the virtue of an anchoret linked, not merely with a thorough knowledge of the Fathers, but with the enthusiasm of youth for the Faith and culture of former days and an intense hatred of all that the invaders had brought with them. No one more capable than he to mould the heart of the young Christian to whom God entrusted the defence of the Mozarabic Church! "He was a shining light of our times," Eulogius in later years wrote of him, "a most eloquent speaker, a distinguished doctor of divinity, a man venerable for his years, and my kindest master."

Esperaindeo taught in a clear and orthodox way in those days of terrible theological confusion. His manner of exposition was attractive and authoritative. His style — rapid, nervous, terse, and occasionally resembling that of St. Augustine — had a twofold charm: one was the number of Biblical texts with which he seasoned it and the other, the similes and comparisons which made clear the most abstract subjects that he touched. Eulogius gave him the name of *disertissimus*.

This gift of doctrinal exposition in a time of so much theological discussion and when the writings of the early Church remained unobtainable, was a great boon for the Christians of Cordova. But the Abbot Esperaindeo was moreover a national hero. When Alháquem so terribly avenged himself upon the conquered race, he had rushed to the fore in its defence. Not content with this act of daring, he wielded a skilled and intrepid pen against the religion of the victors. Beginning with the life of two martyrs of Seville, Adulphus and Juan, who suffered in the earlier part of the century, he aroused the conscience of his coreligionists against the absorbing power of Islam. But the fullest vent was given to the bitterness of his feelings in a violent diatribe against the superstitions of Mohammed.[1]

Eulogius has preserved a few paragraphs from this book by which we can judge of the rest. The author levels a firelock at the prophet, pursues him with his irony, discloses his wickedness, berates his blasphemies, and overwhelms him with the avalanche of his taunts. "It would be no paradise," he says, speaking of the Moslem heaven, "but a harem." Then he adds:

> I do not want to remember how that unclean dog yelped against the most Blessed Virgin, the Queen of the world, the holy, venerable Mother of our Lord and Saviour. O brainless head and devilish heart; O vase of perdition and dwelling of the infernal spirits! O tongue worthy of being cut off by a keen-edged knife! O chorus of Satan and organ of the devils! Who, O foul sewer, lake of perdition, abyss of iniquity, and sink of all the vices, so deprived you of all feeling that, not content with the perdition of so many nations immersed by you in the abyss of impurity, you dare, infamous slanderer, so to insult your Creator, soiling with the filth of your blasphemies that heavenly palace,

---

[1] The only treatises by the Abbot Esperaindeo that have been preserved are in the *Patrol. Lat.* of Migne, Vol. cxv, 959 sqq.

the tabernacle of the Holy Ghost, immaculate, most pure, most holy, and most chaste?

Apostasy from the Faith to seek temporal shelter in the unclean religion of the conquerors was the supreme temptation for the Christians of that day. The quotation given here suffices to show what must have been the lectures of this terrible ascetic in his efforts to stem that evil. Fortunately, the viziers of the alcazar and the alfaquíes of the mosques did not understand the language of the schools and books. Esperaindeo could tranquilly continue to form the minds of the new generation of apostles and combatants. Yet some of his violent diatribes seem to have reached the public. About the year 850, near the end of his life, Esperaindeo complained of the severe tribulations he endured:

> Annihilated by the darts of my enemies, overthrown by their persecutions, I suffer the wounds of pain and sorrow. My brain is inflamed and my soul is consumed. My mind, flooded with bitterness, is tossed to and fro like a skiff on a stormy sea.

We know nothing more of this great master of the Mozarabic teachers, but a calendar compiled a century later by Bishop Aben Zeid gives his name for May 7:

> On this day the Latins commemorate the feast of Esperaindeo and his martyrdom at Cordova. He is buried in the church of the suburb of the Tiraceros.

When Esperaindeo died, Eulogius, who now possessed great influence in the Church of Cordova, succeeded in stealthily carrying away the martyr's body and buried it in the church of San Zoilo, where he prayed every night. It was the disciple's last homage to the master whose words had awakened in his soul a conviction of the mission assigned him by Providence. The master's voice was silenced but he would be his successor.

His sacred relics rested beneath the altar, in one of the apses of the church. For his disciple they were a constant reminder of the ardent exhortations he had heard and they communicated to him in a mysterious manner the ardour of the martyr's faith. Eulogius, too, could now say with his instructor: "My mind, flooded with bitterness, is tossed to and fro like a skiff on the stormy ocean." But a supernatural strength came from the sepulchre of the man whose life had shown like a light in the midst of darkness.

CHAPTER IV

EULOGIUS AND ALVARO: *A FRIENDSHIP FOR LIFE*

HIS MASTER was not the only person whom Eulogius met in the school of Abbot Esperaindeo. Whenever he entered the lecture room his eyes fell on a handsome and aristocratic looking youth, absorbed in the abbot's instruction. His questions, answers, and whole attitude made plain to Eulogius that here was a young man who shared his own thirst for knowledge. The unknown student did not wear a cleric's garb, but evidently wished to learn all that clerics should know. One day the gaze of the two met and in a glance they understood each other. There and then, beneath the eyes of the aged teacher, took root in their souls one of those touching friendships that can be found among the saints alone.

"There," years after wrote this newly won friend, "I had the happiness of meeting him for the first time. There I started the most delightful of friendships and first knew the charm of his conversation." Surely, here was evident a special design of Divine Providence — *respectione divina*. God called them both for the same purpose. They would pass through the same struggles, triumph in the same fields of battle, and their names would be associated in life as their memories remain united in death.

The friend of Eulogius, Paulo Alvaro, was a worthy member of one of the most distinguished families of Cordova. His contemporaries named him Aurelius Flavius, which, with the Visigoths, was a royal title. In his veins there ran both Gothic and Hebrew blood. Though he was proud of that, he was prouder still of being a Christian. "I am descended from Abraham," he said, "and I glory in it; but I do not call myself a Jew, for I have received a new name from the mouth of God Himself."

The culture of letters was traditional in his family, as was hatred of Moslemism in the household of Eulogius. His father was distinguished not only by his rank but by a knowledge of Christianity and its doctrines before which even Abbot Esperaindeo bowed. Uncertain whether he had always treated correctly the great problems of the Trinity and the Incarnation, the humble abbot sent him the rough draft of his lectures, that his lay friend might "instruct and set him in peace (but secretly)," the abbot added discreetly, "so that his errors might not extend to the public." No doubt Esperaindeo's humility impressed this learned nobleman, and when he sought a teacher for his son, his choice fell on the abbot.

Alvaro's father was known for the purity of his faith. He had intervened in the theological dissensions started by Elipando of Toledo and brought many back to the right doctrine.[1]

Alvaro, who inherited his father's tastes, devoted himself enthusiastically to the study of philosophy, as it was then called, which included all that was taught in the schools of Cordova about grammar and theology. He and Eulogius became closer friends than ever. "We listened to the truth," he said, "and searched for the truth, maintaining our friendship until at last our youthful inexperience and presumption led us into depths that engulfed us. We, who could not have guided our skiff on the calm waters of a lake, launched out upon the rocky fury of the Euxine Sea."

Setting out for home when classes were done they amused themselves with what Alvaro called "the delightful game of

---

[1] See Esperaindeo's letter to Alvaro, *Patrol. Lat.*, Vol. cxv, 961.

discussion." They thus continued their study as they passed through the tortuous streets of the city, regardless of the peddlers crying their wares, the almuédanos shouting from the ramparts, the slaves who talked in groups with loud laughter and coarse words, the women whose eyes shot glances at them from above their ample veils, or the fanatic alfaquíes who flung at them their insolent jokes.

Sometimes Alvaro went with his friend to the suburb of the Tiraceros, and again Eulogius returned the visit. "We had our little doctrinal disputes," says Alvaro. Seated together near the fountain of the patio, with the scent of orange blossoms in the air, they argued with one another until nightfall, or until the head of the household, the former defender of the faith against the fatal errors of the Adoptionists,[2] came to decide the controversy.

But sometimes the question remained unsettled. Then, after parting, each took up his wax tablets, or parchment of leaf or linen — the paper which at the time was made in Játiba and Ceuta — and sturdily defended his own opinion in writing. Sometimes these letters, instead of continuing discussions on grammar and literature, contained rhythmical poems. "We wrote each other rhymed verses," Alvaro said, "and the practice was sweeter to us than honey and the honeycomb; every day we progressed until we had the audacity to try our wits, immature as they were, on Holy Scripture, composing whole treatises." Unfortunately these verses and other writings have not come down to us. As they grew older Eulogius and Alvaro agreed that it would be better to destroy them, as they did not wish their childish writings and intimate affections to be made public.

And yet enough is known to show the nobility of character

---

[2] The heresy which sought doctrinal compromises with the Mohammedans and therefore was the most serious temptation to the Mozarabic Christians.

possessed by the two lads. It has been said that the saints lose by degrees the finest natural feelings of the heart, but it would be difficult to meet anywhere with a more human and touching friendship than this, which had it existed in Greek or Roman days might well have been renowned. Unselfish, constant, and unclouded, the years could only strengthen it; persecutions and adversities never dimmed its lustre. It grew with their love of study and with their reading of the Holy Scriptures. Alvaro later wrote of it:

> True concord, disinterested love, and gratitude spring not from the need of perishable earthly goods, but from whatever is connected with the blessing of eternal reward. It is nourished on the banquets spread for it in Holy Scripture and flourishes on the love of sacred learning. It is this true friendship which knows no setting; which can shine forth in full brilliancy in the good alone; which death cannot terminate; which will stand out still more resplendent when this world disappears. Then, indeed, shall its wonderful sweetness surpass all that mortals here can well imagine.

After the death of Eulogius, this friendship remained a great consolation to Alvaro. Amid the troubles of old age, he was able to draw from it new courage by thinking of his friend and looking at the remaining mementoes of their friendship, that could never die. The best beloved of these was a parchment on which the priest of San Zoilo had revealed the sincerity of his fraternal love. Perhaps it recalled the tranquil days of their youth when together they listened to the teaching of the Abbot Esperaindeo.

To enhance the value of this present, Eulogius, an expert in calligraphy, had beautifully written it so that his friend might preserve it like a treasure in a magnificent silver frame. The letters were of gold on purple parchment, and each sentence — said Alvaro — was a pearl. One of them ran:

> Let not Alvaro be distinct from Eulogius, nor let the

love of Eulogius be set elsewhere than wholly in the heart of Alvaro!³

These relations between the two future defenders of the Church of Cordova give us an insight into their souls. They are revelations of a friendship in which the successes of the one were regarded by the other as his very own. They had the same cares, the same aims, and travelled through life by the same road, sharing one another's fortunes.

If in true friendship a person could speak of the greater advantage and profit of one over another, it might be said that in the present case the advantage rested with the privileged Alvaro. The two friends did not move together; one revolved around the other like a satellite about its planet; one received the light and movement transmitted by the other. This seems best to explain the relations between Alvaro and Eulogius. From Eulogius proceeded the initiative. His direction predominated; that of Alvaro is hardly apparent. He admired and delighted in his friend, longed for his company and pined for his presence when Eulogius was called away from Cordova. The latter, in return, consulted his friend in all the events of his life. It was Alvaro who threw him into the fray and persuaded him to publish his writings.

Alvaro seems never to have thought about himself. He lived for others and attended more to his brothers' interests than his own. One of the things he most admired in Eulogius was his love for the Church, while he, himself a fervent Christian above all things, had consecrated himself to her service with all the impetuosity of his character. He felt the stratagems of heresy and the persecutions of the infidels as though they had been directed against himself, and with a zeal that

---

³ "Ecce, Domine, testimonium tuum prae manibus habeo, litteris aureis et sententiarum gemmis depictum. . . . Non sit, inquis, alter Alvarus, quam Eulogius, nec alibi quam penes intima Alvari totus sit conlocatus amor Eulogii." (*Vita vel passio B. Martyris Eulogii, Esp. Sagr.* X, 558.)

even in old age kept its youthful ardour he defended the truth with all the weapons of his eloquence. Brilliant though this often was, it was naturally affected by the decadent literary style in vogue at Cordova in his day.

His religious campaigns brought him many enemies and sorrows. At the end of his life he was poor and had lost his former influence among the Christians of Cordova. Opposed to any kind of compromise with the enemies of the Church, he became an organizer of resistance. All the agitation of his time surged within the man's nature: his soul was a volcano in eruption. When affected by the shocks of this life he could not control the fire within him; he became angry and broke out with burning diatribes against the foes of the sacred principles that he had embraced with a divine enthusiasm. Roused by the force of events, he continued fighting with an astonishing stoical tenacity for the ideals of his youth. His enthusiasm for them never failed.

Alvaro was born to wrestle, and reminds us in some ways of Tertullian. He was a disputant and apologist like the great writer of Carthage. His heart boiled with all the restlessness of the Jewish race whose blood ran in his veins. Yet, though his character was passionate, he showed toward God and man a tenderness and amiability that charm us. He was a precursor of modern devotion characterised by love, so that in one of his last writings, the *Confessio,* in which his natural vehemence is lessened, he appeals with greater freedom than could have been expected in his era to the merciful heart of the heavenly Father.

The character of Eulogius was very different. Inclined by nature to the repose of the contemplative life, he found himself, he knew not how, dragged by the force of circumstances into the field of battle. But when once his sword was unsheathed, and he was recognised as the champion of persecuted truth, he continued fearlessly though prudently to defend his cause to the last hour, and so, consistently shed his blood for it. Two forces urged him on: the tradition of his house and his own conscience. Besides, Alvaro was at his side to uphold him in moments of misgiving and to communicate to him some of the enthusiasm that upheld his own courage. The character of Eulogius resembles that of Cyprian rather than Tertullian. In the golden age of the Visigoth monarchy he would have been another Eugenius of Toledo. He would have sought the quietude of a monk's cell, to spend his life in meditation and study, praising at one time the joys of friendship, at another the charm of nature or the bliss of solitude, and teaching the young what he had learnt in his former travels. Perhaps some prince might have obliged him to rule a diocese: if so, the bishop's palace would have been for him a second monastery.

Eulogius was above all contemplative. His soul was possessed by a profound longing for peace. His eyes turned to the mountains of the north, to the frontiers that separated Spain enslaved from that other Spain where God was served in peace, under the protection of Christian kings. His small body, like that of St. Eugenius, contained the same exquisite sensibility as the Toledan archbishop's. His heart gave echo to the most delicate impression, like a crystal goblet, but its resonance was drowned by the uproar of battle.

Eulogius' letters are serene and peaceful, especially when compared with Alvaro's. Nothing shows so well the character of the two writers. That the most tender and delicate affection could be felt by Eulogius is proved by the deep and silent love he felt for the virgin Flora. The feelings of a man and a saint could not be more closely united than they were in his heart. But, in accordance with the sacred duties of the priesthood, Eulogius was forced to cut down the flower that bloomed in his path. He did so joyfully. Strong as was his yearning for peace, his will was stronger still, for he seems to have renounced all satisfaction to obtain complete freedom from earthly ties.

When there sprang up around him an ardour for voluntary martyrdom, and he felt the conviction that God called him to maintain and kindle it, he calmly deliberated first, as though distrusting the voice within him, lest he should mistake his own for a divine locution. Alvaro was beside him to relieve him of his doubts and vacillation. Alvaro was the first to perceive that a glorious death is better than shameful servitude and a hypocritical protection that would end in the extermination of the Christianity it guarded. Eulogius realised this, and henceforth threw himself with his whole heart into the conflict, throwing all the weight of his sanctity and learning into the scales of the oppressed.

If it was long before he gave his life to consecrate the cause that he defended, it was because he was persuaded that the death of martyrs ought to be decreed by God Himself; and God chose to preserve him until the worst of the troubles had passed. He did nothing to accelerate it, but when the time came, he knew how to die like a hero. It is the character of the race throughout all the ages that reveals itself in the life of this great Spaniard. Devoted to an ideal, it knows how to serve it with heroic tenacity and calm enthusiasm while still keeping a firm grip on realities. It fights for the two titles of which it is most proud — that of a Christian and a Spaniard, which in this case were closely united. For them the martyr gave his life, not only lawfully but gloriously.

In former times, when Caesar with his victorious host encamped before Cordova, Escápula, one of its foremost citizens, prepared a banquet to which he invited his friends. He was robed in purple richly perfumed. After the feast, he bade a slave run a sword through his heart and throw his corpse into the Betis, that he might not fall, living or dead, into the hands of the conqueror. The death of Escápula was that of a pagan. Eulogius died the death of a Christian. But the temper of the race is ever the same.

Eulogius and Alvaro complemented one another. Providence destined them to carry out the same task, each in his own state of life.

CHAPTER V

A MARRIAGE AND AN *ORDINATION*

ALVARO PREPARED himself for the legal profession and remained a lawyer all his life.

On a certain Saturday morning at nine o'clock, a priest — perhaps it was his master, Esperaindeo — came to his house. Crossing the entrance he passed on to the nuptial chamber, sprinkled some grains of salt, and recited the liturgical prayers in which he asked the angels to descend on that home.

This was the preliminary ceremony of marriage in the Mozarabic rite, the blessing of the nuptial couch. Vespers were sung for the betrothed that same afternoon. On the next day Alvaro appeared at the porch of the church, accompanied by his father and friends, among whom Eulogius held the first rank. Shortly after, the bride's relative arrived, leading her in and presenting her to the priest. The air was scented with the fragrance of white orange blossoms as Alvaro advanced, carrying a goblet in which shone two rings. When the priest had blessed and sanctified the wedding rings in the name of Christ, Alvaro, taking up one of them, put it on the forefinger of the bride's right hand. She in turn took up the second ring and placed it on the outstretched finger of Alvaro. The wedded couple then gave each other the kiss of peace, which, as the rubric says, is the real testament.

But that was only the beginning of the ceremony. Alvaro and his betrothed now approached the chancel rails. The priest covered them with a cloth of symbolic colours — purple and white. He then recited the sacramental prayers, took a particle of the Bread of Love, which he had consecrated that same morning, divided it, and gave to the newly wedded pair the Holy Communion. This was followed by the nuptial blessing:

> May the Lord bless you by these words of my lips and unite your hearts by the perpetual bond of sincere love. May you enjoy abundance of temporal goods. May you bear children prudently and enjoy eternal bliss with your friends. Amen.

The time had now arrived for the priest to give the bride to her bridegroom. The choir sang the final antiphon, the happy company left the church, and rejoicings began. Old acquaintances congratulated the newly wedded pair, kissed and embraced them, while the children of the quarter broke out into a prolonged song that lasted until the bridegroom's house was reached. It was the wedding hymn sung by Spanish children in the times of St. Isidore.

> Marry the damsel: play on the oaten pipe,
> Make the glad lyre and flute sound forth a canticle.
> Voices with instruments bring forth sweet melody,
> Strike the strings jubilant.
> Sweep the harp joyfully, loud let the cymbals clash,
> *Nabla* and *zither* sound, dance the *tripudium*.
> Glory to God on high, King of the universe,
> Praise Him for ever, to ages unending.[1]

While the air still vibrated with the childish voices, Alvaro received other greetings that pleased him still better. Among the letters of congratulation was the nuptial poem by Eulogius, written in gold letters and composed in a form of rhythmic verse resembling that used at the time by the Princess Leodegunda, a nun living among the northern mountains.

---

[1] The *nabla* was a kind of harp of Phoenician origin, played with both hands; the *cinera* was probably the zither; the *tripudium* was a solemn religious dance.

> Pour forth plenteous streams of sweetest praise, like arpeggios from the flute, and let us give forth psalms of jubilee.
> Rejoice, blest families! Rejoice again and once again! Sing a song of smoothest rhythm.
> Let the skilled players of the zither draw near and fill the air with lovely harmonies in tetrachords.
> It is the festal hour. The cupbearers prepare in crystal vessels the sweetest nectar. A fitting goblet holds most delicious nectar that shall bring a glow to the cheeks of the bride.
> The singers enter the presence of the distinguished guests and consecrate to God, by whom we live, the first fruits of their lovely strains.
> Far from them be immodest songs with barbarous melodies. Let us praise the Lord while we eat and drink.
> Let the lyre and cymbals sound first for the King of kings, and for Him be the foremost hymn in the supper room.[2]

Alvaro was now occupied with family cares though he did not neglect study. Especially was he devoted to pondering over theological questions. He would be a lay theologian, like his father.

Alvaro's wife seems to have been a native of Seville. It was here, at all events, that her father lived and that Alvaro had many close friends. Among the new relatives acquired by him through his marriage was another literary man of whom we shall hear more and with whom he spent pleasant hours in discussing sacred learning and practising rhetoric. This was

---

[2] The beautiful ceremony of the Sacrament of Marriage in the Mozarabic liturgy, with its corresponding prayers and blessings, is given in the *Liber Ordinum*, p. 433 sqq The *Carmen de Nubentibus* is contained in the *Hymnario*, published by H. Gilson, from an old manuscript at Silos (London). The epithalamium of Leodegunda is to be found in the famous codices of Meyá, written in the tenth century, of which two copies exist in the library of the Academia de la Historia, Madrid.

his brother-in-law, Juan, a grammarian of Seville, who was very "Donatist," as it was called, that is, he was an enthusiastic partisan of Donatus, the famous author of a grammar called *Ars Minor*.

Meanwhile, Eulogius was preparing himself for his ordination as a priest. He was rather younger than Alvaro, and the canons strictly forbade the ordination to the priesthood of anyone under the age of thirty. Before this age had been reached, however, the rector of San Zoilo sent for him, and in the presence of the whole college asked whether he willingly embraced the life his mother had chosen for him. He was thus given the option of accepting or refusing to fulfill his parent's wishes. The granting of this liberty had been decreed by the second council of Toledo, and the Church of Spain observed what seems only natural to us, but what was then an exception in the Christian world. But Eulogius saw the will of God in the desire his parents had expressed regarding him. His own inclination drew him to the priesthood, that he might instruct others, save souls, and awaken men's consciences to the voice of God. Without hesitating, therefore, he answered in the affirmative to the question put to him by the rector of San Zoilo.

Alvaro was delighted at seeing him draw near the altar, although he felt his friend's fortitude as a reproach to himself, and exclaimed: "It is he, not I, who is happy, for I am wallowing in the pleasures of this world!"

Shortly after this Eulogius was ordained subdeacon. He was then nearing the twenty-eighth year, the period which St. Isidore considered as the beginning of youth, when he might be permitted to receive that Order which enabled him to wear the *orario*. This was an ample stole, hung over the left shoulder, so as not to impede the movements of preaching. Now at length free scope could be given to his evangelical zeal, to his quiet eloquence, his knowledge of the Holy Scriptures, and all the learning he had acquired during twenty years of devoted study. To the Christians of Cordova it must have appeared at times as if the happy days of St. Isidore and St. Julian had returned.[3]

At last the morning of his ordination to the priesthood arrived. The church of San Zoilo was decorated as for the greatest festivals. A rich Oriental tapestry covered the tomb of the martyr, and the walls of the church were similarly draped. Above the altar — a simple table covered with linen cloths, with neither retables, statues nor candles — glittered the crowns and the chests in which were kept the Body of the Lord, the relics of the saints, the *evangelaria,* and certain liturgical vessels. They were suspended from the roof, and made of the most precious metals: gold, silver, and plate, incrusted with glass and adorned with pearls. Brazen and glass candelabra of various shapes, resting on brackets, lighted the apse with their many flames. The crowd surged into the three Byzantine naves built by the good Bishop Agapius, and there patiently waited until the curtains of the *iconostasis,* which hid the splendour of the altar, should be withdrawn.

Two boys now appeared and drew back the great folds of the curtains, thus revealing the bishop seated on his throne of precious wood inlaid with ivory and decorated with silver nails and knobs. He wore the ample chasuble, with pointed hood, introduced by St. Torquatus and his companions who, we are told, received their consecration from the Apostles and were sent as missionaries to Spain.

Bishop Recafredo, who had come to ordain the young levite, was equally well acquainted with the ceremonies of the

---

[3] St. Julian, like St. Isidore, belonged to the seventh century. He was archbishop of Toledo and guided the Spanish Church from A.D. 680 to 690. He has not merely left us valuable writings, but has revised and developed the Mozarabic Liturgy used in Spain at that time.

Church and those of the Moslem Court. Eulogius was to meet him again under less pleasant circumstances. But now the two choirs of the clergy, with major and minor Orders, broke into a jubilant melody:

> What shall I offer to the Lord that is worthy? Wherewith shall I kneel before the high God? (Mich. 6:6.) Alleluia, alleluia.

Eulogius appeared, vested in a brilliant chasuble, embroidered by his mother and sisters with all their art and devotion. He was accompanied by the priests of San Zoilo and many others who had come to take part in the ceremony. They remained in the apse, before the altar, in a large circle, their hands pointing to the centre where Eulogius knelt on his right knee, deeply affected, overwhelmed, and abased. The bishop prayed:

> Sanctify, O Lord, this Thy servant Eulogius whom we consecrate by our hands to the honour of the priesthood. . . . May he be the teacher of the faithful, the guide of his subjects. May he hold inviolate the Catholic Faith and teach true salvation to all. May faith rule his life, chastity preside over his office, and peace crown his humility.[4]

While the bishop spoke, the priests repeated his prayer, appealing with extended hands for the grace he asked. Some further magnificent Mozarabic orations now followed. Then the bishop was silent, the circle of priests quietly dissolved. But Eulogius drew near the episcopal throne and there received the Sacramentary. It was the symbol of his new office. In a low voice Bishop Recafredo spoke a few words of prayer over him and so dismissed him with the kiss of peace. Would that this were never to have been withdrawn!

But the kiss of divine grace had marked his forehead, and

---

[4] The rite of the ordination of priests is given in the *Liber Ordinum*, pp. 54 sqq.

from among the crowd came forth a woman who gently pressed upon his brow her own warm mother's kiss, the kiss of an undying love. Then she wept for joy. Doña Isabel knew that, compared with the priesthood, the rank of his noble ancestors and all their senatorial line was but as dust and ashes.

CHAPTER VI

GLOWING *IDEALS* OF PRIESTLY LIFE

> I invoke Thee, Eternal and Omnipotent God, Father, Son, and Holy Ghost; God of justice, God of mercy, who seest all things; incomprehensible, unspeakable, eternal, everlasting, blessed God from whom all things come, to whom all are subject, and for whom they all exist. Cleanse my soul, remember not my sins, forgive my faults, erase my evil actions and crimes. Send Thy help to the weak, heal the sick, restore him who suffers. Give me a heart that fears, a mind that understands, eyes that see. Give me a spark of Thy wisdom to show me Thy ways and teach me to avoid the gulfs that the enemy opens in my path.[1]

THUS IN the Mozarabic liturgy, that splendid liturgy, so theological, so rich, and yet so human, began a Mass that the priest was to say for himself. No doubt it was one of the first said by St. Eulogius. It reveals the feeling of the newly ordained priest, but Alvaro has left us nothing on the subject. Possibly on the day of his ordination Eulogius may have felt tempted to take flight, like other saints, including St. Eugenius of Toledo. No doubt he remembered the words of his former teacher, Esperaindeo, preserved in an ancient manuscript:

> Tremble and fear, for you hold in your hands Christ's Body. Kindle your faith by the divine word: "Be ye clean, you that carry the vessels of the Lord" (Isa. 52:11). There is more in the Eucharist than in the vessels; there is the Word of God who enters it.[2]

---

[1] *Liber Ordinum*, p. 266.
[2] These words with others of the Abbot Esperaindeo, quoted later on, are taken from the *Samuélico* manuscript. They were published by P. Fidel Fitea, with a careful study of the codex, in Vol. V of *La Ciudad de Dios*.

Eulogius himself tells us how profound were his reverence and awe as he ascended the steps of the altar. Over a thousand years have passed since his words were written and yet they appeal to us with all the freshness of youthful conviction.

> O my Lord God, I fear because of my misdeeds! My crimes torment me, and though I still delay amending them, they are ever before my eyes. I see how monstrous they are, I think of the judgment to come, and feel beforehand the punishment they deserve. I hardly dare look at the heavens, overwhelmed as I am by my burdened conscience.
>
> Yet it pleases Thee to make use of my tongue, as though it were fit to take part in the heavenly Sacraments. I have dared to touch that which is most sublime, I, poor and contemptible! I have handled what is pure, though I am impurity itself, and weighed down by iniquity, I have ventured to enter the Holy of Holies. Yet I have done this, not borne up by pride, but realising my abjection and humiliation, filled with vehement desire of earning the rewards and the intercession of the saints. Thou knowest this, O Lord.[3]

The same misgivings beset him in public. He wished to preach, but the remembrance of his sins choked him. What were his sins? Paulo Alvaro who knew all his secrets was ignorant of them; he could only say that: "All Eulogius' actions were straightforward; the love all showed him testified to his goodness, humility, and charity; his daily endeavour was to draw nearer heaven, while the burden of his body wearied him."

Eulogius said to the Christians of Cordova: "It is our duty to preach; it is yours to listen. That I live a disordered life and crawl slothfully in the mire gives you no right to despise the word of God." Remembering the great work of canalisa-

---

[3] These beautiful words are contained in the prayer with which St. Eulogius ends the second volume of his *Memorial of the Martyrs*. Those that follow are from the first pages of the same work.

tion then being carried out by Abderrahmán to supply the city with water from the sierra, he continued: "Do you not see how lead serves the emperors of the world to bring water to their palaces? And here in the church beside the vessels of gold and silver, decorated with cameos, turquoises, and amethysts, are earthen vessels that must not be despised."

The citizens enjoyed listening to such language. They delighted to look on his radiant face. And, to say the truth, Eulogius knew how to speak words that came home to their hearts and influenced their lives. In a few lines he has traced for us the plan of his sermons: "Cry out, saith the Lord, rebuke the people for breaking the divine law; set before their eyes the severe judgment due to sinners; treat of repentance, of the certitude of pardon, of trust in God."

In Cordova the number of believers was constantly growing less. Moslem sensuality enervated Christians who were weak of faith. The fear of persecution made cowards of men. Eulogius foresaw a dark future for the Church and resisted the evil with all his might. "I will not be silent," he exclaimed, "I will be like a dog that never tires of defending his master's interests; that only barks and attacks the more when he is struck and hurt."

Alvaro Paulo speaks of his burning eloquence, his fine diction, his brilliant learning. This learning was, above all, the knowledge of Holy Writ. For Eulogius, Holy Scripture held the first place. He had studied it eagerly from childhood, as he studied it still. Whenever he visited Alvaro, it was to discuss the Scriptures, and together they would practice the golden advice given them by their teacher Esperaindeo:

> Let him who reads the Bible know that the letter is the body that contains the spirit. Without the letter, which is the body, the spirit cannot be understood. But if, while reading the letter you cannot attain to its spirit, then pray, saying: "Our Father, who art in heaven, give us this day our daily bread." Pray until you understand, and when

you do, go to the Fathers and ancients to see whether it is the spirit of God or no, and do not preach it until you have so proved it. Remember how deserving of awe is the Divine Word you receive in Holy Communion. If a particle falls from the priest's hands, all present are thunderstruck, and give place that the divine particle may be searched for and restored to the paten, for the Eucharist is the Body of Christ. "Eucharist" signifies grace, and the Gospel is also called grace. Thus, though you understand the Gospel, you may have let fall some particle, and you must ask God to show it to you.

With such religious reverence these two disciples of the venerable abbot investigated the "Divine Library," as the Scriptures were called. Eulogius spent whole nights in prayer, Alvaro tells us, keeping his vigils in the church of San Zoilo. His studies were followed by long and fervent meditations, and these by austere fasts and severe penances, so carrying out his master's aphorism: "If you wish your prayer to fly to God, give it two wings: fasting and alms."

Though naturally inclined to the delights of the contemplative life, Eulogius did not forget that he had received the grace of ordination for the sake of others. With the fire of contemplation there burnt in his heart a divine zeal "by which he drew men forth from their miseries to raise them to the kingdom of light."

Abstractos barathro sublimat aethere. Simple words these, that explain how Eulogius understood the laborious and marvellous alchemy performed by the sacerdotal ministry: to help souls, to withdraw them from their despondency, to uplift them, to give them light, love, and joy! Behold the duty of the priest of God!

Sometimes the parishioners of San Zoilo came to him with their lawsuits and quarrels. The *Fuero Juzgo* gave priests and bishops a social prestige that the Arabs had not yet completely uprooted. They were, by their office, the judges for all difficulties that might arise in their parish or diocese, and the civil power recognised their decisions.

Alvaro speaks of his friend's prudence as a judge. In judging and preaching, in rebuking hardened sinners, and in drawing chosen souls to a more narrow way, Eulogius was always courteous, having *affabilitatem usualem officii,* as one who saw in men the image of God, keeping all his harshness for the infidels, and for the Pharisees who were their accomplices, who sought to mislead and cause the loss of souls. For him, to be a priest meant self-surrender, and his whole life was a gift: first by action and speech, later on by struggle, and ultimately by the oblation of his life.

This explains his power of attracting his contemporaries and of drawing so many to the very heights of sacrifice.

The feeling of his unworthiness ceaselessly tormented him. Neither long hours of prayer, fasts, nor macerations contented him. He felt within him the ardours of youth and his memory was disturbed by the thought of certain levities of his past life. In order to overcome the former and atone for the latter, he wished to make a pilgrimage on foot to Rome, the city of the martyrs and the centre of the Faith, the home of his filial love.

But in those days a journey from Andalusia to Rome was all but impossible. Even in time of the Catholic kings of Toledo, correspondence with Rome had been very difficult. Not until ten years after the event did Pope St. Gregory learn that the Visigoths had been converted to the Catholic Faith. Isolated by nature, by politics; isolated to a certain extent by national pride, the Church of Spain had now further fallen into the isolation of servitude.

Besides that, the roads were almost impassable. The Arab chiefs, engaged in fighting one another, had filled the country with military stations that were centres of robbery and disorder. Several cities persisted in refusing to acknowledge the emir's authority. Beyond Saragossa the roads became impassable. Anarchy stalked through the land. By sea there was peril of tempests and pirates; and over the land extended the ferocity of the turbulent foreign foe.

His friends set these difficulties before the young priest in the most vivid colours, but they could not shake his decision. His mother wept and called him an undutiful son, his sisters hung round his neck, Alvaro told him he was mad, and the clergy of San Zoilo alleged his duty to the parish. They were almost forced to resort to violence. "We all opposed this plan and at last succeeded in stopping but not in convincing him," said Alvaro, who had been greatly distressed at his friend's resolution.

Eulogius surrendered, but from time to time entered into prolonged retirement when this was possible for him. A longing for solitude beset him continually. Each day he felt called more strongly by its mysterious, subtle voice. It was the symptom of the sacred, delicious restlessness that often occurs unexpectedly in great souls. Two contrary forces struggled for the mastery and tormented him. He wished to be both in his parish and in a monastery, to save souls and be alone with God. At last he succeeded in combining the two and in enjoying the divine blessings of the one without quenching the sacred ambition of the other. He entered into retreat and then returned to "adorn the church with his teaching." He trampled on this world's ways and so took up anew his life of priestly charity and apostolic conquests.

CHAPTER VII

MOZARABIC MONASTICISM: A *ROMANCE* OF SANCTITY

EULOGIUS WAS not alone in feeling within himself spiritual longings. Natural causes, in fact, may at times contribute no little to a desire for retirement from worldly affairs, for this is not necessarily supernatural and rooted in God, as was the longing of Eulogius.

Great difficulties and agitations weary individuals as they do the people. In the middle of the ninth century Spanish souls needed rest and solitude. On the fluctuations of the conquest had followed the horrors of the rebellion, to be succeeded by a few years of quiet, which in reality were little more than a truce. In the meantime Christians had witnessed the final destruction of all their hopes, the depletion of their riches, and the complete demolition of all that could satisfy temporal ambition. Well, indeed, might they realise the nothingness of earthly things.

But even the Moslems themselves, in many instances, became tired of war and slaughter. Some there were who sought refuge in meditation and asceticism. Particularly was this noticeable in Cordova as early as the time of Alháquem I.

Islamism was certainly not favourable to the development of monasticism in its followers. The Koran never mentions monks except to abuse them. It proceeds further and issues the express prohibition: "Let there be no monkhood in Islam." The prophet of war and polygamy could not speak otherwise.

Yet the Moslems were impressed by the wonderful examples

given by the Christian ascetics, and even during the time of St. Eulogius there were, in Cordova, a multitude of devout men who strove to realise under Mohammed's law the ascetic principles springing forth from Christianity. Some fled from cities to fast and keep vigil more freely, others sought mortification in pilgrimages, still others divided their goods among the poor and lived in extreme poverty. Extraordinary instances of chastity and startling penances are recounted. Some men passed their lives beside the mosque or marabouts. These were the religious sages. As in earlier days Eulogius and Alvaro had together prolonged their vigils to meditate on the Holy Scriptures or recite the psalms, so these men forewent sleep, endeavouring to read through, in the course of the night, the entire Koran.

During the youth of Eulogius some of the judges of Cordova were model ascetics. Mansur ben Mohammed, son of the famous Aben Baxir who scandalised good Mussulmen by his magnificent apparel, used to knead his own bread every day and take it to the oven to be cooked. Jahya ben Maamar, his successor as judge, lived in the strictest poverty. All the furniture of his house consisted of a wretched heap of straw, a cup, a pitcher, a porringer, a rush mat, and a large earthen jar, in which he used to put flour to give to the poor when his office was done.

Many of these ascetics acquired the outward semblance only of Christian monks. The virtue of humility was the last thing they learnt.

Perhaps, while Eulogius was young, he heard of Abulachanas, who lived enclosed in a cell near the city. People talked of his rigorous fasts, which he broke only three times during the month of Ramadán. The prince admired him, and when passing along the road to Almodovar used to rein in his horse to salute the hermit. One day he merely waved his riding whip. The ascetic, who was on the flat roof of his hut, answered by shaking a cord he held in his hand. "He saluted me with his whip," he said afterwards disdainfully to his friends, "and I answered with the rope."[1]

This eagerness for asceticism in Islam was but an echo of Spanish monasticism, which flourished surprisingly at that time in Cordova. People felt a longing for perfection. Whole families of the highest rank relinquished their riches and enclosed themselves in monasteries. Strangers who had come to the city to study in its schools, felt the contagion of the universal enthusiasm. Monasteries sprang up in Cordova and its suburbs as though by magic. Incidentally, in the chronicles of that age, writers mention a few names that recall the most brilliant heroism. With what generous enthusiasm did the Church of Cordova face suffering and death!

On the side of the river opposite the busy city life rose the monastery of San Cristóbal, to which the Christians resorted on the tenth of July. It was erected in the choicest part of the town, "In a marvellous garden," as St. Eulogius described the scene. There the magnates had their country houses, the sick their hospitals, and Nazar, the eunuch, his *almunia*. The numerous Mozarabs of the suburb of Mediodía, which had risen from its ashes since the slaughter of Alháquem, went to San Cristóbal to receive the monks' blessing and hear them chant the psalms.

In the south, but still on the plain, stood the abbey of San Ginés, and near it arose two more convents: one of monks, dedicated to St. Martin; the other of nuns, under the patronage of Saint Eulalia. Campiña and Assahla were rich in monasteries and churches. To the north and east of Cordova rose the sierra in undulous delicate curves, filled with sanc-

---

[1] On the religious atmosphere of Islam in Spain during the ninth century, see Asín Palacios' work entitled: *Abenmasarra y su escuela. Orígenes de la filosofía hispanomusulmana.* Madrid, 1914.

tuaries and populated by cenobites. The words of a modern poet might here have found their application:

> O'er the beauteous sierra,
>   On the heights above,
> Nestled mid the rocks are dwellings,
>   Milk-white as a dove.
>
> There the lemons shed their odours,
>   Scent the mountain air,
> Rosemary and orange blossoms
>   Yield their perfumes rare.
>
> There the lark its song is trilling
>   High the clouds above;
> There upon the cross, Christ hanging,
>   Stretches arms of love.
>
> There hearts by the world deluded
>   Find oblivion's balm;
> There the hermits chant devoutly
>   Prayer and praise and psalm.

The hermits dwelt in the caves of the mountain, in wattle huts, forming white hermitages. They lived absorbed in their penances and meditations. Some were closed up in their hovels, some wore iron plates fastened to their bodies, others devoted themselves to the study of the Holy Scriptures or passed the days and nights bent over their parchments, making copies of the writings of past ages.

> Sailing o'er the sacred billows,
>   For the port they steer:
> Blessed caravan that passes
>   Through earth's desert drear.

The cenobites dwelt near the hermitages and beside these rose the monasteries — the great monastic beehives, where hundreds of monks served God under the austere rules of the ancient Visigoth reformers. In the west stood the abbey of Cuteclarense, where a community of nuns commemorated by day and night the glories of Mary. Farther up the mountain lay hidden among the cliffs the monastery of San Félix de Froniano, and in the very heart of the Sierra Morena, concealed between rocks and precipices, dwelt the monks of San Justo and San Pastor,[2] a day's journey from Cordova.

Somewhat farther on, perched on the heights like an eagle's aerie, was the abbey of San Zoilo of Armelata, where the monastic cells can still be seen. In the midst of this terrifying solitude two compensations were to be found: the workers dwelt close to the heaven above them, and below ran the Guadalmelata plentiful with glinting trout. But the two most famous monasteries of all were those of Tabanense and of San Salvador de Peñamelaria, both near the Septentrión, and both possessed of that powerful attraction which the mountain heights always hold for contemplative souls. Here most gently the caressing murmur of impenetrable woodlands blended with the psalms of the anchorets.

It was in these sacred fortresses that Eulogius took refuge from the iniquity of the city which grew more sensual and opulent every day and constantly flaunted before his eyes the scandals of its luxurious enjoyments. These he abhorred and sought the society and aid of the saintly athletes whose lives he admired and envied. He climbed the mountains of Roxana to visit his kinsman, the monk Cristóbal, who, though still young, gave evidence of the greatest sanctity. He visited the monastery of San Cristóbal to kiss, through the little window, the fetters of Habentius, the recluse, a wonderful old man who voluntarily spent his life in chains, thus learning to bear those wherewith later Abderrahmán's myrmidons would load him. Nor did Eulogius forego the delicious trout caught by

---

[2] Justus and Pastor were two Christian boys, aged thirteen and nine years respectively, who under Diocletian were scourged and beheaded by order of the merciless prefect, Dacianus, at Alcalá, Spain, about A.D. 304.

the monks of San Zoilo in the Armelata. He listened to the melodious chanting of the nuns in their convents of Santa Maria and San Eulalia, and enjoyed the sweetness of the honey left by the wild bees in the rocks of San Salvador. From this, in fact, the place derived its name of Peñamelaria.

But nothing so charmed him as the melodies that rose to heaven from the spacious woods of Tabanense, when the army of monks and nuns together toiled in "the work of God." There Eulogius met the venerable Martin; Columba, the contemplative virgin; Digna, the humble servant in God's house; Isabel, the "strong woman," who formed grand characters under her rule; Isaac, the valiant monk who opened the path for martyrdom; and many other noble, indomitable spirits whose society inspired him with courage. So it was that Eulogius felt a passionate love for the contemplative religious life. To quote the words of his biographer: "His heart clove to the solitary rocks and was held a captive beneath the leafy shades."

Only when duty called him back to the city did he descend, *gemens et anxius,* "sad and anxious," as Alvaro says. How often, as he approached its bustling suburbs and passed by its palms and orange trees, must he have felt what the poet of Cordova so finely expressed:

> Heavy weigh the weary burdens,
>   Caused by worldly cares,
> On a soul that from the valley
>   To the summit dares.
>
> There the monks with soul and body
>   Prayer and labour blend,
> But how broad the footpath widens
>   Should that soul descend!

The monks, too, felt their parting with Eulogius. They loved to look upon his kind face; to see in his eyes the innocence that shone from them; and more than all else, to admire the humility of one who spoke so wisely. In his turn, he told them what he had learnt from the divine and human writings, enabling them to share after their own manner in the feast that his priestly zeal spread for the Christians of Cordova.

His love for the monastic life was providential as it enabled him to prepare souls for the coming struggle and so to supply the finest wheat for martyrdom. Many of the anchorets who looked forward to his coming were his disciples. He had persuaded them to leave the world, for, as Alvaro says in his hymn to Eulogius, he taught men to despise riches. Later on, all the ascetics of Cordova became his followers and friends.

Besides this, as he was learned in monastic law, he perceived the deficiencies, due to ignorance rather than lack of good will, which existed in the Cordovan monasteries, and strove to remedy them by establishing new rules. He was a reformer of Mozarabic monasticism, a reorganiser of communities which had often been started without premeditation.

Not that Cordova lacked a monastic tradition. As we know, there had been formerly a large abbey connected with the church of San Zoilo. Nor was that the only one. Probably, when Eulogius visited the monastery of Armelata, he went a few miles farther into the midst of the mountains and reached the town now known by the Moorish name of Alcaracejos. Wearied by the long walk, he may have rested beneath the olives on the hill which still bears the monastic name of El Germen, "the Germ." The sight must have saddened him. It recalled the time when beautiful basilicas were seen in Spain; now nothing remained but their ruins.

In remote ages there must have been here a *vexilatio,* or Roman garrison, whose soldiers worshipped Jupiter. Even now votive altars exist with the names of legionaries on them. Later on, the temple of the father of the gods served as a quarry to build a church and monastery adjoining it. Time has disclosed the tombs and names of many who served God there — Asper, Columba, Uguerico, Eustadia. We know nothing of them save that they were servants of Christ, lived there for a certain number of years, and slept in peace. Eustadia's epitaph, however, is less laconic:

> Eustadia, a virgin and servant of Christ, lived in this world, preserving the chastity of her body, for thirty-six years, more or less. Joyfully mounting to the courts of heaven, she left her body to rest in this tomb, on November 21, in the year 649.

This was rather later than the time of St. Isidore, the Doctor of Spain. But war disturbed this holy peace, the war of the invaders. It was not only in the church of San Acisclo that the Christians of Cordova resisted. Traces of the fray are still to be seen here. On the fine pavement, until a short time ago, lay the bodies that were buried beneath the roof which had been thrown down by the violence of the flames and machines of war. Near the skeletons, blackened by the fire, lay broken columns, fine jasper capitals, fretted cornices, square tiles, liturgical vessels of various materials, ornaments of precious metal with jewels set in roughly chased gold.[3]

The monks either died or fled. During the disturbed years of Moorish occupation it was impossible to restore abbeys that had been abandoned, so the monastic tradition was lost. This explains what was the work done by St. Eulogius in the religious houses of his time. The new monasteries had sprung up suddenly in consequence of the ascetic enthusiasm of that generation. A lady of high birth or a powerful magnate, inflamed with religious ardour, would draw after them a number of friends and members of their household. Men and women might simply transform their own dwelling into a monastery, and so a community was founded.

The two most famous abbeys of Cordova had arisen in this

---

[3] P. Fidel Fita wrote of this most interesting monastic basilica which has been recently discovered in the *Boletín de la R. A. de la Historia*, Vol. 65, pp. 563-572.

way. Their founders, friends of Eulogius, asked him to direct them in their new life. In this, as in his other activities, the mission of Eulogius was to restore former practices. A strong and thorough reformer of Christian life, of patriotism, of ancient poetic and literary traditions, he was called upon to retie the thread that bound the Mozarabic monks to the Visigoths.

No doubt he had recourse in this work to the encyclopedia of St. Isidore, rich in instructions on the religious life. St. Isidore had written his Rule for the monks who lived on the banks of the Guadalquivir, but it was intended for beginners and did not satisfy the holy enthusiasm felt by the Mozarabs. Eulogius rather chose as his guide St. Fructuosus,[4] the Castilian, who during the seventh century went through the Peninsula, sowing his monasteries everywhere, until they formed a long chain extending from Contábrico to the Isle of Cádiz.

From the Rule, *Regula Communis,* of St. Fructuosus, we can best learn of the life of those times, which differs no little from our modern practices. He legislated for double monasteries, such as those of the best known abbeys of Cordova. Men and women shared them, living under the same roof though separated by thick walls. The women could communicate with outsiders through a little window only. An abbot held supreme command over both communities. Very young children lived on both sides, but the Rule had provided against all abuses. Thus St. Fructuosus decreed:

> When anyone enters with his wife, and little children under the age of seven, the holy rule decrees that parents and children shall leave it to the abbot to arrange what

---

[4] A Visigoth prince who on retiring from the world, sold his goods, giving part to the poor and devoting the rest to the building of monasteries He was made archbishop of Braga in 656 and died in 665, having been stretched on ashes before the altar, as he requested that he might so yield up his soul to God. (Translator.)

they are to do. Out of compassion for the little ones of so tender an age, we allow them to go from their father to their mother whenever they please.... Older persons are completely separated, so that except in the prayers and chants their voices may not mingle. If a monk is found talking to a nun, he shall receive a hundred strokes.

St. Fructuosus was a resolute, severe Goth. Scourging, hair shirts, fasts, imprisonment, fetters, were in his eyes the best means of curing delinquents. He held a very strong idea of obedience:

> No one may extract a thorn from his body without the blessing of the superior; nor cut his nails without permission from the head of the monastery; nor may anyone put down the bundle of faggots he bears on his shoulders until he has received a blessing from the ancient.

The Divine Office of St. Fructuosus,[5] the same as that preserved in the monastic breviaries of the Mozarabic rite, comprised a number of psalms and hours that are not found in any other liturgy, yet they allowed for many hours of out-of-door labour. The food was austere: herbs and vegetables, fish on feast days, with a little wine, of which a double quantity was served on Saturdays and Sundays. Sleep was short and interrupted. The first night hour, from six to eight, was sanctified by a long service of prayers and psalms.

> The brethren shall then disperse, forgiving one another their negligences and dislikes. Being now united in perfect peace, they shall go to their beds, singing three psalms and reciting the Creed, so that if the soul of any one of them leaves his body that night, he can present to God a pure faith and clean conscience.

The *Miserere* was then recited and the monks could sleep

---

[5] Silos possesses a *Breviarum Antiquissimum*, written in the ninth century, in which the Divine Office is regulated in agreement with the Rule of St. Fructuosus. This Rule is to be found in the *Patrol. Lat.*, Migne, Vol. 87.

tranquilly. Meanwhile the *vigiliario* watched the stars, or if it rained, consulted his sand hourglass. Shortly before twelve he interrupted the monk's sleep to keep the second vigil with twelve psalms. This was followed by another brief slumber, broken by a continuation of the midnight Office: twelve psalms, four responsories, a reading from Holy Scripture, a sermon by the abbot, more or less lengthy according to the preacher's eloquence, followed by another twelve psalms as at the beginning. The brethren then took their third sleep, which was cut short by the cocks of the monastery. Thus ended the monastic night.

It ended thus for Eulogius very often. His body must have felt weary, but his soul must have been very keen and fresh to begin the new day. And it is the soul that matters. He must have missed the wooden rattle of the *vigilario* when the tyranny of daily duty held him prisoner in his cell in the suburb of the Tiraceros. But his nights did not vary greatly from those of the monastery. When he left San Zoilo, he opened the large codex with gilt initials, read, meditated, or copied. The nightwatch patrolled the streets gabbling unintelligible words. Eulogius looked out of the window as Eugenius of Toledo used to do. The hours had passed unobserved. The Dog Star shone in the east and the Scorpion had set in the west. The two Ursi gleamed over the sierra. The monks there were singing the *mesonictio*. Eulogius suppressed a sigh.

> On the crest the cross is stationed,
>   High its summits soar!
> Thence how short the path to heaven;
>   'Twere but one step more!

CHAPTER VIII

ARDENT SEARCHERS AFTER *TRUTH*

WHILE TREATING of the religious disputes that disturbed the early days of the Mozarabic Church, we must not omit the mention of an important theological misjudgment, that should not surprise us if we bear in mind the disordered state of the country.

The wonder is that truth managed to survive after a century and a half of Mussulman rule. A thousand opposing forces strove to attack and overthrow it. On one hand, we find the unitarian tendencies of Islam; on the other, the remains of that former Gothic heresy, Arianism; while paganism still survived to some extent among the country folk. During the first century of Arabian rule, Sabellian heresy combined with Mohammedanism had arisen. Besides this attempt to harmonise Christianity with the Moslem faith, fanatics appeared upon the scene who claimed to be the Messias; ignorant, foolish teachers who strove to pervert others more silly than themselves. Then came the well-known theological case of Elipando of Toledo and Félix of Urgel, who, crossing the frontiers, kept the more learned men of Charlemagne's dominions hard at work.

The orthodox were shocked and disturbed at the rage for discussion. Elipando fell from the Faith after combatting the errors of Migecio with the best will in the world. Egila, Bishop of Iliberis, became a Migecian after having been approved and praised by the Pope. On the other hand, there were few books in which to search for the truth, since these had been burnt by the invaders or carried by the fugitives to the mountains of Asturias, France, or the banks of the Rhine.

The splendid library of liturgical volumes composed by the Spanish Visigoths bore magnificent evidence of the faith and devotion of these men, but was an object of misgiving to many because the authors of the Adoptionist campaign believed that their own errors were confirmed in the fine prayers contained in them, of which the people were justly proud. The same cause had impaired the authority of the Spanish theologians of the seventh century, whose writings formed the nucleus of the national libraries of the country.

This partly explains the inaction regarding theology and the liturgy which followed the brilliant epoch of Isidore and Ildephonsus.[1] The Spanish clergy considered that under these circumstances, purity of doctrine could only be preserved by blind adhesion to a traditional standard, expressed in the Nicene Creed, the work of a Spanish prelate; and in the Creed of St. Athanasius, a genuine, clear, and authoritative summary of learned Spanish theology.

To preserve these ancient treasures without changing or touching them was the sole care of the Mozarabic Christians. They had a profound distrust of reason on account of its dangers. While on the other side of the Pyrenees that same race took part in the difficult disputes concerning transubstantiation, predestination and free will, searching into the psychological and human aspect of the question, in Spain, ecclesiastical science confined itself to a positive, antiphilosophical view. It was understood, indeed, that we must be ready to give an account of our faith, as St. Eulogius said, but this presupposes a knowledge of Holy Scripture and tradition. Esperaindeo and his disciples had learned the sacred writings

---

[1] St. Ildephonsus, like St. Isidore, belonged to the glorious seventh century in Spain. Abbot of Agli and later consecrated bishop, in 657, he gave us among other works a treatise on *The Spotless Virginity of the Mother of God* and a study on *Ecclesiastical Writers*. (Translator.)

almost by heart, and with them the commentaries made by the Fathers best known in Spain: St. Augustine, St. Jerome, St. Gregory the Great, St. Isidore, St. Ildephonsus, and St. Julian. But the Bible, though interpreted by these famous doctors of the Church, yet studied without subtle dialectics or daring metaphysics, left them very hesitant as to their own understanding of it.

A certain scrupulosity, mingled with distrust in themselves, is noticeable in the prudence recommended by Abbot Esperaindeo. He advised his disciples to study Holy Scripture for some time; then, in order to understand it, to meditate and pray for a long while. Having learnt during prayer the meaning of the text, they must compare it with the writings of the Fathers and trustworthy teachers. Only after this long process should the priest instruct or preach. It was best to keep silence on certain matters. Said the abbot speaking of the mystery of the Incarnation:

> It is useless to try to explain our Lord's nativity. The Evangelists themselves could not do so fully, though inspired by the Holy Ghost. Therefore silence is best. It is better to believe the simple meaning of the words than to lose time in searching and writing about them. We believe in the Father, the Son, and the Holy Ghost, three Persons and one God. As for the Immaculate Son of the Virgin and why, after His birth, He chose to suffer, we are forbidden to meditate upon or discuss it; blind faith is here our sole attitude. And if we are to set a limit to our thoughts on such subjects, how much more should we control the language of our pen?[2]

Docile to his master's teaching, Eulogius adopted his motto: "Believe and keep silence," and it was only when impelled by a strong impulse of divine charity, as he says, that he decided to break silence. Rarely did anyone ever wield the pen with a greater regard for truth. It is difficult to be the leading

---

[2] Letter from Esperaindeo to Alvaro: Migne, *Patrol. Lat.*, cxv, 961.

actor in an event and at the same time its impartial historian, yet St. Eulogius filled both roles. His books combine the enthusiasm of one who in the conflict pauses to write with a convincing sincerity of the struggle in which he himself is engaged.

Addressing our Divine Lord he says:

> If I speak falsely art not Thou the Witness of my dishonesty? If I pervert the truth, am I not beheld by Thee? Thou seest all, dost investigate all. Thou knowest all secrets and whatsoever is hidden, since all things are present to Thee. Past and future are written in the book of Thy wisdom. To Thee are known all the thoughts that arise in us by the impulse of Thine inspiration and all that our mind brings forth through divine grace. Known to Thee are our boasts when egged on by the spur of vainglory and our weakness when involuntarily we slip and fall.

"Flawless truth," he says elsewhere, stating a principle of philosophy, "walks with a firm step, however homely her clothing; falsehood, though richly adorned, cannot stand for long. Nor would Christ allow the defender of truth to go unrewarded, but the liar is guilty of homicide."[3]

But it was divine truth that this conscientious champion cared for chiefly. He was tormented by the fear of erring from the Faith, and when he decided to write a book he did not dare to publish it without the censorship of Alvaro, his master and safe guide in matters of faith. "Perhaps," he says at the end of the *Apologético de los Mártires,* "some error contrary to the Faith may have slipped into this book, but God will forgive me through your intercession, O glorious saints, who know my heart is innocent! I am aware that even prudent men often speak incorrectly though their souls are far from a shadow of error."

An even more touching prayer stands at the end of Volume II of *The Memorial of the Saints.* It is the strongest evidence

---
[3] *Vida de Santa Flora,* Prologue.

of the love of truth which ever possessed the soul of St. Eulogius and of the fear inspired in it by the limitations of human reason.

> I turn to Thee, O my Lord and my God, oppressed by my sin, full of crimes and iniquities, begging Thee to look down from the throne of Thy unspeakable mercy and cleanse my heart, freeing it that it may be at liberty to confess and praise Thee. Purify this little work of mine, lest by stratagem, against my will, the tempter may have sown his tares in it. Purify, cleanse, sanctify it. Root up all that might suggest error, all unseemly and unfitting language, all that is unworthy of Thee or offends Thy holy will or lacks unction and devotion, that so this work may be acceptable in Thy presence and pleasing to Thy holy angels.

These words reveal the aim of the saint in all his writings. Though personal misgivings and timidity prevented him from joining in the theological controversies of his day, yet to them is chiefly due the charm of simplicity as well as the perfect truth and justice always characteristic of his works.

His friend Alvaro saw things in a very different light. He must often have reproached Eulogius for his excessive prudence and have playfully told him that he was a coward. Though not a priest, Alvaro had all a priest's zeal, and there was no religious question of his time on which he did not state his opinion. He loved to argue on theology with friends and foes, in speech or writing, and it was he who urged both Abbot Esperaindeo and Eulogius on to do battle. He was right in saying: "Wordily I begin, continue, and end the discussions," *et primus, et mediator, et novissimus scriptor accedo verbosus*. It was his restless spirit that engaged him in these disputes in which he did not always prove himself overcompetent.

Nothing could be more interesting, as showing the spirit of the times in which Eulogius lived, than these discussions in which he and Alvaro mutually engaged. As the latter remarked, their arguments only increased their love for each other, "learned discussions are the delight of future generations; foolish quarrels only shock them."

Since both lived at Cordova no record, by way of letters, remains of these discussions. From Alvaro's letters to his brother-in-law, the grammarian of Seville, we know, however, the subject of their arguments.

Preoccupied one day with the doctrine of the origin of the soul, as treated by the ancient doctors of the Church, Alvaro consulted Eulogius, who cited the Councils and holy Fathers. Of the five doctrines familiar to the theologians of Cordova, one only is actually acceptable: that of the soul's creation by God. Alvaro thus stated it in his own way:

> That is our belief and the most correct one. God daily creates human souls and sends them into bodies, according to the Gospel: "My Father worketh until now; and I work" (John 5:17).

But in this creationist doctrine Alvaro saw the same difficulties St. Augustine recognised. How explain original sin, if the soul came from God? Which part of man received the grace of baptism, the body or the soul? If, as seemed more natural to him, it was the body, since it was that which descended from our first parents, why were the dead not baptised? Alvaro became involved in a multitude of difficulties which filled him with perplexities, though they did not affect his faith. These difficulties are stated in a letter to his brother-in-law.

Juan of Seville also saw the difficulty of this problem, but his answer threw little light on the subject. He concluded by saying that we must agree with the words of St. Paul: "By one man sin entered into this world, and by sin death." This might be called begging the question. Juan, however, agreed with Alvaro that the creationist doctrine was the safest. Of the explanation Eulogius must have given him we have no record.

Alvaro was not always so successful in securing from Juan a reply to the theological question. While the latter was at Cordova they began a violent argument about the mystery of the Incarnation. This was some time after the year 840. Juan returned home and soon forgot all about it, but Alvaro had a better memory for such matters. In his eagerness to learn the truth, he wrote a long letter on the subject to Juan, who evidently feared these discussions and prudently refrained from answering. Soon afterwards he received this characteristic note from Alvaro.

> Hitherto I have written to you affectionately. Now I shall see whether threats influence you more than love. Truly, O most cruel of men, your heart is of stone, or you must have been suckled by some Hyrcanian tiger. You deserve rather to be met with knotty cudgels of oak than addressed in the polished sentences of Donatus. If you still persist in shutting yourself up in this Pythagorean silence, you are either a log or a lump of metal.

Juan knew his man, and even this half-humorous and half-serious pleading made no deep impression on the Sevillian's heart.

But a great grief now came to Alvaro. One by one he lost his three daughters. Sorrow for the time obliterated all other considerations. Then at last came the answer, from his friend Juan — a letter of condolence enclosing the theological argument.

> I have heard through our father of the death of your daughters. Do not mourn as one who has no hope. We must go to Christ through much tribulation, for He Himself said: "The world shall rejoice: and you shall be made sorrowful, but your sorrow shall be turned into joy" (John 16:20).

Alvaro tells us that when the letter came, he was oppressed

with grief, sunk in deadly anguish. However, he found strength to return to his books and write a long treatise on the Incarnation.[4]

---

[4] This theological correspondence is found in the collection of Alvaro's letters, published by Padre Flórez, Vol. XI of his *España Sagrada*, pp. 81 sqq.

CHAPTER IX

THE ENDLESS *STRUGGLE* WITH HERESIES

THE EAGER search into the most sublime doctrines of Christianity we have witnessed on the part of Alvaro was most praiseworthy, especially in the circumstances under which the Mozarabs lived. We can forgive the faulty expressions sometimes used, due to devout curiosity. Juan, however, was really a partisan of the Adoptionists, among a group of whom he dwelt at Seville. Alvaro warned him of this error and confronted him with the authority of Beatus, the chief adversary of Elipandus.

The heresy of Elipandus, Archbishop of Toledo, was an effort to reconcile Christianity with Mohammedanism. If Christ, as man, was only the adopted Son of God, the Koran was right in saying that the Word of God, the Messias, was a great prophet, but nothing more.

Alvaro, a controversialist and extremist, could not brook this, but his hatred of Islam ran the risk of involving him in the opposite error. In fact, in opposing the semi-Nestorian separation of the Adoptionists, he fell into an implied Eutychian doctrine of the fusion of the two natures.

In opposition to this, the formula of Sansón of Cordova, contemporary with Alvaro, is clear and correct: "The Catholic Faith confesses that the two natures (*substantiae*) of our Lord and Saviour Jesus Christ exist in one Person, teaching that one is Creator, the other created." Eulogius was right in saying that the wisest men are liable to err when they least expect it.

Fortunately Alvaro's mistakes, as Eulogius said, were only the weeds sown in the field while the owner slept. No one was more prompt than he to submit to the teaching of the Faith. "If your letters teach me the truth," he wrote to Juan, "I beg pardon at once." What he greatly needed, as he confessed, were opportunities of hearing the words of God. He loved the doctrine of the Church, the Bride of Christ, and longed "that it might shed its light on men's minds."

He was the first, indeed, to give warning of a heresy that was beginning to make proselytes among the Mozarabs. Mistrusting himself in his arguments with the heretics, he spoke to Eulogius and went to see Abbot Esperaindeo, his "dearest master, venerable father, and holiest of priests." The abbot soothed him and quoted texts from Holy Scripture which Alvaro used to advantage in his future controversies. The abbot himself, embittered by the persecutions and jealousy from which he had suffered, did not perhaps feel strong enough to leave his cell to defend the Faith. Shortly after, however, he received a letter from Alvaro who was more disturbed than ever by the virulence of the sectaries and the multitude of souls they were dragging to perdition. Then his master decided upon publishing two small works, full of comparisons and Biblical texts, confuting the principal errors of the new sect.

Chief of these errors was the negation of the doctrine of the Blessed Trinity. All the heresies of that epoch were anti-Trinitarian, an evidence of Mohammedan influence over Christianity. Denying the Blessed Trinity, it was logical to deny the Divinity of Christ, whom they looked upon as merely a man, a prophet. Since the tradition of the Fathers stood in opposition to this they renounced it altogether, as well as that of the prophets, taking the Gospels, interpreted in their own way, as the sole source of truth.

This sect was connected with a group that ravaged the country south of Cordova and which was probably identical with it in doctrine.[1] It claimed that its doctrine was a return to pure evangelical teaching, especially in regard to public worship. Its followers, therefore, cast aside many observances not found by them in the primitive Church. This agrees with Alvaro's opinion that these heretics had a special predilection for the Gospel, but as a theologian, he noted only their doctrinal errors. In matters of discipline they strictly forbade anyone to partake of food with infidels, abstained on Christmas day if it fell on Friday, renounced honour to relics of the saints, passed the chalice from one to another at Holy Communion, omitted anointing with oil at baptism, and introduced the ceremony of moistening the eyes of the sick with saliva, as Christ did in the instance of the man who was born blind.

The sect centred in Epagro, the Poley of the Arabs, in the province of Cordova, was evidently of puritanical, evangelical tendency. Its members would not receive Communion from other Christians, even at the hour of death. This, however, did not prevent them from joining other heretics who authorised bigamy, in imitation of Lamech, and equally, incest — although we do not know whose example they pleaded for this. They allowed mixed marriages and gave priests full leave to enter business, open taverns, participate in commerce, and practice surgery, which then was another name for bloodletting, since it consisted in performing the bleeding undergone by both sick and sound at stated seasons of the year.

These heretics further maintained that they were sent from Rome, leading us to infer that they were a branch of Migecianism, a puritan and anti-Trinitarian heresy, which fifty

---

[1] The author believes the heresies of Epagro to be those spoken of in the letters of Alvaro and Esperaindeo (*Patr. Lat.*, cxv, p. 961). His opinion is shared by Count von Baudissin in his book *Eulogius und Alvar*, pp. 71–77. He does not consider as certain, however, the dates assigned to the letters by Flórez and sometimes differs from him in this point.

years before had sprung from the barbarous mind of Migecius. This heresiarch, too, had anathematised those who eat with infidels and insolently asked the priests: "Why call yourselves sinners though you are holy? And, if you are sinners, how do you dare to mount to the altar?" His god was a person who had manifested himself first in David, then in Jesus, and finally in St. Paul. He thus understood the Trinity. The perfect church was in the city of Rome, where all were saints. It was the new Jerusalem of St. John's visions. Egilanus, the papal delegate, as foolish as Migecius, thought that the best way he could show his gratitude to the Bishop of Rome was to accept all these absurdities, and became one of their most ardent propagators. Elipandus saw both the faith and authority of his Church threatened. He vigorously assailed the senseless defendants of a material Jerusalem and easily routed them with his impetuous abuse and arguments. But the seed remained, and fifty years later sprang up in the strange sect of Epagro.

The true Church, amid its isolation and servitude, found an effective remedy. It called a council. Learned prelates came from the provinces subject to Abderrahmán II, under the protection and safe conduct of the emir. Wistremirus of Toledo presided. Ariulfus of Mérida sat on his left, while on his right was Juan of Seville, a venerable old bishop who in his youth had fought gloriously against the Adoptionists, and whom the Moors called Sil Almatram, "the metropolitan." Near them sat five other bishops, and lower down a large number of priests and clerics.

No doubt Eulogius, too, was there. He was still young and had just been ordained priest, but his learning and virtue were too brilliant to escape the notice of the council. His friendship with the bishop of Toledo dated from that time.

The whole assembly agreed that the church of Epagro was no church, but *a cave of thieves and a synagogue of Satan;* and further, that its leaders, Cassiano and Cunierico, were ignorant deceivers and murderers of weak and innocent souls. This they stated in their Acts which were not lacking in canonical and theological knowledge, but were written in a Latinity that must have caused no slight qualms to men who, like Esperaindeo and Eulogius, were trying to raise the level of Mozarabic culture.

Recafredo, Bishop of Cordova, was commissioned to convert by his exhortations all the heretics, whether Cassianists, Acéfalos, Simoniacs, Jovinianists, or Vigilancians, with authority to consign them, if they persevered in their heresy, to the eternal fires of hell with Judas, the traitor. The document was signed by bishops and priests, on February 21, 839.

There was living in Cordova, at the time, a strange person named Samuel, addicted to study and attached to Christian tradition. He was a cleric, probably a monk, and one of a group of devout and learned men who devoted themselves, like Eulogius and Esperaindeo, to preserving the purity of the Faith and of ecclesiastical knowledge. Probably he was a disciple of the abbot, and familiarly signed his name, SPdo.

Samuel collected in a book whatever struck him most in his readings and in his master's lectures, leaving us a delightful anthology of religious knowledge among the Mozarabs. Writings of the Fathers of the Church alternated with the Councils and Scriptures. Following a chapter of Cassian on monks came a law of the country on bees; beside a treatise by St. Augustine or St. Jerome stood a scheme of philosophy or strange theories about some such subject as wildfire. It is all written in a firm hand, but with more care for science than for the art of calligraphy. The last sentence of each extract is generally illuminated in red, blue, or yellow.

Samuel lived in the days of turmoil in which the heresy of Epagro assailed the Mozarabic Church. In the first pages of the book he gives us a proof of his orthodoxy. He begins his notes with the significant verses of Proverbs (6:16–10) that speak of "the heart that deviseth wicked plots . . . the deceitful witness that uttereth lies, and him that soweth discord among brethren." There follows a stanza by St. Eugenius on the plagues of Egypt. After these two exordiums, we find the Acts of the Council of Cordova and certain treatises of Abbot Esperaindeo. Samuel had access to some special letters of the abbot which had been lent him by Alvaro.

Besides the original Acts of the Council, in order to lend additional authenticity to his copy, he made a facsimile of the bishops' signatures, so that we can recognise their handwriting to this day. It is a pity that Samuel did not give us the priests' names, for we should have that of Eulogius among them.[2]

At a somewhat later date, about the year 900, the codex, completed by Alphonsus and Recafredo, received a new inscription which needs no comment. The ancient manuscript literally speaks for itself:

> I am a book belonging to the monastery of SS. Cosmas and Damian, founded in the territory of León, near Torio, in the valley of Abellar. May he who banishes me hence be banished from the Catholic Faith, from paradise, and the kingdom of heaven; and may he who restores me or says where I have been put, have part in the kingdom of Christ and of God.

---

[2] P. Flórez copied from Samuel's codex the Acts of this Council of Cordova, published for the first time at the beginning of Vol. XV, in *España Sagrada*.

CHAPTER X

THE *JOURNEY* THAT TOOK A YEAR

EULOGIUS WAS a dutiful son. Neither his priestly duties, nor his literary work, nor even the mystic longings that drew him to the communities of the sierra could make him forget the interests of his family. Being the head of the household he was bound to take care of his mother, brothers, and sisters. An important event in his life shows how he understood and performed this sacred duty.

Eulogius had two sisters: Niola and Anulo, and three brothers: Alvaro, Isidore, and Joseph. Anulo consecrated her virginity to God without leaving home. Eulogius allowed Joseph, his youngest brother, to study from childhood the Moorish language and literature in order to provide a career for him. Though Christians were ineligible for any honourable, lucrative office in direct communication with the Mohammedans, the Moslem law did not exclude them from the army nor from purely administrative offices, and the emirs were past masters at interpretating the law as suited them. Later on, Joseph became *catib* or government secretary, an important post that Eulogius calls "brilliant."

Isidore and Alvaro seem to have entered commerce, in which the position of *dımmies* (Jews and Christians) was inferior to that of the Moslems, since they were obliged to pay special tithes and imposts. Commerce with Christian countries was centred in the hands of the *dimmies* who sent rubies to the north from Beja, and Malagon, and bartered in Levantine pottery, skins from Cordova, praised by Theodulphus the Spanish poet of Charlemagne's court, weapons from Cordova and Toledo, woven stuffs from Almería and Seville, and many other goods produced by the growing industries of Andalusia or imported from Egypt, Syria, Byzantium, and Bagdad.

Urged by the interests of business or, as Eulogius says, by the state of the times, Isidore and Alvaro went to the northern frontier, crossed the Pyrenees, and entered the empire of Charles the Bald. At first their family received news from them. Following the *Via Heraclea* of the Romans, they had safely reached the domains of Louis the German. After that nothing more was heard of them. Isabel and her children questioned the merchants from the most distant Spanish frontier, the many northern Slavs who constantly enlisted in the Sultan's armies, and the eunuchs whom the Jews brought from France to serve in the royal palace and the houses of the chief Moorish aristocracy. Nothing was of any use.

Isabel began to feel all a mother's anxieties, and Eulogius endured her grief together with his own. At length he could remain at peace no longer and resolved to go in search of his brothers. The responsibility for their disappearance weighed upon his conscience and nothing could stay him from carrying out his resolution.

The undertaking of such a journey in those days was no small matter. The roads were unknown to him and filled with bands of soldiers and highwaymen, between whom there was little choice. The Mozarabic liturgy properly provided its ceremonies and prayers for such an occasion, and when these had been completed and the necessary recommendations secured, Eulogius set out with his faithful deacon, Teodomundo.

It was apparently in 845 or else in the following year that this journey was begun. Mounted on mules the two travellers joined one of the caravans such as were constantly leaving the capital for different parts. Doubtless he first struck into the *Via Heraclea* to make for the other side of the Pyrenees.

But on the frontiers of Gothia rumours of war reached him and every kind of violence and outrage was being perpetrated. A fierce struggle was going on. Far from losing courage when thus face to face with danger, he changed his route and took the pass of Roncevalles — the Bort Xezar, or "crooked pass," as the Moslems called it, thus finally reaching Pamplona.

But new wars and rebellions had now broken out in this direction also and made it impossible at first to leave Spain. With the help, however, of the saintly bishop of Pamplona, Wiliesindo, and the escort he supplied, Eulogius passed over the rugged mountains, on the southern side of which the men of Navarre were fighting the Moslems, to the north of which was a massing of French forces, and on the west were taking place the incursions of the Asturian kings. Surely this was a world in turmoil, giving an excellent picture of the times.

With this danger successfully passed, Eulogius visited the sanctuaries and monasteries of Navarre. Thence he passed through the fertile valleys of Aranguren and Izagaonda, which were just recovering from destruction and pillage by Abderrahmán's troops. So wars and rumours of wars and the desolation of war were the order of the day. But the traveller continued with his caravan until at last they saw below them a savage sierra.

"Those are the mountains of Leyre," said one of the company. "Behind them is the sierra of la Peña, with the abbey of San Juan, the refuge and citadel of the brave Aragonese. Lower down stands Sangüesa, a heroic town that bravely resisted the Moor's assaults. That cluster of houses, near the rock, is Javier, a place of little importance. Rather higher up, at the foot of the Peña Mayor, standing on arid ground, but well cultivated, is the monastery. It is easy to see that monks have worked on it. No Moors dare venture there."

The monastery of San Salvador was surrounded by mountains, the natural defence among which the anchorets had enclosed themselves, lest the turmoil of invasions should interrupt their prayer and work. But the world was conscious of their sanctity and learning. When Wamba's army marched past in his campaign against Paul the rebel, the servants of God were already here and their psalmody echoed among the mountains.

The travellers called aloud, and a voice answered, *Benedicite*. A moment after, the door was opened. Eulogius gave the bishop's letter of introduction to the porter. It spoke of the dignity, learning, virtue, and birth of the illustrious visitor. The news caused a commotion in the Leyre community. What a surprise! A Mozarabic priest, one of the chief representatives of the clergy of Cordova! It was many a year since anyone had come from thence except to sow death and desolation.

The abbot, Don Fortún, with most of his monks, came to the entrance, and monks and travellers walked in procession to the oratory, led by the abbot. After praying awhile, the usual acts of charity were gone through. The abbot washed his guests' hands and gave them the kiss of welcome. Steaming dishes of beans from the monastery garden and delicious trout from the Aragon awaited them in the refectory. After supper came the ceremony of the *Mandatum*, the most touching expression of Christian charity and monastic hospitality. Eulogius and his companions took off their shoes, Don Fortún and the guest-master knelt before them, and washed and kissed their feet. Meanwhile the monks chanted: "Let us love one another; for charity is of God. And everyone that loveth, knoweth God and is a child of God."

Then the cantor took up the chant and continued:

> Behold a woman that was in the city, a sinner, when she knew that he sat at meat in the house of Simon the leper, brought an alabaster box of ointment; and standing behind at his feet, she began to wash his feet with tears, and wiped them with the hairs of her head, and kissed his

feet, she broke her alabaster box and anointed them with the ointment.[1]

The cantor narrated this event in a simple, syllabic tone, and the choir afterwards repeated the antiphon, breaking forth into a jubilant, trilling chant expressive of the delights of love.

The monks then drew near their illustrious visitor, listening eagerly to what he said. They wished to hear his spiritual teaching, so highly praised by the good Bishop Wiliesindo, and to receive as well the news of the times. In the Middle Ages it was in the cloisters that political and religious affairs were discussed and their chronicles written. The community of Leyre shared the interest felt by others. They wanted to hear of what was happening in Cordova, of the position of the Christians there, the conduct of their conquerors, and the adventures of their guest along the way. Eulogius tells us he found among them souls far advanced in the fear of God, whose conversation pleased him greatly.

But these saints were also ardent patriots. Leyre was beginning to be known as the cradle of Navarran independence. The abbot, Dom Fortún, was related to Iñigo Arista, the commander who led the people of Navarra against invaders both from the north and south, and who formed the first link in a glorious dynasty. His wife, Queen Oneca, liked to make her retreat at Leyre, and Iñigo Arista was wont to go there for means to maintain his warfare. So, too, did his successors later on. When he died, he was laid to rest from his labours beneath the shelter of the church, and many other kings were to lie beside him. Leyre would be the royal Pantheon of Navarra. The venerable crypt, a record of heroic times, may

---

[1] At Leyre and the other monasteries of Navarra visited by St. Eulogius, the Rule of St. Benedict was kept, but the ritual of the Visigoths was retained until the eleventh century. The above example is to be found in *The Mozarabic Psalter and Hymnary*, by Gilson, p. 326.

THE JOURNEY THAT TOOK A YEAR

still be seen, as also the splendid Romanesque basilica, with its beautiful front decorated with saints and fabulous animals.

From Leyre, at the extreme east of Navarra, Eulogius set out for the abbey of San Zacarías, at the extreme north of the country, visiting once more many religious houses along the road, until he stood before the snowy summits of the Pyrenees. Here, in the western district, a little more than a three hours' journey off, rose the walls of a monastic building. It was the abbey of San Zacarías "which enlighteneth all the west with its learning and regular observance." The saint found here the ideal abbot, Odvario, a man of sanctity and learning, with a hundred monks serving God under his fatherly guidance. Speaking of these men Eulogius waxes eloquent. They were as stars shining in God's firmanent, each with his own particular excellence.

Since the monastery was on the route which the travellers from France, on their way through the narrow pass of Roncevalles, were bound to take, the monks had erected here a *hospederia* for their reception. No better place could have been found by Eulogius to obtain the information he had come so far to seek.

News, good news, was quick to reach him. Alvaro and Isidore, his two brothers, had already returned to Spain by way of Saragossa in company with a merchants' caravan. Without delay he therefore set out to overtake them and reached Saragossa before the merchants had departed. His brothers, he learned from them, were safe and sound, doing excellent business no doubt at Maguncia, beyond the Galia. His worries now were past.

In the meantime Saragossa itself must have had for him a peculiar interest. It was called by the Moors, Madina Albaida, on account of the dazzling whiteness of its houses. A miraculous light, it was said in Cordova, hovered over it, which could be seen day and night by all. This the Moslems attributed to the virtues of two of their recluses who were buried there, but the Christians declared that the city had been illuminated by it ever since its foundation.

Mohammedans admired its marvellous mihrab, unlike any other in the world, that had been cut from one block of solid marble and decorated with carvings. What Eulogius admired was the lofty walls of forty cubits that surrounded the entire city, the fertility of the soil, the gardens, the bridge over the Ebro recently constructed and fortified by Abderrahmán, the magnificent buildings, and above all, the fine Christian mementoes. He had read in the *Etimologias* that Saragossa was the healthiest city in the world for body and soul: for the body, on account of its equable climate; for the soul because of the intercession of its martyrs.

From Saragossa he happily directed his steps homeward, starting for the capital by way of the Alhambra, the ancient Laminium of the Romans. Such was the famous journey which had taken over a year. No wonder he remarks: "After this long pilgrimage my forsaken family received its head as if he had arisen from the grave." Soon their joy was to be increased by the arrival also of his two brothers. There was but one event that clouded their mutual happiness. Abderrahmán at this period, deprived Joseph of his office in the palace. The emir became greatly incensed with him, perhaps because of his brother's journey, since Christians were strictly forbidden to go into any other countries.

But Eulogius had gained much valuable information. Conditions in the north of Spain were utterly unknown in Cordova, and more serious for the Moslems than anyone believed. Thus on the frontier of Aragon a leader of Gothic descent, brave and daring, was planning and conspiring against Cordova, ready to throw off the mask when the right time came; Gothia was fighting for its independence; the kings of Asturias were increasing in power within the shelter of their mountains; and the men of Navarra laughed at Abderrahmán's threats, in spite of the periodical raids made by his troops who often got close to Pamplona.

The traveller was disgusted, however, with the individualism that disintegrated all these efforts for freedom. In Toledo alone he found great grounds for consolation. There the Christians were in the preponderance, and love for liberty, restrained for the moment by the Cordovan forces, inflamed all the citizens, Mozarabic and Muladíes.[2] No doubt the fire was fed by the presence of Eulogius, and in fact soon afterward Toledo rose against the emirs.

---

[2] A Moorish tribe.

CHAPTER XI

A NINTH-CENTURY CLASSIC *RENAISSANCE*

ON ENTERING Cordova Eulogius might have quoted the words of Sansón, his contemporary and to a certain extent his disciple: "The time will come in which Latin will be spoken correctly once more in Spain," a phrase equivalent to saying: "A time will come in which this foreign rabble will disappear."

Learned men in Cordova understood that the traditional language was the best support of religion and patriotism. The Hispano-Gothic soul would live in the spirit of the idiom of Isidore of Seville. In the spirit of defence, a campaign had begun to restore the ecclesiastical language which had become extremely decadent. The Acts of the Council of Cordova, in 839, give us a very poor opinion of the Latinity of the Mozarabic bishops of the first half of the ninth century.

Teachers of the Arabic or Chaldean language drew away their pupils from the Latin masters. Arabic was the official tongue, and those who spoke it were sure of state employment. Latin, on the other hand, had been forbidden, and was tolerated only on account of force of circumstances. Not all Moslems knew the language of the invaders, but a great number of them and many Christians, especially of the higher classes, spoke it, though this did not interfere with their genuine profession of the Christian Faith. Many who were afterwards martyred spoke Arabic. It was spoken in the family of Eulogius and known to him. Alvaro praises its harmony and large choice of words, so that he must have studied it; but he was angry at its absorbing influence and immoral effects upon the Mozarabic people. It was easy and even frequent for an Arabic linguist to become an Arabic believer. In his burning zeal Alvaro asks:

> Who is there in these days, among the faithful, who studies the Holy Scriptures and the writings of the doctors of the Church in Latin? Who is kindled by the flame of the Gospels, by the longing of the prophets, or the fire of the Epistles? See those fashionable youths, with handsome faces, polished and eloquent in speech, distinguished in dress and deportment, learned in Moslem subjects, consummate in their knowledge of Mohammedan literature — how eagerly they search for Chaldean books, how attentively they read, and with what ardour they explain them, with what avidity they purchase them, and repeat their teaching with extravagant praise, all the while knowing nothing of ecclesiastical literature and despising as vile the streams of the Church that flow from Paradise! . . . Alas! Christians know not their law; Latins are so ignorant of their own language that few can write a letter in decent grammar. Yet a numberless crowd can explain in learned terms the grandeur and beauty of the Chaldean tongue.[1]

Such people could allege in excuse the bad Latin that was then in use among the Mozarabs. Elipando, archbishop of the metropolitan see of Toledo, employed in his letters a language nearer to popular Romance than Latin. Besides this, most of the copies of Latin literature had disappeared at the invasion, while Moslem books, brought from the East or written in Spain, had begun to fill the libraries, schools, and shops. It was urgent that traditional language and literature should be restored to aid the new movement.

Eulogius began this task with Alvaro's help, and he worked with renewed enthusiasm when he learnt in his northern journey how strongly the national spirit was aroused, though

---

[1] *España Sagrada*, XI, 274. The *Historia crítica de la literatura española*, by Amador de los Ríos, Vol. II, Chap. XI, gives a short but incomplete account of Mozarabic literature.

in Cordova it seemed crushed. His position at San Zoilo helped him in the struggle. From the time of his ordination to the priesthood, he had taken his place among the professors, but now he was at their head, the *archischolus* of all the teachers in Cordova. The college of San Zoilo became the most famous in the city. Alvaro had exaggerated — it was in his character to exaggerate — when he said that none of the Mozarabs studied Latin or the Holy Scriptures. In Eulogius' school a group of young laymen joined the clergy, attracted by the distinguished precentor of San Zoilo. Some were from Cordova, others from various parts of the kingdom. Students came even from the foreign legion whose members called themselves *esclavos*, "the slaves." Later on we shall behold some of his pupils yielding themselves up joyously to martyrdom.

Eulogius taught piety as well as learning, so that his instruction bore double fruit, for his chief endeavour was to win his scholar's hearts by kindness. Hence his words made torture welcome and death sweet; hence came the confidence placed in him by Cordovans in the hour of fear and danger. We have as an example the deep devotion shown him by his deacon, Teodomundo, who faithfully followed Eulogius and shared the punishments he endured. Eulogius called him *filius meus*, "my son," showing the paternal character of his authority, in keeping with the old Isidorean tradition. "Papa," says a glossary of the time, "is the schoolmaster by whom the scholars are taught."

Perhaps Eulogius may have received the *nefrenditium*, the present of a visor, which the students used to give on certain occasions to their professors, but he was never mercenary. Alvaro says that he was severe as St. Jerome, modest as St. Augustine, gentle as St. Ambrose, patient as St. Gregory in correcting mistakes. He encouraged the little ones, incited their elders, and bore with the faults of his people, adapting himself in a marvellous way to all.

His teaching was not the same that he himself had received thirty years ago. His journey, especially, had brought him in touch with new methods. Thus, he had visited at Pamplona one of the imperial schools — *scholae dominicae* — established by Charlemagne in the principal cities of his empire, resembling that founded by Alcuin at Tours.

New books, too, had been acquired in Cordova. To the psalms and metrical sentences of the pseudo-Cato, from which he had learnt Latin, could now be added three or four of the classic volumes of the best European schools of the time: the *Grammatica* of Elio Donato — the *Ars Minor* — which had not been unknown to the Andalusian Mozarabics in the beginning of the ninth century but which neither Eulogius nor Alvaro had been permitted to study in their childhood because of the contacts with paganism; the fables of Avienius which, after the psalms, was the book chosen for analysis and translation; the *Eisagoge* of Porphyry, with a large number of explanations, the only book of Greek philosophy, except for a dialogue of Plato, known in the glorious Middle Ages; and finally the *Aeneid*, which was very difficult to obtain in Andalusia, and then probably only in fragmentary form. With these elements of learning, the school of San Zoilo found nothing to envy in the school of St. Gall, then beginning to rank as foremost in the West.

But Eulogius was not satisfied with this. He continued his work of renewal outside the precincts of the church, consecrating all his spare time to restoring Latin literature, which had been forgotten, corrupted, dispersed, and to a great extent lost. He aimed at a resurrection of the past, at reforming Visigothic learning, at making such a library as Isidore had made at Seville.

He began to seek everywhere for manuscripts, to buy and copy, or have them copied. From Navarra, besides the *Aeneid*, Avino's fables, and Porphyry's works, he obtained Juvenal's poems, the satires of Horace, St. Augustine's *City of God*, the

Epigrams of Aldhelm, an Anglo-Saxon monk of the seventh century; a collection of hymns and a miscellaneous codex of Scriptural questions by various authors, Alvaro says: "Every day he showed us new treasures and wonderful things unknown to us. One might have said that he discovered them among the ancient ruins or dug them out of the earth."

Many of these manuscripts were in a lamentable state; some were faded with age and incomplete; others mouldered by dampness or injured and disfigured by being written over. To restore them, as Alvaro states:

> [Eulogius] corrected what was amiss, mended what was torn or deteriorated, renovated what was old and worn, and renewed the works of ancient authors. I have never known anyone with such unwearied zeal, and such a thirst for learning and teaching as adorned his soul. Of what volumes was he ignorant? What authors were unknown to him, whether Catholics or heretics, or even heathen philosophers? Of what poetry does he not know the harmony, or what hymns or foreign works has he not read? And his generous soul never keeps these things to itself but shares them with us. . . . He gives us his enlightenment and will leave it for posterity. This servant of Christ is a light to others in all his ways; whether he goes out or whether he returns, he is always frank, delightful, and kindly.

Alvaro, affectionate and grateful, recalls his friend's energy in restoring Latin culture. He finds him devoting to this his pen, his speech, his actions, and his time spent in the schools and monasteries.

The library he had got together with such pains was open to all who would help him in his work. He loved and guarded his books; each codex that he kept so carefully represented the life's work of some writer.

Juan, the rhetorician of Seville, wanted information on rhetorical composition and remembered that Eulogius had a treatise on the subject. He wrote to Alvaro: "If you cannot

A NINTH-CENTURY CLASSIC RENAISSANCE 93

send me Eulogius' volume, or the part that speaks of this subject, which is known to you, copy it and send it to me, and may Christ give you joy in return! But if you don't Eulogius will lend it to me, and tell me how many days I may keep it." We do not know what action Eulogius had taken. Perhaps Juan was afraid that even Alvaro's intercession would not persuade him to allow a manuscript to be removed from his collection. It was a fine library, since Alvaro, an ardent lover and collector of books, says so, but we must not exaggerate. Two hundred volumes would then have been an extraordinary number, remembering that they were all handwritten. We can partly reconstruct it by the names of books then known in Cordova and those cited by Alvaro, Sansón, and Eulogius. The reader will find in the appendix this list and a description of the volumes.

The library of the Escorial contains an inventory of books, probably part of the martyr's library, made ten years after his death. There are about fifty volumes mentioned there, among them are the poems of Adelhelmus, Virgil, and Juvenal, with others brought by Eulogius from Navarra. The manuscript itself seems a valuable relic. It contains geographical, scientific, and theological works; sermons of St. Augustine; fragments of St. Jerome; the maritime *Itinerarium* of Antoninus; the names of the episcopal cities of Spain; the chronicle of Prospero of Acquitaine; a treatise by Euquerius on the topography of Jerusalem and various works of St. Isidore. Among the latter are two new titles; Rufus Festus, with his history of the Roman people, and Eticus with his treatise on the earth's dimension.[2]

Eulogius had given new life to the manuscript. It had been

---

[2] Guillermo, Antolín, *Catálogo de los códices latinos del Escorial*, III, 486. All the authors found in this reconstruction of St. Eulogius' library are quoted in the writings of the Saint or his contemporaries in Cordova. As Alvaro says that Eulogius was acquainted with all the authors known in his time, the list seems rather wanting than exaggerated.

written in the seventh century with handsome capital letters, but when acquired by him parts of it had become stained and illegible. He completed it with elegant Visigoth lettering and large red capitals for the titles. This was the Mozarabic style of the ninth century. He wrote numbers of notes in smaller letters on the margins in Latin or Arabic, and sometimes in Hebrew. In the ninth volume he drew a map of the world; the circular one of St. Isidore, not the square one of Beatus of Liébana. Folio 67 has another map, giving the idea which a Cordovan of the ninth century had formed of the Straits of Cadiz. Within a circle below is written *Fretum gaditanum;* on either side are Mauritania and Hispania; below is Africa. There are other designs, one of these is meant to explain an eclipse of the moon. In Volume VI we read in red letters: *Eulogii mementote peccatoris,* "Remember Eulogius the sinner." Alvaro says that Eulogius not only dictated rapidly but was an accomplished copyist and draughtsman, *peritissimus tractor.*

The most remarkable point in this culture renewed by St. Eulogius is its wide range. While the emirs watched over and censored scrupulously the literature that came from the eastern regions of the Moslems, Eulogius collected and studied all books without exception. Pagan, heretical, and ancient philosophical volumes stood beside those of the Fathers of the Church. Among the pagan writings some were in Arabic. Eulogius knew the *hadices* or traditions of the prophet. Alvaro planned to refute the Koran, and both he and Eulogius show that they were not as mistrustful and fanatical as their persecutors, the Mohammedans.

Eulogius was specially devoted to the ancient classics, which he studied and quoted opportunely. Most of the books he brought back from Navarra as trophies of victory were classics. Sometimes he exaggerated the rusticity of his style: he boasted of despising "the deceptive adornments of rhetoric," that he might strive solely for pure simplicity; he owned that he had never found time to "speak with superb eloquence and weigh the elegance of his phrases"; he understood how rare it was to find in those days great writers to set as models before his students. "Unfortunately," he writes with exaggerated humility, "I am the least of those who have a glimmering of the knowledge of letters." He feared criticism; but was it more to be feared than in our own times? He asked his scholars to "read with simplicity his simple writings and not to make his works the object of criticism and ridicule, like the beasts of the forest who delight in clawing and biting."

Though always simple and candid, Eulogius was ever influenced by his literary work. He often quoted the classics, while his histories of the heroes of the Faith read like poems. He agreed with Theodulfus, another great Spaniard of the century, who lived in the reign of Louis the Pious, and who also read and imitated the ancient poets:

In quorum dictis, quamquam sint frivola, multa plurima sub falso tegmine vera latent.[3]

This is really wonderful, for in the schools there was a great distrust of the classics. Isidore, as we saw, warned men strongly against their charms, and so deterred readers from studying them. Alcuin, too, was suspicious of their influence, and reproached his disciples with preferring the steeds of Apollo to the four-horse chariot of the Evangelists. Such a preference was obviously not in question here. The teachers at Fulda and St. Gall counselled discretion in reading pagan writings. Naturally the classics were to be consigned to their true place and function.

Alvaro, perhaps in faithfulness to the teaching of Abbot Esperaindeo, clung to the tradition of St. Isidore, but Juan of Seville, as a thorough grammarian, differed from him. Alvaro did not despise grammar, which he considered indispensable for preserving the "most sacred language of our fore-

---

[3] "Vain though their sayings are, yet many a truth lies hidden there under a false covering."

fathers," but thought it unnecessary to study Elio Donato's *Ars Minor* in order to write correctly. For him, the poets' songs were the food of devils; he called the philosophers *filocompos,* inventors of lies. To love the venom of the pagan writers was idolatry. "What has Horace to do with David, Maro with the Evangelists, Marcus Tullius with the Apostle?" And again, elsewhere he says: "My letters do not seek favour with pagans or wear the colours of Athens. Their perfume is that of Holy Scripture, their flavour that of the holy Fathers." Juan valiantly defended the pagans with arguments from Holy Writ and ecclesiastical tradition, but Alvaro stood firm. Later on he said that anyone who took pleasure in infidel writings and investigated their teaching, except to refute them, set on the door of his study the sign of the beast of the Apocalypse.

However, his books contradict his theories. No doubt Eulogius converted him to humanism. Alvaro's style is not so quiet and harmonious as his friend's, but copious, violent, and often in the decadent local type; yet he is looked upon as one of the writers of Cordova. He was fond of the foreign idioms and Greek words that abound in the glosses of Isidore. One of his letters begins with: *Engloge emperie vestrae sumentes eufrasia, imo energiae percurrentes epitoma.* He knew classic literature, if only by hearing it; constantly names the most famous classic representatives, Socrates, Antisthenes, Aristotle, Plato, Epicurus, Thucydides, Sallust, Titus Livius, Aeschines, Demosthenes, and Homer; asks his adversary Bodo to read Greek, Latin, and other history; often quotes the classic poets, especially Virgil, and after condemning heathen mythology with all the energy of his temperament and literary powers, calls the moon Cynthia and writes verses in praise of the nightingale, the cock, and the peacock.

There is a touching good will in these efforts to attain classic culture. All barbarisms had not yet been uprooted; the conjugation of verbs troubled our Mozarabic writers; sometimes they employed popular words and expressions familiarly used in the Romance language, while on the other hand a childish effort at culture often marred their language, especially that of Alvaro. Yet it seems almost impossible that they should have written as well as they did within ten years after the Council of the year 839. Their style would naturally be similar to the contemporary Latin of other lands, though it is difficult to find any work elsewhere with the colour, verve, and life of the Cordovan style.

A great renovation had been effected. The correct expression was carefully sought for, and like the learned men of Charlemagne's court, the Cordovans interrupted their theological discussions to solve a grammatical problem. Thus Alvaro asked Juan what part of speech *maturius* was. To prove that it was an adverb the Sevillian quoted Cicero.

No doubt some people did not recognise that times had changed, but their mistakes were not left uncorrected. This was the case with Bishop Hostégesis. He was a bad theologian, a worse bishop, and no better as a grammarian.

Hostégesis, who filled the Church of Cordova with consternation during the last years of Alvaro and Eulogius, had trouble with Sansón, who later continued the work of these great protagonists of the Faith. Sansón, probably a schoolfellow of Eulogius at San Zoilo, was his disciple and imitator. Some of his sentences were framed on those of Alvaro and Eulogius. Perhaps he was not their equal in correctness or force and movement, but he surpassed them in philosophy and theology. Like them, he loved the classics, quoted the poets, and enthusiastically maintained the laws of grammar.

Citing a paragraph from Hostégesis, Sansón says:

> These are his words. If one seeks in them Latin, it is hard to find it, and still less orthography; if one considers their meaning, they will seem to have come from a madman's brain. Who could help laughing at such nonsense? The very children would do so. Yet self-confident and with

an inflated head, foolish though he is, he shouts forth his rancid emptiness, ignorant of the order of words or of verbal tenses — as if everyone did not know him for a barbarian and not a Latin scholar!

The good abbot then quotes another of the bishop's utterances and vigorously continues his process of exposing this "wicked man" and baneful menace to the Church.

> Come, all you who know anything of Latin, and suppress your laughter if you can; we cannot but laugh aloud. Oh, wonderful eloquence! Magnificent speech! How dares he attempt to philosophise when he can not string two words together! Marvel at him, learned men and you who know how to censor scholastic writings.
>
> Where did this man acquire his new tongue? Perhaps he drank of the Tullian fount? Or did he learn from Cyprian, Jerome, or Augustine? Rather was it all dictated by his own ignorance? He calls a man an *idolatrix*. Is this Latin? Stupid! Have you not seen that in our codices, when they treat of pagans, one must say *cultor idolorum* of a man, and *cultrix* of a woman? But if I say more, I fear some one will apply to me the old proverb: "He loses oil and money who anoints his ox." Such a wicked man as he could never speak good Latin, and if he spoke rightly, it would be by chance. Virgil's lines apply to him:
> *Qui Bavium non odit, amet tua carmina, Maevi,*
> *Atque idem jungat vulpes et mulgeat hircos.*[4]

Sansón consoled himself by thinking that the clouds of ignorance would clear away from Spain some day, and the art of grammar would be known again. "Then," he said to Hostégesis, "your errors will be made clear and the stupidity of the men who presume to call you learned."

Long before that day came, the movement was destined to perish in its cradle, blown away by the hurricanes of persecution.

---

[4] The works of Abbot Sansón, published by P. Flórez in Vol. II of the *Esp. Sagr.*, pp 325–516. The quotations are made from Vol. II of his *Apologético*, Chap. VII. The verses are from Eclog. 3 90, 91.

CHAPTER XII

MOSLEM SPLENDOURS AND THE *CHRISTIAN YOKE*

THE FEVERISH eagerness shown by Eulogius to restore religious feeling among the Christians, to raise to still higher levels the monastic life, and to arouse new interest in the Latin language and its literature, had a patriotic as well as a religious purpose. The rector of San Zoilo had constituted himself head of a national group that had no violent or revolutionary aims like those of the renegades of the middle of the last century, but was no less enthusiastic in seeking to promote the ancient Hispano-Gothic spirit in all its manifestations.

His efforts had not been in vain. A strong nucleus of men actuated by the same ideal gathered round Eulogius. To strengthen and encourage him in the fatigues of the struggle, Alvaro stood at his side, together with the band of Christians who had made no pact with Moslem sensuality.

There were others who had fallen in a moment of weakness but looked with horror at Mohammedan doctrines. These now were ready on the first occasion to redeem their fall. They, too, sympathised with the Spanish movement. Besides this, Eulogius had disciples in almost all the churches of the city: young clerics who had listened to his lectures and been fascinated by his knowledge and irresistible sympathy. Many of them would ardently seek martyrdom later on.

Though Eulogius had powerful enemies among the clergy, he had competent aids as well. Cyprian the poet was a *laudator martyrum* like himself, Leovigildo, previously mentioned, was also one of those who accepted Christianity with all its painful privations and humiliations. In nearly all the Cordovan churches were zealous priests who participated in the honour of collecting the bodies of the martyrs.

But the most audacious defenders of tradition were the monks. In the monasteries Eulogius found his best disciples. For years he had lived with them, prepared them by word and by his own example of evangelical perfection, preaching on the virtues of the monk and the Christian, extolling hatred for the world and contempt for life, teaching moral opposition to Mohammedan sensuality.

A profound aversion for all that was Mohammedan characterised this party, whose members constituted the chosen and most illustrious Christians of Cordova. For them, Mohammed was a wicked, impure pseudoprophet; the rule of the Cordovan government, a despotic, ferocious power; Abderrahmán, a hateful tyrant. Eulogius used these expressions. He recalled with longing the time of the Toledan kings, "when religion flourished, magnificent churches were built, and priests were respected." Many persons wondered why God had allowed the infidel barbarians to overthrow the Gothic monarchy. Eulogius, following the philosophy of Paulus Orosius and St. Augustine, argued against them, throwing the blame on the vices of the age manifest in the Acts of the Councils of Toledo. "And to the vices of our fathers," added Abbot Sansón, "are conjoined those of many Christians in these days who live like Mohammedans. This is why, after more than a century, the foreign scourge still strikes us."

The increasing prosperity during Abderrahmán's reign, a scandal to many Christians, strengthened and excited the defenders of tradition, who became more and more threatened. They did not deny the existence of that prosperity and even spoke of its being prophesied in Holy Writ. Alvaro says that the Moslems were proud of their philosophy and literature, and claimed to find an allusion to Cordovan prosperity in

Job's words: "By what way is the light spread?" (Job 38:24.) Referring to this outward splendour he continues:

> It is all too clear to need explanation. That wicked man [Mohammed] was hardly dead when his way began to be alight with so many sects, schools, and vain doctrines that if the Merciful Ruler of all things did not direct by His inspiration the hearts of Heaven's citizens, we should all be deceived by such human splendour. Their exquisite inventions for baths and purifications, their extreme facility in every kind of art and discipline are known to all.[1]

Eulogius himself was amazed at the magnificence of Abderrahmán's court "that surpassed all his predecessors in luxury and pomp, raising the capital city of his rule to wonderful grandeur, bringing it honour, increasing its glory and riches, and filling it with earthly delights unspeakable and beyond belief."

During his reign Cordova began to be what the Moslems describe as the city of two hundred and eighty thousand houses; of seventy thousand, four hundred and fifty-five shops and offices; of twenty-eight districts; of thousands of mosques; of nine hundred baths; of palaces, countryseats, inns, and gardens beyond number.

Abderrahmán was an indefatigable builder. All the principal cities of his kingdom testified to his love of splendour by their palaces or castles, bridges or mosques. But Cordova, especially Moslem Cordova, owed to him the greater part of its beauty. He turned its environs into wonderful gardens, beautified the Rusafa, rebuilt the ancient fortresses, constructed, paved, and set in place the *acicales,* founded and endowed schools for poor children, paved the roads with stones, organised the police, brought pure water from the sierra in leaden pipes, constructed public baths, and placed fountains of marble and vari-coloured jasper in squares. In

---
[1] *Indiculus Luminosus,* No. 31, *Esp. Sagr.,* XI, 268.

his fondness for luxury and elegance, he insisted on pompous complications in court ceremonies, modified the fashion of dress, imposed new fashions, and introduced into Cordova all the wonderful products of Eastern industry. The greater part of the treasures of the caliphs of Bagdad were brought to Spain when, at the death of the son of Haroun al Raschid, the palace was sacked and plundered. A necklace, called by the Arab historians, Axxabé, that had belonged to Zobeida, the mother of Giafar, became the most valuable jewel in the Spanish emir's collection.

Such was the opulent city called by Eulogius *florentissima civitas et regia*, but which he and Mozarabic writers preferred to style *civitas patricia*. Far from loving its splendour, they thought it diabolic; a bait of Satan to catch the unwary. They envied their brethren among the northern mountains who, as Eulogius said, though poor, were free under the rule of Christian princes. Many abandoned their homes to go there. Since the invasion, the emigration had been continual. Most of the Christians were bound by many ties to the land of their birth; they were obliged to stay, but did not love their persecutors.

The yoke became more unbearable every day. The law gave them the right to exist, but made life impossible. They were impoverished, degraded, and despised. All the civilisation, by which they could not benefit, was produced by the sweat of their brow. As Eulogius said: "We are like the Israelites under the thong of the Egyptians." The pacts that had been made were not kept. Every Christian, as we have seen, was subject to the territorial tax and a personal tax, the *jarach* and the *chizia*. When money was wanted for war or to continue the fantastic buildings, extra taxes were levied on the Mozarabs. On one occasion, they were forced to pay at Cordova an overcharge of more than a hundred thousand *sueldos*, equivalent to several million *pesetas* of modern

Spanish money. Any injury done to a Mozarab remained unpunished; if committed by another Mozarab, the latter only had to renounce his religion to be forgiven.

The state recognised the existence of the Church; but only as a means of dominating and tyrannising over it. A bishop, when elected, could not occupy his see without the emir's permission. Sometimes it was the emir himself who elected bishops at the price of a handsome sum, or of a promise of absolute submission. Provided they undertook to fulfill either of these conditions, it mattered not if they were merely laymen, untaught clerics, or priests of very bad character. With such prelates in office within the Church we can imagine what the councils would be — a miserable assembly of wicked or weak men, over whom the intrigues of the sultan or his representatives could prevail, even if crowds of Moors and Jews did not enter to carry a decision by force.[2]

Priests were the greatest sufferers from Moslem fanaticism. Their presence in the street generally caused some disagreeable scene; the children spoke to them insultingly, the young men sang irreverent and indecent songs, older persons shook their heads and looked rudely or angrily at them, while rubbish or stones or filth was hurled on them from the windows. Men looked on them as unclean, avoided speaking to them, or if they were forced to do so, stood at a distance so as not to touch their clothes. It was extremely dangerous for them to enter the Moslem quarters, and they never left their house except when absolutely obliged, so that they might not encounter the barbarous fanaticism of the rabble.

The monthly payment of the *chizia*, humiliating and painful for all the Christians, was doubly so for them. They

---

[2] This was the case later on when the religious discussion between Hostégesis and Sansón was raging. The Christians of Cordova gave way before the heretic who was protected by Servando. The latter sent to the council every sort of vagabond of whatever religion, the first he met in the streets.

often feigned to be ill or remained in bed for the day, less for the sake of saving a few gold pieces than to avoid the blows and insults showered on them while making payment. Such was the condition of the Church under the Mohammedan yoke.

CHAPTER XIII

THE RELIGIOUS *CONFLICT* DEEPENS

GRIEVOUS AS was the suffering and humiliation of the Christians, the Mohammedans were not satisfied. They believed that the existing treaty was excessively tolerant and seriously proposed, as Eulogius states, that it should be abrogated. In making this statement the saint possibly had in mind the intrigues against the Christians carried on in the palace of Abderrahmán by the Jew, Bodo, himself an apostate from the Catholic Faith.

On returning from his long journey, Eulogius had found the Church at Cordova in a state of perturbation owing to the influence exercised over the emir's counsellors by this man. His history, therefore — sad as it is interesting — deserves a special place in this narrative.

Educated from childhood at the court of Louis the Pious, he acquired a theological and literary culture rare at that time, which raised him to the dignity of deacon of the palace. In 838 he asked permission to make a pilgrimage to Rome, which the emperor granted, entrusting him with valuable presents. To these the deacon added by seizing the rich altar vases from the imperial chapel, thus violating the consecrated building. Bodo then apostatised from Christianity. Soon after leaving the court he became a Jew, took the name of Eleazar, and sold his travelling companions as slaves to some Jewish merchants, with the exception of his nephew, whom he forced to receive circumcision. To conform to Jewish customs, Bodo let his hair and beard grow and married a Jewess.

He must have been in communication before this with the

Jews and dazzled by the favour they enjoyed in the Frankish kingdom. The Empress Judith, who tyrannised over the weak Louis the Pious, openly protected them. Wide liberty of belief reigned in the court, and still wider liberty of morals. Bodo owned to having met there members of fourteen different sects, and did not blush to tell of shameful doings within the very church itself. He was still the crude peasant, under the varnish of his literary training.

In the middle of August, 839, he appeared in Saragossa, much to the scandal of the Spanish Christians, and shortly after this presented himself at the emir's capital. The Jews greeted him with delight. He seems to have written at the time an apology for his conduct in which he bitterly vilified Christianity. Alvaro, who had Jewish blood in him, thought he could convert the apostate, and in 840 began a correspondence with Bodo. It is interesting on account of the ideology and character of the writers. A medieval monk later copied their letters, but an overscrupulous reader afterwards tore from the folio the barbarous answers of the Jew so that only a few short passages remain.

In the first letter Alvaro treats the apostate (his "dear Eleazar") with affection and mildness. He openly states that he wishes to win him for our Lord and offers to change his own belief if he is convinced that it is not true. He interprets the Messianic prophecies, shows that the doctrine of the Trinity is already contained in the Old Testament, and tries to overcome Bodo's repugnance for the dogma of the Word Incarnate.

Eleazar replied, pleading the obscurity of the Sacred Scriptures, and the various interpretations put on them. He strove to justify his apostasy by alleging the immorality of many Christians of which he gives a harsh picture. "Farewell," is his closing taunt, "be you with your Jesus forever." To this Alvaro replied in truly beautiful words:

Amen, and again, Amen! Amen in heaven and on earth! As I embrace Him willingly with faith, by means of His grace, so may He hold me fast, and may nothing ever drag me from His arms either by violence or magic.

Alvaro's second letter was stronger and more ironical, resembling rather his adversary's in tone, but the latter was far inferior to the Mozarabic doctor of theology in learning and the power of reasoning. Bodo's second letter, especially, is as poor in argument as it is rich in sarcasm.

Once more Alvaro responded, driving him into a corner with the force of his reasons. His style became hard and aggressive with its subtle irony, and expressions occurred that are too strong for our delicate palate. His explanation of the Holy Scriptures shows no ordinary knowledge of classic writings. "Your law," he says, "announced Christ even more strongly than did mine. Thousands of Jews hoped for Him; through thousands of years they prepared themselves for His sacred advent. . . . We are the true children of Israel who looked for the Messias, but when the fullness of the time was come, according to the prophet's vision, the glory of the Lord filled the whole earth."

However, Alvaro found he was wasting his time. There are things which are not set right with reasoning or quotations from Sacred Writ. "It was not logical difficulties that made you a Jew," he told him. "Do you know what it was? The same thing that drove Adam from Paradise; that led Solomon, the beloved of the Lord, astray; that blinded Samson. . . . Who was the author of all this evil? Woman, the moth of soul and body. . . . But if you were so fond of pleasure, you might have become a Mohammedan and had many wives instead of one, and revelled to satiety in filth. Why did you lose this world and the other?" But elsewhere, repenting of this irony, Alvaro writes: "I am sorry to see you in this state. God knows I pity you with all my heart."

As was to be expected, Eleazar took no notice of these friendly advances. He clung to his opinion and cut short the discussion in an easy and trite way by saying that he took no notice of the barking of mad dogs. Alvaro congratulated him on his prudence: "It would never do for the fox to bark when the dog yelps."[1]

The Jew dissembled his anger for the moment, but not for long. Like all apostates, he made every effort to depreciate his former coreligionists. He urged the Saracens not to tolerate the Christian religion and lost no opportunity of stirring up a persecution. He knew the emir disliked the Mozarabs, also that the Jews had rendered him no small service. A few years before they had succeeded in opening the port of Barcelona to him in an expedition he made to the frontier province.

The better to carry out his projects, Bodo took the military badge and enlisted in the troops that defended the emir, in the hope that it would help to introduce him into the palace. He had the audacity to propose that a decree should be published commanding that all Christians should be forced to become either Moslems or Jews.

This was the state of things when Eulogius returned from Navarra. But Abderrahmán knew that this was not the moment to create internal difficulties. The Normans had been making great havoc on the southern coasts and had succeeded in entering Seville, so that it was feared they would land again; the kings of Asturias were continually harassing the frontiers; a new focus of resistance was forming in Navarra; the loyalty of the governor of Aragon was suspected, and to top all these evils, Andalusia was undergoing a drought so fearful that the animals died and the parched ground cracked.

Far from listening to Bodo's plans, the emir resolved to

---

[1] The statements about Bodo are taken from the *Anales Bertinianos* (A.D. 849) and from what remains of his correspondence with Alvaro, *Esp. Sagr.*, II, pp. 171–218

make peace with Charles the Bald whose incursion into Gothia he had long resisted. In 837, he sent therefore an embassy to Rheims, which was well received by the emperor. No doubt it included some of the chief Christians of Cordova with a letter from their coreligionists begging Charles to recall the apostate, the veritable scourge of the Mozarabs.

Henceforth no more is heard of the Jew. Probably he became a Moslem as Alvaro had advised, or died in a French dungeon.

In his last days Alvaro wrote a hymn in praise of the cross, celebrating the triumph of the Church over infidels and especially over the synagogue, probably in remembrance of these troubled days. The cross, reared among the stars of heaven, laughs to scorn the enemies of the Faith and recalls the day when Christ died on its arms and heaven celebrated, with a thousand prodigies, the sublime feast of the dead. In any case, Bodo's frustrated plot furnished the first spark of the conflagration kindled soon after by Mussulman fanaticism.

As time went on the lower classes, and even the alfaquíes who made them fanatical, were delighted at the rumour that a descendant of Fátima, after conquering Constantinople, the capital of Christendom, would reign as monarch in Spain, kill all the Christians of Cordova and the neighbouring provinces, and sell their wives and children so cheaply that a boy could be bought for a spur and a girl for a hat plume. This prophecy is contained in a book written by the celebrated theologian, Abdelmelic ben Habid, a contemporary of St. Eulogius and a renegade of Granada.

Some years afterwards there returned to Andalusia Ibn-Hocal, an emissary of the Fatimites, who had been victorious in Africa and wished to set foot in Spain. In his book of travels, after having stated that the Christians were very numerous and troublesome to the Government, he proposed a very simple way of getting rid of them — to exterminate every one of them. The only drawback he saw to such an expeditious means was that it would require much time to carry it out. But after all it was nothing but a question of time.[2]

The royal council saw things from another point of view. The luxury of the court needed funds, and the people who filled the treasury must not be wanting. Besides, the Christians worked hard: they swelled the ranks of the artisans of Cordova, and all the stonemasons and builders in the palaces of the great were Christians more or less Islamised. If these Christians become Mohammedans, Abderrahmán III would have to import thousands of workmen from the north to Spain to finish the fantastic buildings of his predecessor.

Evidently this moderation, even as regards religion, was inspired by policy, an art of which Abderrahmán was a past master. His courtiers counselled no tolerance.

Among them was Ziryab, a Persian musician, pupil of the famous singer Ishac Maucili. Driven from the court of Bagdad by his master's jealousy, he came, together with his wives, children, and slaves, to seek his fortune in the West. Alháquem had just died; but his son received the musician enthusiastically, giving him large sums of money and a magnificent palace.

From the first time that Ziryab sang before him, he would listen to no one else. The Persian had so large a repertoire that he could have sung every day for years without repeating himself. He was a brilliant, clever talker, extremely cultured, and of matchless charm. Abderrahmán was enchanted with his songs and descriptions of the countries and peoples he had seen. In Cordova he was the glass of courtly fashion, determining court manners and ways in the smallest details for the aristocracy, and was looked upon as the model of good form. Perhaps his hair was not fine, for he cut it to the

---

[2] Dozy, *Historia de los árabes de España*, translated by Castro, Vol. III, 28.

roots; as a consequence, the once long hair of the courtiers, parted in the middle, was henceforth seen no more.

Ziryab, a man of tact, did not interfere in politics; this task was left for Jahya and Nazar. The former, as we remember, had been the chief instigator of the riot in the suburb, but was convinced later that it was better to curry favour with the head of the state than to conspire against him. The ruler was fascinated by his cold, churlish virtue, and handed over to him, with the direction of his own conscience, the religious and political jurisdiction, and the administration of justice. In order to dismiss a judge, Jayha had only to ask him to present his resignation. The alfaquíes flattered him, the public revered him, and the authorities feared him. Jayha died in 849, and then, says Aben Adhari, "the alfaquíes were freed from his venom." Unfortunately, many of them were infected with it.

If Jahya was a fanatical Arab, Nazar was even worse. He was descended from apostates. His father, of pure Spanish blood, did not even know Arabic. From a simple eunuch of the harem, Nazar had risen to be prime minister.

By his intrigues he had become close friends with the Sultana Tarub, a selfish woman devoured by a thirst for wealth. From time to time she took a fancy to shutting herself up, and locked herself in her dwelling place. Abderrahmán persuaded her to open her door by sending her a necklace or blocking it up with little bags of silver coin. Like most women in the emir's palaces, she was a slave from the north of Spain, and must have troubled herself little about religion since she entered the palace; but Nazar, her right hand, showed profound hatred for his ancestors' coreligionists.

The emir had succeeded in making himself loved by his Moslem subjects and feared by his enemies. St. Eulogius, always impartial and just, recognised in him great capability and success in war, indomitable energy, fine political tact, and a regal generosity by which he subjected his enemies better than by his arms.

Nazar's capability enabled the emir to neglect politics in order to indulge his sensuality. Either he was in his harem — he left nearly two hundred children — or at table, enjoying the matchless banquets prepared by Ziryab. He composed verses celebrating his victories or the charms of his favourites; enjoyed listening to recitals of his two favourite poets, Aben Xamri and Algazali; heard with reverence the canonical-religious dissertations of Jahya; was ravished with the melodies of the Persian singer, or played at chess with another favourite whose company pleased him wonderfully: Mohammed ben Said ben Gamri, walí of Sidonia.

His life, worthy of a follower of Epicurus, equally fitted a follower of Mohammed, and Abderrahmán, though he had studied philosophy, was a good Moslem, indeed a pious Moslem, who submitted with docility to the penances imposed on him by his director, Jahya ben Jayha. Doubtless he had to see that the two fundamental laws of his religion were kept: that no Moslem or son of a Moslem should renounce Mohammedanism, and that no one should speak profanely of Allah or his prophet. The Koran punished with pain of death whoever broke these laws, and Abderrahmán knew how to make the word of God's messenger obeyed. "Beneath his yoke," Eulogius declared later on, "the orthodox Church suffered almost to the point of extinction."

Not that he was bloodthirsty; he easily forgave his enemies and rather despised than hated Christians. He would never have provoked a religious conflict. A struggle was bound to come; the Christians feared and foresaw it, but it would result from the intolerance of the people of Cordova, a mixed class of renegades, natives of Barbary, Arabs and Syrians, united in defending the Koran. The populace were fanatically addicted to men like Jahya, who was prejudiced against learned Andalusians versed in the studies of the East, and who therefore spoke with horror of the daring spirits who in the courts of the *abásidas* disputed on all questions, sacred and profane, setting aside all revelation and ridiculing the Koran. The rabble of Cordova hated these philosophers, called them impious, insulted them, and more than once stoned and burnt them.

This intolerance daily showed itself also against the Christians, especially against the fervent followers of Eulogius. At the end of Abderrahmán's reign there was a resurgence of fanaticism that filled the measure of the sufferings undergone for the last century. The Christians resisted valiantly, defying their oppressors in a manner unknown to history. They could wield the sword, join the movements of revolt preparing in all quarters, but they sought to die in a more glorious manner.

CHAPTER XIV

BEGINNINGS OF MARTYRDOM – *PERFECTUS AND JUAN*

THE CONFLICT broke out during the early part of 850. Many Moslems were perplexed by the Christian revival that was taking place in their midst. They wanted to know what these more fervent Christians really thought and spoke about in private, and what they preached about Christ and Mohammed. A group of Moslems one day accosted a priest who was passing in the street in order to satisfy their curiosity. The priest, Perfectus, belonged to the church of San Acisclo, and was probably the procurator of the community, as business often took him to Medina and Axarquia. He had spent almost all his youth in the episcopal college studying science and ecclesiastical literature, and spoke Arabic fluently.

In answer to the Moslems' questions Perfectus fearlessly affirmed the divinity of Christ. "As for your prophet," he added; "I dare not tell you what Catholics think of him for you would make me pay dear for it, but if you give me your word that I have nothing to dread, I will tell you, in confidence, where the Gospel speaks of Mohammed and of the fame he enjoys with us."

The infidels, increasingly curious to hear in what Gospel Mohammed is mentioned, promised on oath all the priest had asked. "Well," continued Perfectus, "there is a text that says. 'There shall arise . . . false prophets, and shall show great signs and wonders, insomuch as to deceive (if possible) even the elect' (Matt. 24:24). Of all these the chief is Mohammed, the enemy of God, seduced by the devils and the prey of evil enchantments, who after having sunk you into the filth of uncleanness, seeks to fling you into the torments of hell."

The poor priest had fallen into the trap. His questioners let him go free that day, without losing sight of him. A short time afterwards, as he was passing through that district, a furious crowd, compared by Eulogius to an angry swarm of bees, threw themselves upon him and dragged him before the cadí's tribunal with such violence that his feet hardly touched the ground.

"This man," they cried, "has blasphemed the prophet (may the blessing of peace be on him!) you know what punishment his crime deserves."

The judge of the Moorish assembly of Cordova was a man after Jahya's own heart, whom the terrible alfaquíes had set at the head of the tribunal. His name was Mohammed ben Ziad el Lajmí. He was said to be honourable and good, and to tell the truth he was not noted for strictness, yet he had to carry out the law of the Koran: whoever blasphemed Mohammed was to be condemned to death.

Perfectus was afraid and denied the blasphemies he was accused of, but it was useless. The rabble clamoured with threats for his death. The capital sentence was confirmed by the first minister and the emir, and Perfectus laden with chains, was taken to the filthy cavern in which the worst criminals were confined until their execution. He had been imprudent enough to trust to the oaths of the Moslems who had betrayed him.

The courage that had failed him in the cadí's presence came back in prison. Nothing could save his life, but he sought to prepare for death, atoning for his cowardice by a life of penance and ceaseless prayer. He hardly let sleep close his eyes, but confessed his faith aloud, and angrily blasphemed Mohammed and his teaching. He thus spent two months in profound joy. Nazar seemed to have forgotten him; perhaps he wished to prolong Perfectus' sufferings. In this surmise the priest was mistaken. The eunuch had his plans. By a refinement of cruelty he resolved that the priest's punishment should take place during the solemn festivity that followed the feast of Ramadán.

The feast fell this year on Friday, April 18. For thirty days the streets of Cordova had been silent and deserted, but the moon of Ramadán had set and the month of fasting was followed by the festival of Xaual. All was joy and animation. The crowd hastened to the mosques, some by foot, others on mules, camels, or horses superbly caparisoned. Even the women, shut up during the whole year in harems, went out that day to pray in the mosques, laugh in the gardens, and weep in the cemeteries. Masters and slaves, women and children, all went with their new clothes and festal ornaments. Joyful retinues of the nobles crossed the streets carrying palms; bread and wheat was given to the poor at the gates of the palaces; men drank until they were tipsy; in every place there were songs, flowers, greetings, congratulations, a thorough outbreak of men's primitive instincts.

In the afternoon, the crowd crossed to the other side the Guadalquivir, where the most solemn moment of the feast would be celebrated. An enormous multitude filled the flat plain that is now called the Campo de la Verdad. Countless boats filled the river, picturesque groups met beneath the trees for their annual rejoicing. Among the devotees, clothed in the white pilgrim's robe — the sacred *irham* — passed visitors from all Islam's dominions to behold the lofty Al-Kobbat, the vast dome of the mosque of Cordova, which although it did not yet possess its twenty-eight naves, was already known as one of the most famous structures.

The leader of prayers arrived, mounted on a superb chestnut horse. The Moslems followed. He was to preach the sermon for the feast. Making the ritual prostrations and invocations, he said repeatedly: "God is great," accompanied by a chorus of murmured approbation. He then read some pages from the Koran, and after having bowed to the East with profound reverence, gravely pronounced the sacred formula: "In the name of Allah, clement and merciful." With this done, he continued: "Ye faithful, we commemorate a great day, the sublime anniversary of the revelation made by God to his prophet. So long as the sun shines, and the moon grows and diminishes, it will be celebrated by men on earth and angels in heaven."

He then praised almsgiving, which the law bade them practise daily, exalted the disciples and companions of Mohammed, and remembering the Christian priest who was mourning in prison, hurled furious anathemas on the infidel dogs who blasphemed and vilified the prophet.

That sufficed to arouse the fanaticism of his audience. Drunk with wine, they now wanted to be drunk with blood as well. "Let the blasphemer appear," they howled, like mad dogs. Perfectus was led in, accompanied by the executioners, and brought into the very midst of the revellers. He was calm, ripe for martyrdom. Regardless of the threats and jeers of the multitude he had said on the way: "Yes; I spoke against your prophet and I do so now. He was an impostor, an adulterer, possessed, and his religion was the religion of Satan. All of you will go to hell."

The idea of furnishing sport for his enemies had disturbed him on one account.

"I assure you," he told his fellow-prisoners, "that this Nazar, this haughty man before whom the heads of the most noble families bow down, this eunuch who wields sovereign power in Spain, will never again see the festival that he has chosen for my death."

Perfectus walked to the scaffold, blaspheming Mohammed before the angry crowd that surged around him, curious and enraged. With a firm step he mounted to the block where the executioner beheaded him in sight of the multitude.

During the acclamations of the Moslems, a boat that was crossing the river sank, drowning two Mohammedans. Six more who were with them saved themselves by swimming. The Christians looked on this as a judgment from heaven. St. Eulogius said: "God remembered His martyr. Our cruel persecutors sent one to Paradise; the river ingulfed two of them to send them to hell." This damped the joy of the Moslems; their rejoicings ceased; the groups dissolved and an atmosphere of tragedy took the place of the noisy, bustling mass of revellers.

Taking advantage of this unexpected event, the bishop, accompanied by some priests and devout laymen, carried away the body of the martyr enveloped in his own blood. It was borne by them to the episcopal basilica, and reverently placed beside the relics of St. Acisclus. No one doubted that Perfectus was a saint.

Some time afterwards the Christians suffered again from Moslem bigotry. There lived in Cordova a shopkeeper named Juan,[1] a good Christian but not one who was expected to be called by God to suffer martyrdom. He was an intelligent, bustling merchant, acute enough in all lawful means of selling his goods. As he had many Moslem customers, he had got into the habit of swearing, as they did, by the prophet.

"By Mohammed," he used to say, "you could not buy anything finer! I assure you of it by your prophet, may God bless him!"

In the Christian merchant's shop everything sailed with the wind, right aft. Not so in his neighbour's case. They were Moslems and saw in the lucky shopkeeper a rival of whom they must get rid. They tried in vain for some time, and at last went up to him saying: "You can't be allowed to swear by Mohammed every time you tell a lie." Juan answered that he had meant no harm. But his neighbours were so pertina-

---

[1] *Memoriale Sanctorum*, Vol. III, Chap. IV.

cious that at last he said: "Very well; I won't name your prophet again, and accursed be he who does so!"

That was precisely what his enemies had wanted. Hardly had he said the words than they laid hold of him violently, and with shouts and cries took him before the cadí, who sentenced him to four hundred stripes. After this, setting him, half dead, upon an ass, with his head to its tail, they took him through the city, accompanied by the town crier, loaded him with chains and threw him into a dungeon.

The Moslems were disgusted at this sentence. If Juan was guilty, he should have been beheaded; but the judge, seeing the envy of his accusers, acted like Pilate: "I will chastise him therefore, and release him" (Luke 23:16). Mohammed ben Ziad could not easily bring himself to sign the death penalty; these scruples brought about his dismissal.

A nephew of Achab, one of the emir's wives, made an irreverent remark on a rainy day about God. He was imprisoned and Achab interceded for him in vain. A tribunal consisting of the six most famous alfaquíes was formed to judge him. Among them were Mohammed ben Ziad and Abdehuelic ben Habid, the great teacher of the time. The cadí and three others said that the accused, though deserving severe punishment, should not be condemned to death, as he had spoken without intending to be blasphemous. But Abdehuelic, breaking into a flood of tears, exclaimed: "May his blood be upon my head! The Lord whom we serve has been blasphemed, shall we not defend him? We should not be faithful servants but wicked slaves." The case being brought before the sultan, he decided that the blasphemer should be crucified and the cadí dismissed.

But Nazar's hour had come, thus "fulfilling to the letter," as St. Eulogius said, "the inspired prophecy made by Perfectus in prison." The all-powerful minister died a victim of his insatiable ambition.

Abderrahmán, though not very old, was exhausted by

self-indulgence. With his constitution, a fit of apoplexy might carry him to the grave. He was aware of this, and had appointed as his successor his eldest son, Mohammed, the child of Bohair, one of his favorite wives. But the Sultana Tarub wished to secure the throne for her son Abdalá. Nazar, who hated Mohammed, was of the same mind. The sultana and the eunuch concocted a plot by which a catastrophe was to be brought about by poison, the weapon commonly used in the Byzantine court.

There dwelt in Cordova an oriental doctor named Hairani, famous for a remedy against gastric disease, which he sold at fifty *monedas* the flask. The eunuch went to him, and after having satisfied the man's greed for money, told him to prepare a poison, the very name of which was of evil omen: "ambrosia of kings." Hairani sent the potion to Nazar, but was seized with scruples, and, by means of a woman in the harem, advised the sultan not to drink any ambrosia of Nazar's giving.

When the minister visited his master, the latter began, as usual, to complain about his health. "I know of a remedy that will cure you directly," said Nazar, "I will bring it to you tomorrow morning, for it must be taken fasting." Next day, Nazar presented himself with the flask of medicine, saying: "Here it is, my lord."

"I do not feel sure about it," answered the emir with a malicious smile: "try it first yourself."

Nazar drank it with perfect calm; he rushed back at once to his palace, sent for the doctor, and after telling him what had happened, asked for an antidote. Hairani prescribed goat's milk. But it was too late; the poison had burnt up Nazar's entrails. This happened in the year 851.

Every effort was made at court to hush up the plot, in which important persons were concerned besides Nazar and the sultana. Perhaps someone may have spoken of it to the assembly of cadís and rulers summoned by the sultan a few months later to swear fealty to his heir, Mohammed, but the populace knew nothing of what had happened. There was only a vague rumour that the minister had been poisoned. St. Eulogius mentions it without attaching great importance to it, stating that violent heat had devoured the eunuch's entrails, and applying to him what Sedulius sang of Arius; *Visceribus fusis, vacuus quoque ventre remansit.*[2]

---

[2] The history of Perfectus and Juan, as well as the narrative of the other martyrs, is told by Eulogius (*Memoriale Sanctorum*, Vol. II, Chap. I).

CHAPTER XV

A FEARLESS BAND OF *MARTYRS*

THE LAST days of Abderrahmán were characterised by increased rigour and intolerance in religious matters. The public opposed the revival of the Christian spirit which they realised was directed against Moslem tyranny and oppression, as exercised in every field against the Christians.

But popular opposition grew also against certain Moorish schools of philosophy whose members had little regard for established authority, even when they were not spies sent by the politico-religious sect of Ketamianos, who were becoming alarmingly powerful in Africa.

The intolerance of the orthodox Moslem clergy, encouraged by the Government, was sternly set against any innovation, however harmless, in their religion. They regarded as heresy all arguments concerning Allah's revelation, even when used to confirm it by the natural light of reason. All books were prohibited without examination, excepting those that were traditional, and all schools of law were persecuted if they did not follow the traditional interpretation of the *malequens*, officially adopted in Spain.

Any complaint unconsciously uttered by the suffering sick fell beneath the rigour of the law, as did any irreverent speech, though uttered with no wrong intention. This intransigence reached an incredible degree; it produced an atmosphere of impeachment and a carefully organised system of inquisition.[1]

At the same time that the Christians were troubling the minds of the cadís, the state ministers took by surprise a Moslem missionary who was preaching an esoteric theology founded on a symbolic interpretation of the Koran. The ignorant populace willingly listened to the austere, penurious-looking preacher, with tonsured head, uncut nails, and a beard that reached to his waist, worn under the pretext that it is not lawful for a man to alter what God had made. He was probably only a harmless fanatic, but Abderrahmán put an end to his sermons by having him crucified. While lifted on the cross, he asked his judges: "Do you kill a man who says: 'Allah is my Lord'?" This confession of faith availed him nothing. But neither did such severity avail to stop the progress of philosophy, which soon spread in Cordova as it had in Bagdad.

The same was the case with Christianity. "This frightful crime," said Eulogius, alluding to the death of Perfectus, "made many who were tranquilly enjoying their Faith in divine contemplation among the craggy rocks of the mountainside and amid the vast solitude of the forests, come down among the crowd to show their hatred for the wicked prophet and curse him with their tongue, inflaming souls with a violent longing to die for justice."

These generous spirits were the anchorets from the mountains of Cordova. Accustomed to penance, they were prepared fearlessly to face torture by the grace of God; free from all family and worldly cares, it was thought little by them to exchange their secluded toilsome life for the open hatred

---

[1] Asín Palacios, in his book *Abenmasarra y su escuela*, describes with his usual mastery the hostile feeling in Cordova against philosophical discussions during the reigns of the first emirs (pages 18–30). The history of the extravagant anonymous dogmatist is given by Abenandhari, translated by Fernández y González into Spanish, p. 180.

and contempt of men. During their long vigils and meditations they had thought of the grandeur of faith, the vanity of error, the eternity of future bliss and the evanescence of present things. They read the books that told them of the eternal promises of God and studied the Holy Scriptures which they loved so well, especially the passages which Eulogius was wont to dwell upon:

> Go and teach all nations. . . . That which I tell you in the dark, speak ye in the light; and that which you hear in the ear, preach ye upon the housetops. . . . Behold I send you as sheep in the midst of wolves. . . . You shall be brought before governors, and before kings for my sake, for a testimony to them and to the gentiles. . . . Fear ye not them that kill the body, and are not able to kill the soul: but rather fear him that can destroy both soul and body into hell.[2]

These men were hated and despised, but they rejoiced, like the Apostles, to be persecuted and held in contempt for the name of Christ. The grace of God on which alone they relied, rendered them firm, strong, and invincible against all this world's powers. Their mission it was to react against the persecution which was sometimes violent, sometimes crafty and perfidious. On them the Church could depend to protest against the disappearance of the true Christian spirit, and to arouse the Mozarabs when sunk in the enervating voluptuousness of Islam that surrounded them. Their protest was a rebellion that had a character entirely its own. They sought not to rule, but to suffer. They came not to slay, but to die, they wished that the words of the Gospel might be fulfilled in their regard: "He that shall lose his life for My sake, shall save it" (Luke 9:4). No one should say of them what a traveller in Andalusia recorded at the end of that same century: "The saddest thing witnessed by foreigners in this country is that it is entirely under the sway of tyranny, for its in-

---

[2] Matt. 10: See *Memorial de los Santos*, Book I, Chap. V.

habitants have neither dignity, nor brains. They are cowardly and unable to defend themselves."[3]

They were no cowards. All were ready to shed their blood for the Faith; all longed to be martyrs. But St. Eulogius, who had instigated this outbreak of enthusiasm, knew how to control it. "A martyr, like a monk needs a vocation," he said, "This grace is given only to a few, not to all. Those who are to be martyrs have been chosen from eternity." Eulogius stressed this idea repeatedly; traces of it are constantly found in his writings. But he added, lest he should betray the mission God had entrusted to him: "Nothing can stop those who go to martyrdom inspired by the Holy Ghost." Great purity of life and ardent zeal for the Faith are the best indications of a true martyr, and if to this were added a supernatural sign — a vision, words from heaven, a revelation — so much the better.

Eulogius discovered these marks in Isaac, a young cenobite of the Abbey of Tábanos. He belonged to one of the richest and most aristocratic families of Cordova, had been highly educated, and spoke Arabic perfectly. This, together with his uprightness and business capacities, won him, while still very young, the favour of Abderrahmán who entrusted him with a high position connected with the royal revenues. But at the age of twenty years, whether embittered by the insolence of the Arabs with whom he had daily contact, or impelled by conscientious scruples, he left the court and all his brilliant prospects to bury himself in the monastery of Tábanos. There he found several members of his own family, among whom were Jeremias and Isabel, founders of the monastery.

It so happened that this was the favourite abbey of Eulogius on account of its nearness to the city, its isolation, and the religious enthusiasm of the community. He enjoyed the society of the two founders, who after a most luxurious life

---

[3] Dozy, *Historia de los árabes de España*, Vol. III, p. 23.

in the world gave themselves up to the strictest penance. Many in the monastery, both men and women, looked upon him as their spiritual father, and he launched them upon the perilous path of contemplation. The venerable Abbot Martin was happy to take advantage of his thorough knowledge of divine science. Isabel, the abbess, consulted him about the supernatural experiences of her daughters. All received him as their father whenever he came there.

Among his most attentive hearers, besides Isaac, was a young priest named Fandila, from Guadix, who had come to study in the famous schools of Cordova, but while still young had left his teachers to live under the direction of Abbot Martin. Among the virgins was a young girl named Digna, not yet twenty years of age. All admired her for her humility, devotion, and obedience. Delicate as a flower, she was unbending as steel in the practice of penance. Having learned to despise the world, she would one day despise life.

Eulogius, further, had the highest admiration for the holiness of the virgin Columba, described as "most beautiful and noble, the mirror and standard of sanctity for all." With her sister Isabel she ruled and directed the nuns, taking special charge of the young. Before entering the monastery she had for a long time opposed the plans of her mother, who had wished her to marry one of the richest, most fashionable young men in Cordova. Columba procrastinated, and meanwhile her mother died.

Once in the monastery, the young girl set herself to redeem the lost time. Eulogius, who only discreetly alludes to her beauty, cannot find words to describe her virtues. She surpassed all in grace of soul. Her conversation was praiseworthy, her humility sublime, her chastity perfect, her charity constant. She prayed devoutly, obeyed with docility, was quick to sympathise, ready to forgive, eager to teach, and eloquent. She never gave way to anger. When the children were naughty or a sister was negligent, a humble glance from her sufficed to correct them. She never gossiped; her heart and lips spoke nothing but Christ. Nor did she ever discuss others unkindly. "I know," she told Eulogius, "the devil's deceit and men's malice which often condemn those who are innocent in God's sight." Blameless as her life was, she keenly felt the sting of temptation. The enemy clouded her soul with sadness and aridity; sometimes he made her weary of life, at others he promised her extreme old age; he recalled to her the faces of the young men she had met at court festivals, and wore her out with worldly imaginations. Hers was a true southern temperament, vehement and impassioned. Unable to suppress these disturbing suggestions, she wept, and seized with panic, mortified her body by penance. She feared lest she might fail to follow her vocation until death and so lose the company of her Bridegroom. "The ardour with which I long for Him," she told Eulogius, to whom she confided these interior struggles, "opens in my body and soul a frightful wound that nothing can cure except His gaze in heaven."

Eulogius felt sure of the courage these brave women might be counted upon to display in the face of death, but he was still more confident about Isaac who bore the visible seal of the elect. It was said in the monastery that his mother heard him speak before he was born. A nun affirmed she saw a globe of light from heaven enter his mouth. A cenobite declared later on that Isaac had received a miraculous letter prophesying his martyrdom. Everything concurred to create a fervent enthusiasm in the young monk who believed that he was called to die for Christ, and nothing held him back.

He went to the cadí and said: "I wish to become a faithful follower of Mohammed if there is anyone who will teach me his doctrine." The judge, not detecting the irony of his words, spoke to him seriously, proud of being able to exercise his zeal for proselytising.

Eulogius described the scene as if he had been present. The cadí cleared his throat, inflated his cheeks, and poured forth falsehoods from the sonorous caverns of his chest. He spoke of the origin of Islam, the life of Mohammed, his relations with the angel Gabriel, the doctrine of the Koran and the joys of paradise, peopled by lovely houris.

"Falsehoods, fables!" exclaimed Isaac, interrupting the judge, "that wretch deceived you so that he might drag you to hell. Why, as you are a reasonable man, do you not forsake these impostures and become a Christian?"

The judge, beside himself, pale and stupefied, tried to refute him, but his surprise at such unexpected audacity made him speechless. Then, bursting into tears of rage and indignation, he rose in fury and gave his neophyte a violent blow in the face.

The Moslem law forbade such an insult during judgment, as the assessors reminded the cadí. But it was characteristic of the man. The description given of him by St. Eulogius squares with that of Aljoxaní. His name was Said ben Soleiman el Gafequi. The people looked on him as a faithful, fervent Mohammedan. He was distinguished particularly for his patriarchal simplicity. When Abderrahmán sent to nominate him as judge in the Cordovan assemblage, the messengers found him ploughing in his farm near Cordova in the plain of the Bellotas. As a rule he held his ecclesiastical court in the mosque, where he appeared clothed in a white jacket and robe, wearing a white pointed cap, for the turban had not as yet acclimatised itself in Spain.

Other judges went to the Court of Judgment on magnificent horses; he went on foot, and when the tribunal was over, used to take a small black loaf from out his white robe and carry it to be baked in a neighbouring oven. Some of those who laughed at his manner of life heaped acorns on the mat he was wont to pray upon when in the mosque, meaning to cast up against him his low birth.

Being a man of independent character, he had the courage to dismiss the father of the all-powerful eunuch Nazar when he found him wandering among the escort of guards who accompanied the judge on his way to close the sessions.[4]

He was kind rather than severe, and, desirous of pleasing everyone, sometimes sacrificed his own interests to those who contended with him. But his religious fervour partook of fanaticism and this fervour had been stung to the quick by the incredible insults of the young monk. Isaac remained perfectly calm.

"Do you dare," he exclaimed "to injure an image of God in this way?"

"Wretch," answered the cadí, "either you are drunk or mad. Do you not know that it is the immutable law of the prophet you have insulted, that he who dares to speak thus must pay the death penalty?"

"Cadí," the monk replied quietly, "I am neither crazy nor drunk. My fervent love for truth made me tell it to you and those around you. If you condemn me to death for it, I care nothing. I should welcome it with joy and would not move my throat an inch to escape the headman's axe. I well know our Lord's words: 'Blessed are they that suffer persecution for justice' sake; for theirs is the kingdom of heaven'" (Matt. 5:10).

The case being a new one, the judge gave an account of it to the sultan, who was furious and ordered that the law should be carried out in all its rigour, and that, lest the Christians should venerate Isaac's body, as they had that of Perfectus, it should be hung head downward for several days on a gallows, then burnt and the ashes thrown into the river.

Thus, says Eulogius, a glorious way was opened which Isaac could justly claim to have been the first to tread. Many others would follow fearlessly in his footsteps.

These events took place on a Wednesday, June 3. On the following Friday a youth from the south of France, named

---

[4] See the sketch of his character in Aljoxaní's book on the judges of Cordova, translated by Julián Ribera, pp. 137–139.

Sancho, a disciple and admirer of Eulogius, was similarly put to death. Sancho belonged to the slaves' legion, so that to his impiety was added the crime of high treason. They threw him down, drove a large stake through his body, raised him up and left him to endure the convulsion of a prolonged agony in the terrible torture of impalement.

Next Sunday six monks from different monasteries presented themselves, led by Jeremias, the pious founder of Tabanos, and Habentius, the ancient hermit who spent his life weighted down by iron plates and fettered with chains.

"We say the same as our brethren Isaac and Sancho," they told the judge, "we are very sorry for your ignorance but we are bound to tell you that you are poor dupes, deceived by a perverse, possessed man. Pronounce your sentence, invent your tortures, let loose the rabble to avenge your prophet."

They all were beheaded.

The Feast of St. John the Baptist, the Mahrachan, as the Moslems called it, had formerly been celebrated everywhere with joy, music, and flowers. Both Mohammedans and Christians rejoiced and their religious and social differences seemed appeased for a time. In their churches the Mozarabs prayed:

> O God, who hast been pleased that we should all rejoice on this, the natal day of Thy precursor, grant that we may one day all enjoy in Thy presence the bliss that never ends.

Meanwhile in their mosques the Moslems sang:

> See the Mahrachan delight the morn while the cloudlets weep and let fall their tears. The earth clothes itself with perfumed flowers and is covered with a carpet of green silk. The breeze fans the waters of the fountain, and wafts perfumes of musk from its wings. Men send to one another greetings and gifts, and the poor do not gaze with envy on the rich.

This had taken place in former times. But now the joys of St. John were stained with hatred and blood. The Christians entered their churches timidly; the Moslems viewed them with disdain and wrath.

A few days later another martyrdom took place. Sisenando, a deacon of the church of San Acisclos, dreamt that two of the martyrs came down from heaven to bid him suffer for the Faith. He accepted their invitation, and bravely followed them in their confession and sufferings. He was beheaded on July 16, after a few days' imprisonment. Paul the priest, a relative and disciple of Eulogius, died on July 20; and Theodemirus, a monk of Carmona, still a mere boy, on July 25.

Eleven martyrs in less than two months was a startling triumph for the Church of Cordova. The Christians were full of enthusiasm at these scenes of heroism, listening in religious silence to the details told them at the doors of the monasteries, in the vaults of the churches, in the squares and streets. A chorus of praise of these heroes of the Faith rose from all quarters. The sultan might burn the remains of the victims — their fellow Christians held their memory enshrined in their hearts and inscribed their names on the lists of the saints. A few voices were raised in protest, but were drowned by the murmurs of universal praise. It was the spontaneous manifestation of Christian sentiment.

In the monasteries, especially, the enthusiasm was indescribable. The monks were proud, with good reason, of having given new heroes to the Church. The thought that those who had a short time before chanted with them in choir were now in heaven, filled them with joy. The glory of the confessors of the Faith was theirs as well.

Eulogius also claimed a share in it. Far from being alarmed at this sudden outburst of religious enthusiasm provoked by his words, he looked upon it as his strongest recommendation in God's sight. "Allow me, dearest brothers and devout sisters," he said to the dwellers in the monasteries, "to share your joy. You are not so jealous as to reserve for yourselves the patronage of these martyrs who underwent the trial of torture for all the members of the Church. . . . They are both yours and ours. They came from among you, but we are all born of the same baptismal font. All are one in Christ.

"On my part, I have urged several of them on to the combat and if I have not fought myself, I have armed them for the struggle. Let us all share in rejoicing, and jubilantly, indiscreetly, if you will, celebrate the glorious memory of these blessed men. Let us sound forth our voices in unison and offer with a like enthusiasm our sacrifice of praise to that Lord who has brought back to us the blessed times of past ages, by whose grace the saints fight and conquer, go to meet death, and live and grow so valiant as to despise with manly courage all the torments that the impious infidels can invent."

CHAPTER XVI

THE ARDENT CHAMPION OF THE *MARTYRS*

WHILE THE Christians were celebrating the glory of their martyrs, the Moslems were perplexed and stupefied. Good Mohammedans lamented such scenes, which always began by blaspheming their prophet. The court, too, felt undecided; the sultan did not know what measures to take with men who mocked at torments and death. Mistaking the character of the movement, he suspected political complications and feared for the security of his government.

Recafredo, the metropolitan of Seville, the same whom we met at the ordination of Eulogius, came to deliver him from this dilemma. He was worthy of the emir's confidence, having always been a willing tool of Abderrahmán. The latter had rewarded his docility by giving him first the mitre of Cordova, then of Egabro, of Cabra, and finally making him archbishop of Seville. Recafredo took the emir's part and anathematised the martyrs. He then entered the cathedral of Cordova "like a hurricane," says Alvaro. He came to put an end to these fanatics, disturbers of the Church and society, and reckoned, as he declared, on obtaining full support from the sultan.

His coming filled the Christians of Cordova with consternation and revealed the cowardice of the lower classes, who are naturally inclined to uphold what is good so long as they run no risks by it. "Dismayed by the tyrant's wrath," Eulogius wrote to Alvaro, "they changed their opinion with incredible fickleness, and began to abuse the martyrs, saying that both they and their abettors were guilty of a great crime."

The former opposition that had divided Spanish Christians,

of which we find traces in the legends of the last Gothic kings, now returned with renewed embitterment. Since the invasion, there had been two opposing parties among the Mozarabs. One was that of the Biscayans and their descendants, composed principally of Gothic nobles, who after having made a compact with the conquerors were given public charges, both civil and ecclesiastic, and retained their high social position, with its riches and hereditary rights. Their chief preoccupation, and that of their clients, was to keep on good terms with the Moslems. Hence their Christianity was lax, accommodating, and sometimes halting. The other division included those who had upheld King Rodrigo in 711 and still honoured his memory. They were consequently hostile to the invaders. Foremost among them were the great Hispano-Roman families. At present, however, their contention did not go beyond a show of secular antipathy.

Recafredo, heir to the See and also to the traditional emulations of Don Oppas, was not averse to accepting the mission entrusted to him by the emir. He presented himself armed with scimitars and arguments — the scimitars being the most convincing arguments for cowardly Christians, but his texts from Holy Writ making many others vacillate.

"The sultan," said the partisans of the archbishop, "gives us the free exercise of our religion; there is no persecution, no oppression to justify your action. Those you call martyrs are suicides, enemies of their brethren, the scourge of the Church. Such martyrdom is new and unheard of; it springs not from true virtue but from a subtle pride. If these rebels knew Holy Scripture well they would not abuse Mohammed, for it says that evil speakers shall not possess the kingdom of God. The Gospel says in words that contain the essence of Christianity: 'Love your enemies: do good to them that hate you' (Matt. 5:43). The Moslems are right in saying: 'If God had inspired these fanatics to rush to their death, He would have performed miracles to show that Mohammed is not a prophet.' And what miracles has He performed? The relics of your pretended martyrs have been burned, cast to the winds, thrown in the river, or else they decay like other corpses. These martyrdoms do good to no one: the martyrs are simply madmen."

These words were repeated triumphantly in the markets and streets. They were preached in the churches over which the archbishop had been able to impose his authority. The partisans of the martyrs, those who upheld the Christian tradition, shunned and terrorised, dreaded more than ever the fanaticism of the Arabs that was aroused by the recent victories and bitter recriminations of their coreligionists.

Eulogius and Alvaro were still the leaders of this party, but were now strengthened by the authority of Saul, the bishop of Cordova.

Saul had been nominated to the See a year before and was a true ascetic, though impulsive and obstinate. He had not become a bishop with altogether clean hands. Though legitimately elected by the clergy of Cordova, he was refused approbation by the sultan, who knew how upright and irreconcilable he was. Saul could obtain this only by promising a sum of four hundred gold pieces to the eunuchs who surrounded the monarch and who, on that consideration, promised to obtain the royal consent. Once made bishop, Saul, interpreting the canons as he chose, ordained clerics and priests without the clergy's consent; appointed two rectors for the same church without convoking the necessary synod; absolved many persons who had been excommunicated by other bishops, and committed other excesses that the Cordovan clergy did not forgive. The defence of the martyrs suited his puritanical character and afforded him a welcome occasion for restoring his good name in the eyes of faithful Christians.[1]

---

[1] The statements about Recafredo and Saul are to be found scattered through the writings of Eulogius and Alvaro. The latter speaks of Saul's appointment and his arbitrary actions in Letter XIII, *Esp. Sagr.*, XI, 169.

This attitude of his bishop greatly encouraged Eulogius. There were moments when even he had seemed to doubt, moments when he lost courage under the burden of responsibility weighing on him in the campaign of which he foresaw the consequences. He may have wondered whether, after all, it might not be best to be silent and remain quietly at home. But then, as in all the decisive moments of his life, Alvaro came and thrust him back into the battle. To retreat now would have been to condemn the work of his whole life.

It was then that Eulogius determined to write his defence of the martyrs, refuting the sophisms brought against them which had frightened the souls of many who did not fear physical violence. There was need to calm the monks and all good Christians, and at the same time to give them a weapon against detractors.

Eulogius was engaged in this work during August and a great part of September. He had almost finished it when, one day in the beginning of October, 851, the police came to his house and, in spite of the cries of his mother and sisters, carried him off to prison. There he was soon after joined by Bishop Saul, some fellow priests of his diocese, and several abbots of the Cordovan monasteries. Recafredo had taken this means of warning the chiefs of the party that still resisted him, though unfortunately its numbers had greatly diminished.

Alvaro tells us: "Bishops, priests, clerics, and learned theologians of Cordova all took the crooked path, denying by their attitude, if not by their speech, the Faith of Christ. Fear of the sultan's vengeance had subdued their spirit."

None but the captives were at liberty. Eulogius was so uncurbed that he had the courage to publish the first copy of his defence of the defenders of the Faith, entitled: *A Memorial of the Martyrs*. At first he thought the manuscript had been lost in the confusion caused in his house by the entrance of the sultan's emissaries, but fortunately they had taken no notice of the wax tablets and heap of parchment on which he had inscribed it.

When a few days later his family visited him in prison, Eulogius heard, to his great joy, that the papers and tablets had been saved and asked to have them brought to him together with some books from his library. He thought that by reading and writing he would forget the trial of imprisonment and relieve his solitude.

Soon he had finished his book. Making a clearer and more legible copy he sent it to his "dearest brother in the Lord Jesus Christ, Alvaro." "In the past," Eulogius told him, "I was at rest and at peace. Calm and love reigned in my house, and I was happy there. But suddenly fear filled the hearts of all; we were struck with alarm and the whole city trembled."

Eulogius then draws a vivid picture of the situation, gives an account of the motive and history of his book, and adds:

> I think of publishing it. Future generations will decide whether I am waging a shameful war, as detractors say, or whether it does me honour. But first, to deprive my adversaries of any motive for complaint and abuse, I send the book up to you, my dear brother, the trustworthy arbiter of my feeble knowledge, so that if you approve of it, the work may be published: if not, it may be condemned to perpetual silence. If it is silent, no one will laugh at it: if you bid it speak, it can defy the wrath of slanderers and appear triumphantly in the sight of those who will greet it with gratitude.

Alvaro was beside himself with joy on receiving the manuscript. He did not know which to admire most; the literary skill of his friend, the strength of his arguments, the elegance of his style, or his courage in daring so to speak at such a time. He read the book eagerly, entirely approved of it, and wrote a letter full of enthusiasm to the author. For him, Eulogius was not only a friend, but a martyr, a teacher, a guide for God's people, a veritable reappearance of St. Cyprian. Repeatedly he kissed the volumes, written with a trembling hand in the dim light of the dungeon, and affectionately told the holy prisoner:

> You recall to me, my master, the grandeur of the ancients. You have hurled the lightnings of Catholicism through the night, and have opened the fountains flowing from the rich veins of Christ's heart. He who inspired the martyrs for the battle, has also inspired the great teacher to write their praise, when all abused them. Your strength is heavenly, your eloquence both divine and human. With these, as with an invincible weapon, you have been the first to defend the Church, to glorify martyrdom, to fight the Lord's battles. . . . You have wrested light from heaven, giving us in these days the example of fair truth-telling, which both for us and for those after us will be as the perfume of a blossoming bough, sweet as nectar, so that our age may be celebrated in years to come and your name may be known to the uttermost ends of the earth.
>
> You do wrong in disparaging yourself so much; be careful in future lest you err against the truth. As you have submitted to my judgment, listen to my sentence patiently. It is that, for the good of my souls, you should consign to an eternal life this codex, brilliant as the stars. It is a magnificent poem you have given us, so that, enchanted by its melody, we may lose the fear of death; that this inveterate stupor of the soul may disappear, this coldness which freezes our hearts; that the living fervour, the divine fire which Christ brought to earth, may live in lifeless bodies, that the spark may be rekindled that has been quenched and the light restored that has been extinguished by Moslem falsehood.
>
> What joy and triumph for you not only to have praised the confessors, but by your defence to share their torments. Sowing the word of the Kingdom behind prison bars, you amass more glorious victories.
>
> You deserve the praise of all ages to come, for with the axe at your neck, you do not curb your speech, and when all are silent, you speak for all. May your light shine more brilliantly as time goes on. Yours are the reward and the most precious crown.

THE ARDENT CHAMPION OF THE MARTYRS 139

There is nothing to add to this magnificent letter of Alvaro's — the finest he ever wrote. He was right. In these days, the *Memorial of the Martyrs*, like the rest of Eulogius' later works, are a model of style. But let us not lay the stress on that. It would seem absurd nowadays, to compare them as Alvaro did, to "the milky river of Livius, the classic diction of Cato, the vehement speech of Demosthenes, the opulent periods of Cicero, the florid style of Quintilian."

But there is another thing that can be met with in every literary epoch, even during the period of its greatest decadence: it is the verve, life, and colour, which the competent author puts into his expression, whether plain or polished. Eulogius was a master of colour and movement; his pages palpitate with passion and picture the tortures and insults of the dungeon. Alvaro was right in calling the *Memorial* a poem. In recounting the conflicts of the martyrs, Eulogius recalled Turnus and Aeneas; he gives a profound dramatic interest to his recitals, and raises them to the dignity and beauty of an epic poem. If a quotation from Virgil comes to mind, *he does not hesitate* to quote it.[2]

A true reflection of the author's soul, a triumphal tale of glorious Christian action, this book is no less a striking picture of the society of that period, when the ancient Christian spirit of southern Spain resisted for the last time the growing invasion of the Moslem religion. It gives us a panorama of the religious and civil life of the Mozarabs; takes us into the basilicas and monasteries; tells us the secrets of family life; introduces us into the squares and libraries, the mosques and palace of the emir; and shows us how the magnanimous souls who are the heroes in this moving history felt and spoke and thought.

The earliest edition of the *Memorial* consisted of two volumes: the first apologetic, the second giving the narrative. The first combatted the sophism whose publication had been

---
[2] *Indiculo luminoso*, No. 14.

ordered in all parts by the Archbishop of Seville. Against his anathemas Eulogius intoned an enthusiastic hymn in honour of the heroes of the Faith who, "spurred on by an immense desire of heaven, had hastened to behold Christ's face." Their death was not suicide, because they had not sought death directly, but instead the fulfillment of the evangelical words: "Go and preach the Gospel to every creature" (Mark 16:15). Eulogius found many examples in ecclesiastical tradition to support this doctrine.

To those who upheld the Mohammedan religion, he spoke of the ridiculous legends about Mohammed and the inferiority of his teaching compared with that of the Gospel. Concentrating all his hatred on the prophet he argues that since Mohammed would have been deserving of death for making himself the occasion of "the spiritual loss of so many nations," it could not but be meritorious to abuse this criminal man, against whom Christ has pronounced His curse.

As for the martyrs, it matters nothing that no miracles accompanied the death of these heroes. It is that which exalts them, for their faith shines more brightly because of it. Eulogius believed he was living in the last days, when, according to St. Gregory, extraordinary signs will not be seen in the Church. If God allows the bodies of the martyrs to corrupt and be profaned, what harm, the apologist asks, do their blessed souls receive from that? He recalls the line of his compatriot Lucan, that the heavens cover him whose ashes are contained within no funeral urn: *Coelo tegitur qui non habet urnam.*

To refute those who lay stress on the tolerance shown by the infidels, Eulogius paints in the most vivid colours the vexations by which the Christians are oppressed.

> Can it be said peacefully when they destroy our basilicas, insult priests, and oblige us to pay monthly an intolerable tax? Better die now than live such a burdensome, wretched

life. None of us can go among them safely nor remain with them in peace. None of us can pass beyond the rampart that defends us without being overwhelmed with affronts. When some domestic requirement forces us to leave our little corner for the market or forum, when they see that we are clerics, they break forth, like madmen, into insolent abuse, not to speak of the children, who follow us through the streets throwing stones.

Why should I tell what abominable songs they sing on seeing the venerable sign of the cross, and the curses and filthy words they vomit from their mouth at the sound of our bells? We have to bear with their insolence and their hate for our holy religion wherever we may be. They look upon us as plague-stricken, disdain to speak to us, and if forced to do so, keep at a safe distance lest their clothes should brush against ours.

After painting this sombre picture, Eulogius rightly asks:

Who would dare to say, after this, that we have no right to execrate this wicked man? As for the rest, God's martyrs only tell the truth to their enemies, practising Christian charity and losing their lives to save their enemies from error. Did they speak violently, contemptuously? They did; but it was with devout violence, holy contempt. "So should the martyrs speak," says Eusebius of Cesarea, "humbly with brethren; haughtily with persecutors; meekly with their fellows; fiercely with adversaries; faithful to Christ, rebellious against the devils."

If this be so, know, all you blasphemers, know, you depraved men who dare attack the glory of the saints, that on the day of judgment you will be confronted with them, and then will you blush for your blasphemies. As for me, no one shall ever gag me so that I shall not praise them.

You, brothers and holy sisters in Jesus Christ, leap for joy, for you have sent to God's granary the sheaves of your harvest. The fruit from your seed is in the blessed city of Sion. The heavenly Jerusalem has already peacefully received your triumphant brethren. Travel in safety, hasten on; no one will obstruct your path. When you reach your fatherland, there will go forth to meet you not only this phalanx of the blessed, but all the multitude of the elect as well, among whom will be these brothers of ours, the first fruits of martyrdom.[3]

Alvaro may well have been enthusiastic over this eloquent account of the martyrs. Even in these our days we feel the ardour of the divine fire it kindled in cold and torpid hearts, and are forced to exclaim with the old warrior:

"He is worthy of the praise of all the ages, who, with the axe at his throat, does not refrain his tongue, and when all else are silent, speaks for all. Shine forth more brightly every day! Thine are the rewards; thine is the noblest crown!"

---

[3] The first edition of the *Memorial*, together with the latest works of St. Eulogius, was published by Ambrosio de Morales (Alcalá, 1574). In 1608, Francisco Escoto brought out another more accurate edition, in Frankfort, including it in Volume IV of his *España Ilustrada*. By means of these two editions, without any fresh manuscript, Lorenzana published the work in his *Patrum Ecclesiae Toletanae Opera*, Vol. II. Migne reproduced this in Vol. cxv, 706-870, of the *Patrol. Lat.* All these editions of the works of St Eulogius contain, as introduction, his life written by Alvaro.

CHAPTER XVII

PROSODY AND *PRISON WALLS*

THE AUTUMN of 851 was well advanced. The monks of Cordova had received with enthusiasm the work Eulogius sent them from his prison; they copied it out, read it eagerly. It strengthened their vacillating souls, preparing them for fresh triumphs. Meanwhile Eulogius did not rest for a moment. Alvaro says: "While his companions gave themselves up to idleness and rest, he read and prayed, forgetful of his chains, gathering honey from the books and relishing it with palate and heart."

His chief preoccupation was the restoration of Latin prosody. This may be called one of the finest moments of his life. With the sword hanging over his head, he strove to give new impulse to his literary work. There was the highest purpose, as we have already indicated, in this Latin renaissance that he was promoting and for which he was sedulously seeking to provide the necessary conditions.

In the school of Charlemagne the students learnt Latin by writing exercises, first in prose and then in verse; but before imitating classic poetry, they were taught to compose rhythmical verses, which were classical in style merely by the accent. This was all that Eulogius had learnt in his youth, and it is in this way that the poems he sent to his friend were composed. Nothing else could hitherto have been taught. "Learned men in Spain," said Alvaro, "had lost all idea of what Latin verse was."

In fact, from the invasion until well on into the eleventh century, it is little less than impossible to find any well-written poetry. Vigila de Alelda, the great miniature painter, one of the most cultivated men of the tenth century, tells us accurately what an iambus is; he tries to write it and fails. He had the same ill luck with the hexameter.[1]

St. Eulogius was about to introduce a new discovery of his own into the Cordovan school of poetry. His priestly ministry had prevented his studying the matter before, but there were long and favourable hours in prison life for such a lengthy work of patience and minute scrutiny. In the twilight of his dungeon, the prisoner read and reread his poets, comparing one verse with the other, seeking for the metrical value of the syllables, which was the chief matter he had to explain. Everyone knew that a hexameter consisted of six feet and that the syllables, either long or short, succeeded one another in order, but how was anyone to discover the music that made classical language give longer or shorter metrical value to the syllables? This melody had been irretrievably lost — we do not know it even now.

But with patient and intelligent labour, by reading the classic verses, the laws that regulated the quantity of the words might be rediscovered. This is what Eulogius did. His pupils knew how to write such verses but not how to sing them. Neither do we now know it. His first disciple was Alvaro, to whom Eulogius, on leaving prison, taught the metrical art he had composed there. Naturally Alvaro was

---

[1] On Latin prosody from the seventh to the tenth century, see the author's treatise *Origin de los himnos mozárabes*, Bordeaux, 1926, pp. 4-9. The text of Vigila can be found in the famous *Codice Vigilano*, in the Escorial (G. Antolín, *Catal. Cod. Lat.*, Escorial, 1910, I, 371, 402). In the above-mentioned book the author treats of the hymn of St. Zoilus, p. 48, and on p. 161 of a Mozarabic hymn to St. Euphemia, the first eight strophes of which give the acrostic "Eulogius." This seems to be the name of the author of the poem, but it is so badly written that I do not dare to attribute it to the martyr of Cordova. The work of St. Eulogius on Latin prosody is lost, if he ever wrote one. Possibly he taught prosody orally only. Verse by the Mozarabic poets of the ninth century can be found in Vols. X and XI of *España Sagrada*.

enthusiastic about this new way of writing poems and utilised it in composing obscure poems, forgetting that a few years before he was the declared enemy of antiquity. He took to singing to the nightingale, "with its voice sweeter than are organs or harps"; to the cock, "the sonorous watchmen of the night"; to the peacock, "that shines with lustrous plumes, that gazes on the east, and when it turns kindles a thousand lamps."

These and many other things he wrote in perfect Virgilian or Eugenian verse. He would have nothing to do henceforth with the unpolished poets who followed the former fashions. He wanted everyone to write verses in the mode discovered by his friend, and said to the very peacocks and swans:

> Come, sing with my sweet nightingale, but let your songs be metrical, not in such hateful rhythm, the fruit of sloth and error, that mars the Church's chant and sounds forth in the temples like the roar of bulls.

Abbot Sansón also approved of Eulogius' discovery, though he wrote nothing in verse except a few epitaphs. His own epitaph was written by Cyprian, the Archpriest of Cordova, at the end of the century. The latter wrote other poems on less religious subjects. One of them thanked Count Adulfo for his gift of a precious silver urn to contain the Holy Scriptures.

One day Cyprian saw a beautiful fan adorned with gold letters in the hand of Count Wilfred and wrote on it in cumbrous spondees. When at last, after long delay another such fan appeared in the white hand of the Countess Guisanda, the archpriest composed the following distichs: "Adorn, precious fan, the right hand of the illustrious Guisanda; create a wind, illusive though it be, to refresh her during the summer heat and thus fulfill thy twofold office."

Eulogius was the first to put in practice this method which he taught to his contemporaries. Alvaro mentions his hymns, but we do not know where they have disappeared. There is one in the Mozarabic hymnal that seems to have been his; it is dedicated to St. Zoilus, the saint to whose service he consecrated himself from his earliest years, and was written for the days of martyrdom. It was inspired by Prudentius. The poet felt proud of belonging to a city in which Christ had found so many heroes. "He is ours, and was taught in our arena how to conquer with all his might the terrible enemy." Then, recalling the archbishop's partisans, he exclaims: "Protect the martyrs, crown this thy devout city, whence rises on its march to heaven a snow-white choir of senatorial nobles."

Eulogius had one more desire to fulfill while in prison. For some years he had been in debt to the bishop of Pamplona, Wiliesindo, who had received him so hospitably when passing through his diocese in search of his brothers. The good bishop had asked in return nothing else than a relic of St. Zoilus. But communication between Navarra and Andalusia was very difficult on account of the war then dividing the two countries. "Besides this," Eulogius said, "I could not entrust so precious a treasure to anybody by hazard."

At last a propitious occasion occurred. Among those who visited him in prison was Galindo Iñiguez, a nobleman of Navarra, who was delighted to give Eulogius news of the bishop and other people he had known years ago. Don Galindo, as Eulogius calls him, was about to return home, and the prisoner, who trusted him implicitly, confided to him the promised treasure, together with some relics of St. Acisclus, another Cordovan martyr, and a long letter. In this, after recalling the happy days he had spent with the bishop, he told him of the difficult position of the Church of Cordova. He wrote:

> Most blessed Father, I will not hide from you the trouble that we are suffering for our sins in these days, so that, defended by your prayers, we may escape from this abyss of miseries by means of your intercession which has so high a value in God's sight. The fact is that this year, the

tyrant's fury, kindled against the Church of God, has caused a mighty commotion. It has been devastating in its wrath and has dispersed all around him, imprisoning all the clergy he could capture — bishops, priests, abbots, deacons — who are now fettered in loathsome dungeons underground. Among them is this beloved sinner of yours, suffering the same trials and privations.

The Church has been deprived of the sacred ministry, of prayer, sermons, and the Divine Office; we have neither oblations, nor sacrifice, nor incense, nor place for offering whereby we might placate our God. With mournful souls, in the spirit of humility, we offer Christ our suffrages of praise, so that if the choir of psalmody is silenced in the churches, the sacred chant of hymns may resound in the prisons.

But Don Galindo will give you a fuller account of this; I can say no more because I do not wish to trouble you with my unpolished speech — also because my heart is full of anguish.[2]

Eulogius dated this letter November 16. His mind had been filled with a serious preoccupation for some time; he may have been alluding to this in the last sentence. He had met several confessors in prison whose presence encouraged him to suffer. Among them was Juan, the unfortunate shopkeeper who had been forced to undergo the ignominious punishment of scourging through the jealousy of his Mohammedan companions.

It was at this period that a new and remarkable episode took place in his life.

---

[2] This strange letter is found in all editions of Eulogius' works. It is impossible in these days to doubt its authenticity, as did certain writers of the eighteenth century, who had been made unduly suspicious by the recently discovered fables of the apocryphal chronicles

CHAPTER XVIII

THE VIRGIN MARTYR *FLORA*

ONE OF the most beautiful stories in the annals of the Church's history of martyrdoms is that of the virgin martyr Flora.

Her mother was a Christian, a woman of wealth from the mountains of Cordova. Her father was a Moslem, an influential Arab of Seville who made his home in the capital and died while she was still very young. Left to her mother, Flora was brought up in the Christian Faith, though held by the law to practice the religion of Mohammed as the daughter of a mixed marriage. Particularly was she taught to cherish fervently her ascetic practices. At the age of ten she gave all her food to the poor each Friday.

Eulogius had seen her years before when she had just passed through a great public trial, a sanguine martyrdom for Christ that made her sacred to the Christians of Cordova. Her image had remained indelibly impressed upon his memory. In her person he saw united all the outward grace of a chaste, strong, womanly beauty, combined with the indefinable charm of the grace of God, as one whose goal was higher than the world's allurements. Blended with these qualities was her marvellous discretion, firmness of will, and that natural keenness of intellect, characteristic of Andalusia and Seville. But Eulogius, the impassioned historian of the martyrs, was touched to the quick, above all, by her historic past.

Her story up to the present moment was nothing short of romantic. Condemned by the law to follow the Mohammedan religion, she had been secretly watched at every step by her elder brother, a fanatical Moslem. In consequence of his unflagging espionage the child could not attend the Christian church. She knew the meaning of the Mass, but only in so far as her mother had instructed her. Often in her home, instead of following the devout practices of Christianity, she was forced to keep to the usages of Islam, recite the prescribed prayer when the muezzin called from the minaret, perform the legal purification on Fridays, take part in the sacred Moslem fast, and begin the day with the liturgical ablution that the Koran imposes on its devotees.

It was not in Flora's nature to live a life of such dissimulation. She realised that it was cowardice, and her opinion was confirmed by the clergy whom she consulted. The text from the Gospel engraved itself in the depths of her soul: "Every one, therefore, that shall confess Me before men, I will also confess him before My Father who is in heaven. But he that shall deny Me before men, I will also deny him before My Father who is in heaven" (Matt. 10:32,33).

This teaching induced her to make a desperate resolution. She did not hesitate. It was not in her character to do so. She was incredibly courageous in carrying out a purpose and her constancy was unshakeable. One day, in spite of her brother's vigilance, without saying a word to her mother, she disappeared, taking with her, her sister Baldegotona. Her brother sought for her in vain in all the convents of Cordova. In vain did he order the imprisonment of the clergy who he believed had been in communication with her, because he had seen them enter her house to bring her Holy Communion every day. All his inquiries came to nothing, until the magnanimous girl, seeing that God's Church suffered on her account, came forth from her hiding place, went to her brother's house and said to him: "I know how eagerly you seek me and how keen you are about it: well, now you have me! I come, like a good Christian, armed with the sign of the cross. Now, tear this Faith from me, separate me from Christ if you can. I think it will be very difficult, for I am ready to suffer every torture for Him. I speak strongly — do I not? Well, during martyrdom, I shall speak still more strongly."

Cajolery and threats failed to shake the maiden's determination. The most savage blows seemed to make no impression on her. At last the Mohammedan seized his sister and dragged her before the cadí.

"Judge," he said, "this is my youngest sister who always practised our holy religion with me; but the Christians have perverted her, making her hate our prophet and believe that Christ is God."

This happened in the year 845, when Moad ben Otman el Xabani presided over the court of justice at Cordova. Moad was very different from his brother Yojamir, who had filled the same office some years before and earned a bad reputation by his rudeness and bad manners. It was said in Cordova that he had, as a joke, summoned before his court as litigants Jesus, Son of Mary, and Jonas, the prophet, son of Amathi. Moad, on the contrary, was discreet and gentle, and always disposed to think the best of those who appeared before him. But with Flora he assumed a most severe tone.[1]

"Does your brother tell the truth?" he asked her.

"Do you call that wicked man my brother?" she answered. "All he said was a falsehood. I have never been a Moslem. From my infancy I have known none but Christ: He is my God and I have consecrated myself to Him as His bride."

This defence was insufficient against the law, which decreed that the daughter of a Moslem must be a Moslem or die. But Moad, out of pity for Flora's youth and beauty, thought that punishment would correct her. The punishment was severe: two men held up the girl's arms while a third lacerated the nape of her neck with lashes. When the victim had fainted, the judge said to her brother: "Now, cure her and instruct

---

[1] Aljoxaní treats of Moad ben Otman in his book on the judges of Cordova (Ribera's translation), pp. 119 sqq.

her in our religion, and if you can do nothing with her, bring her before me again."

The Moslem lifted her up and carried her to his house to be cured and taught by the women of his harem.

In a few days, before her wounds were healed, Flora began to think of flight; but she noticed that her brother shut the door with the greatest care, and the house was surrounded by a high wall. However, she was not a person to be easily deterred by obstacles. One night, favoured by the darkness, she climbed up a building near the patio and thence on to the wall, and, taking a daring leap, reached the ground unhurt. She walked for some distance without knowing where she was going until she fortunately came upon the house of a Christian of her acquaintance.

There Eulogius saw her for the first time. The priest was much moved by the sight of this wonderful young girl. Her vigorous type of beauty, her captivating manners, the charm of her speech which was enthusiastic and animated, her firmness of resolution, fervent religious zeal and quenchless courage during sufferings and injuries — all these were as an inspiration to him. Henceforth a light shone in his life — a perfectly human light, though divinised by his virtue and the habit which had cost him dear, of repressing and overcoming himself.

Flora was for him the ideal woman, the heroine of Christianity, the type of the strong, prudent woman, pictured in Holy Scripture. He felt for her a spiritual friendship in which admiration and respect were joined to a love that was pure and intellectual, such as must be felt in the mansions of the blessed where souls are inflamed with sacred longing only. Ten years later he recalled this first meeting as one of the most fortunate events of his life. He remembered it more vividly; his love had become even more supernatural. A glorious martyrdom had come, not to break, but to crown the bond of friendship and set it higher, for it had germinated in the heart of a saint. "And I, a sinner," he would say in after years, "I, rich in nothing but iniquities, who enjoyed her friendship from the beginning of her martyrdom, had the joy of touching, with joined hands, the wounds of that most sacred, delicate head, despoiled of its girlish locks by the force of her scourging."

After that, the maiden, taking the direction of Seville, hid in Osera, a town in the diocese of Accitana (Martos), while Eulogius continued working at his Spanish and Christian ideal in the very centre of iniquity. More than once the memory of Flora cheered him in discouragement; perhaps he did not know where she was, but her example aroused in him a secret joy and enlightenment that consoled him. One day, while in prison, he heard her name mentioned. The poor prisoner trembled. At first he could obtain only fragments of news, for he was shut up in the underground, damp portion of the dungeons where the seclusion was most severe. Soon his visitors were able to tell him the whole glorious truth which filled his soul with joy.

In the mountains of Cordova lived a devout family that had already given a martyr for the Faith, Walabonsus, one of the six who suffered with Jeremias, the founder of Tabanos. María, a nun of Cuteclara, the martyr's elder sister, was inconsolable at his death. Sorrow preyed upon her and she could find no comfort until another nun told her that the martyr had appeared to her and said: "Tell my sister to cease weeping for me, and that she will soon be with me in heaven."

From that moment María ceased to mourn; her grief was changed into an impatient longing to die, as he did, for Christ. One day, leaving her convent and the mountains, she started for Cordova to present herself before the cadí. On the way, she entered the church of San Acisclo to commend her enterprise to God. She knelt beside another young girl who seemed in an ecstasy of contemplation, and in whom she thought she recognised Flora, the fervent virgin whose courage had aroused the admiration of the Christians of Cordova some years before.

In fact, it was Flora. In the solitude of her retreat, Christ had said to her: "I go to be crucified again." Animated by His voice, she was on her way to Cordova and by prayer was preparing herself for death.

María, beside herself with joy at meeting her, took her aside and told her of her own resolve. The two maidens, embracing one another, vowed not to separate in life or death. María was eager to rejoin her brother: Flora only thought of the eternal embrace of Christ, her Bridegroom. Full of enthusiasm, they left the church and set off in search of the cadí.

"I, the daughter of a pagan father," Flora said to him, "was ill-treated some time ago in the most cruel manner by the Moslems because I refused to renounce Christ. Since then I have been weak enough to hide myself; but today, full of confidence in my God, I am not afraid to come forward to declare, as resolutely as before, that Christ is God, and that your supposed prophet is an adulterer, a magician, and an evildoer."

"And I, O judge," María said in her turn: "I, the sister of one of the six courageous men who died on the gallows for having mocked your false prophet — I say, with the same daring, that Christ is God and that your religion was invented by the devil."

The good judge, Said ben Soleiman was shocked at such blasphemies, and in his fit of anger could only break forth into wild outcries, coarse insults, and horrible threats, to which the young girls listened in perfect calm. Seeing that he prevailed nothing, he ordered that the two virgins should be thrust into prison with women of bad character.

Eulogius learnt this in October, the second month of his imprisonment. His heart felt a supernatural joy that made him forget the trials of his confinement. But soon after this, less consoling news filled him with anguish. "Flora," they told him, "is on the point of abjuring the Faith. The emissaries of Recafredo, of the cadí, Said ben Soleiman, and her own family never leave her a moment's peace. It is difficult for her to resist this constant siege. María's case is the same."

Unfortunately this was but too true. The archbishop had promised the sultan that he would see to it that there were no more martyrs, and here were two women making his words a mockery. He must make every effort to break their resolution. Let them be told that their obstinacy was doing great harm to the Church; that they need only tell a venial falsehood to prevent these evils and deliver themselves from death; that those who advised them to rebel were dreamers, fanatics, and some of them cowards, who liked seeing others commit suicide while they themselves were afraid of death.

The judge was advised to content himself with a simple declaration that they had not abused the prophet in any way. He agreed to this and made known that otherwise he would have the two girls taken to the market and sold as slaves.

This sentence filled the two maidens with terror. To be taken to the market meant prostitution — to go to the foul harem of some powerful Moslem. Dishonour was worse than death. From that moment the courage of Flora and María weakened. At first they had been firm and valiant; they prayed, meditated, fasted, and sang hymns of joy. Now they never ceased weeping. "What is your final decision?" asked their bad counsellors, and they continued sobbing, trembling, and hesitating.

Eulogius knew of this, and he too trembled. He thought of the disgrace it would bring upon the Faith, the exultation of its enemies, the shame that would be felt by himself and his party. Above all, he thought of the girl herself, Flora, his ideal heroine, the strong woman, whom he always looked upon as surrounded by a halo. And now she was about to renounce this glory! Rather would he see her die a thousand times!

Eulogius would have liked to visit her, kneel before her, implore her, bring back to her heart peace, serenity, strength. But it was impossible. He was imprisoned in his dungeon, she in hers. Then Eulogius took up his pen again, and rapidly, with the heroic decision of a man who throws himself into danger to save the one he loves, wrote a beautiful, touching treatise entitled *Documento Martirial*.

It was a voice of encouragement for those who hesitate to die for Christ, addressed to the two young, undecided girls. He seemed to have forgotten their dismay; his first words were a hymn to their valour in which he still believed:

> You have done great things, my sisters; you have surpassed men and even the clergy; I own it, I feel it, and my pen exalts it. . . . Your praise will be undying in men's mouths. You recall the magnificent example of Judith and Esther; you leave an everlasting monument of your courage, and forgetful of the weakness of your sex, you have scaled the heights to which men dare not rise.

Then, remembering the trials of imprisonment, its tedium, and the company of bad women, he added:

> Keep before your eyes the example of Christ's Passion; think of it continually, and all the pain of this life will become a pleasure. It may be hard and bitter, but it must be short. The greater the anguish, the sooner it ends; and if it is slight, it is easily borne. While we live in the corruption of this life, however peaceful we may be, however great our prosperity, we are far from God and our peace ought really to be called misery. Everything is subject to unforeseen changes while we dwell in this world, and the words of the wise man will always be true: "All things under the sun are evil, and all vanity and vexation of spirit" (Eccles. 2:17).

Eulogius then speaks with the most persuasive eloquence of all that made Christ's virgins hesitate: corporal prostitution was no matter while the soul remained virginal; the only course to take was to leave oneself in the hands of God. And he adds:

> As for us, unworthy though we are, we share in the heavenly grace of suffering — the prisons are full of clergy; the Church remains without her ministers; the Divine Office has ceased; the spider weaves its web in the empty, silent temples; the cantor no longer sings his canticles; the Psalms are not chanted in choir; the lector does not read the word of God from the pulpit, nor does the deacon preach the Gospel nor the priest incense the altars.

It was a sad picture, but no single falsehood must be told to prevent such great evils. Better than all is the sacrifice of a humble and contrite heart.

> You spoke against Mohammed, and you spoke well. Does not the whole Catholic Church abuse him too? If you were to deny it now, you would commit a double sin. But such a thing is not possible. You are caught in the net; do not be one of the worthless fish that the apostle throws afresh into the sea, but be reserved for the heavenly banquet. . . . You must fight till death and leave God to defend His Church: you must fight till death, because in such a struggle as this victory is won by death alone.

The enthusiastic, peaceful style in which he wrote seemed to show that Eulogius had completely overcome his perturbation. His conscience obliged him to speak of sacrifice and separation, but his heart was full of bitterness. He had made a costly sacrifice in speaking as he had; his mission as leader of the martyrs demanded this. But true love has its rights. He had pronounced the word *death;* had spoken of the reward of heaven. In that country "there is great glory and riches, and everlasting justice." But the writer's pulse beat high, his heart was deeply touched, he forgot that there were *two* prisoners who would read what he wrote, his pen ran on impetuously, ardently as he indicted the last word, the farewell. His heart betrayed him:

Now I will enter the port of silence, I have given you your weapons. And now, O my most holy sister Flora, flourishing in virtuous merits, now I wish to speak to you for a little while, so that you may gladly remember my friendly words as the last counsels of a tender father and keep them in your holy mind and heart. "Hearken, O daughter, and see, and incline thy ear: and forget thy people and thy father's house. And the king shall greatly desire thy beauty: for He is the Lord thy God" (Ps. 44:11,12). Your vocation is not that of others. With a wolf for a father and a lamb for a mother, you flourish like a lily among thorns.

By the grace of God, the glory of martyrdom began to enrapture you some time ago: the enviable fame of your name has become known throughout the world, and thanks to you, many heard of our glorious combats. I remember with emotion that period of your martyrdom in which you deigned to show me your flayed neck from which the lovely and abundant locks had been torn by the scourge, for you looked upon me as your spiritual father and thought I was as pure and chaste as you are. I passed my hand gently over your wounds and would have tried to cure them by the touch of my lips, but I did not dare. After leaving you, I could not forget these moments: I thought of them constantly, and sighed.

And when you, in your gracious way, told me how keenly you had suffered, of the risks and dangers you had run, and how, during the silence of the night, the doors of your prison opened miraculously, I thought of the Apostle St. Peter, whom you so closely resembled by your tortures and marvellous deliverance.

And now again you heard the voice of Christ, saying: "Shew Me . . . where thou feedest thy flocks, where thou sleepest at midday, My sister." "I come to be crucified again." Anew, then was kindled within you the ardour for the fray. Descending to the court of justice, you appeared in the midst of the crowd, gave yourself up to the judge, confessing Christ and detesting the enemy of the Faith. Well may you sing with the Psalmist: "I spoke of Thy testimony before kings, and I was not ashamed" (Ps. 118:46).

I remind you of all these things, servant of Christ, my

sister, my lady Flora, so that the thought of them may stay you from trampling on such treasures of glory. Hasten to receive the crown, run to the reward: this is the time to snatch it. Fight the good fight, my sister, happy virgin, and however great the torment, do not give way. Wounds are the gages of eternal happiness. If you die, you are sure of salvation. Death, O sister Flora, gives us life, joins us to the choir of saints, and confirms for ever the state of those who persevere faithfully and manfully in the fight.

In this case, again, Alvaro was the first to reap the fruits of his friend's labour. "I wish you to give me your opinion before I show it to the two maidens, lest through ignorance I may have fallen into any error." But Alvaro thought he discovered in these pages the flavour of apples of paradise.

"I have read it," he wrote, "with my innate love for letters known to you, and have found nothing that was not admirable.... But I read it very quickly. I was tempted to keep the original and copy it, but I thought it would be betraying your love, so I beg you, before you send it to our sisters, to write it out more clearly in another volume and let me have the rough draft to copy."[2]

Eulogius consented, and did his best to overcome his nervousness, writing out as best he could in the darkness of the prison the *Documento Martirial,* which he sent to Flora and María with a final prayer that was to be said daily, offering their blood for the peace of the Catholic Church and for Eulogius. "O Lord, forget not Thy servant Eulogius, whose teaching instructs us, whose letters guide us, whose advice strengthens us, whose preaching enlightens us!" prayed the kneeling virgins, as their tears moistened the ground. "Cleanse

---

[2] The *Documento Martirial,* preceded by the two letters of Eulogius and Alvaro alluded to in the text, is to be found in the *Patr. Lat.,* cxv, 819–835 It is followed by the history of the two saints, Flora and María, and the letters Eulogius wrote after their martyrdom to Alvaro and Baldegotona. These are the principal sources on which this chapter is based.

him from all his sins and make him ever Thy humble, submissive servant, so that one day he may come to the land of the living, even though he may be in the last place of all."

This intimate appeal met with complete success. Henceforth the two young girls showed a firmness and enthusiasm that surprised even Eulogius. On the thirteenth of November Flora appeared in the court of justice for the last time. Her brother, in accord with the cadí, made a last effort to save her. It was as useless as the rest.

"What is your final decision?" asked the judge.

"The same as before," answered Flora. "And if you persist, you will hear worse things said than have been uttered hitherto."

The judge shouted with rage; the girl's brother was horrified. After all, it was his blood that was to be shed. Flora returned to prison as to a banquet, to use the favourite expression of Eulogius.

Shortly after, Eulogius obtained an interview with her. It was a favour that could hardly be refused to one who was about to mount the scaffold. Besides, Recafredo and his party had lost their cause and the advice given by a priest could matter little to them.

"I thought I was looking at an angel," he said afterwards. "A heavenly light shone around her; her face beamed with joy. She seemed to be tasting the joys of paradise already. She told me, smiling, how the cadí had questioned her and what her answer was. After hearing the tale from her sweet lips, I tried to confirm her in her resolution, and spoke of the crown awaiting her. I worshipped her, and bowed low before her angelic face, begging her to pray for me; and I returned to my dark dungeon with renewed courage."

Ten days after, on November 24, the two virgins died on the scaffold. It was a day of rejoicing for Eulogius. To Alvaro he wrote:

My brother, God has granted me an unspeakable grace,

and my heart is full of joy. Our virgins, whom I instructed, weeping, with the words of life, have won the crown of martyrdom. Having overcome the prince of darkness and despised all earthly affections, they have gone to blissful union with the Bridegroom who reigns in heaven. Invited to the nuptials by Christ, they have entered the mansions of the blessed, singing a new song, and saying: "Honour and glory be to Thee, O Lord our God, for Thou hast delivered us from the power of hell, hast made us worthy of the happiness Thy saints enjoy, hast called us to Thine eternal kingdom." The whole Church rejoices over their victory; but no one has greater right to do so than myself, for I strengthened them in their resolve when they were on the point of renouncing it.

The delight felt by Eulogius communicated itself to all the prisoners. The two heroines had been beheaded at three o'clock in the afternoon; shortly after, the captives grouped themselves in two choirs and began to sing with transports of joy the Office for virgin martyrs for the Faith. "The function terminated with the Sacrifice of the Mass to the honour and glory of the new saints," Eulogius tells us. The confessors then remained awaiting their liberation.

Before going to the scaffold, the two young girls had promised that when they reached Christ's presence they would beg Him to free the priests. This liberation took place when five days later the archbishop released his prisoners. But Eulogius had time to write the following letter from prison to the sister of Flora:

> Eulogius, servant of Christ, to my dearest sister in Jesus Christ, Baldegotona. Greetings.
> I make known to you that our lady and patron, your sister Flora, consummated her martyrdom on Tuesday, at the hour of *None,* with her companion the blessed María, nun of Cuteclara, persevering until death in her sacred profession. Therefore, dearest sister, I beg and command you to fortify your soul with the riches of consolation, as one who is certain that our martyrs are enjoying eternal

bliss in the choirs of virgins, singing the new song of the fatherland, with palms of victory in their hands. As for yourself, my beloved, you must adorn your soul with holy actions, so that you may be pleasing to God and reign with Christ for ever in the company of holy virgins. I send you as a keepsake the girdle worn by your sister in prison. Goodbye, dearest sister: pray for me.

CHAPTER XIX

AURELIUS AND *NATALIA*, FÉLIX AND *LILIOSA*

LIBERTY HAD not been bestowed gratuitously. Recafredo required that the imprisoned clergy should obey him and promise not to leave the city. No doubt he feared lest they should promote a rebellious spirit elsewhere. Their promise was vouched for by persons in the confidence of both parties, who became security for them. Eulogius did not wish to cause fresh troubles by his opposition and submitted with the rest. He thought it best to be silent for a time, but had not renounced his opinions. "Never was he seen to vacillate," said Alvaro, "never did he speak doubtingly or timidly."

The Advent of the year 851 had now begun; a more peaceful Advent than men expected. Christmas came, and tranquillity seemed to lend a new note to Christian rejoicings. On New Year's Day, former enemies waited on one another with the usual Christmas gifts. Even the Arabs joined in the merriment. Rich Moslems bestowed on each other costly gifts, delicious masterpieces of the pastry cook's art made of honey, fruit, sugarplums, and the best wheat bread — artistically fashioned to the likeness of walled cities, enchanted trees, castles, dances, religious scenes, and even of grotesque little lay brothers. Then, as now, it was the delicate fingers of the nuns that made these ingenious little models.[1]

No doubt Eulogius took part in the general rejoicings and there must have been on his table some delicacy sent by the

---

[1] J. Simonet, *Historia de los mozárabes de España*, Appendix, p. 82.

nuns of Cuteclara or Tábanos. Yet he felt troubled. For a time he was perplexed as to which course he ought to take. Nearly all the Cordovan clergy sided with the archbishop, and under the circumstances resistance would have been useless or harmful. Eulogius would have liked to leave Cordova, but was prevented by his solemn promises. He was bound; he could neither act nor speak nor continue the chief mission of his life. The lack of certitude as to the future course he should pursue filled him with anguish and he suffered in this uncertainty. His conscience was confused and disturbed; the small number of the flock that followed him made him think his work was doomed to failure.

Alvaro was always with him, and Bishop Saul favoured his cause. One day, when the three were together with some of the clergy, an incident occurred that showed what torments Eulogius was undergoing. They were talking of the Holy Scriptures and the difficulties of the Church, and were reading the works of the Fathers. On that day, Alvaro brought with him the works of St. Epiphanius and purposely chose a letter from the saint to John, bishop of Jerusalem, which he asked a deacon to read. In this letter, St. Epiphanius told how St. Jerome, seeing that he would be obliged to communicate with the bishop of Jerusalem, a violent defender of Origenism, preferred not to celebrate the Sacrifice of the Mass.

Eulogius sighed profoundly as he listened to the deacon; he saw reproduced in his person the history of the anchoret of Bethlehem. Realising this, he did not doubt that it was a message from God, and looked at Alvaro to show that he understood. Then, turning to the bishop, he said: "If the teachers of the Church and the columns of our Faith acted in this way, what should we do, oppressed as we are by the weight of our sins? I shall not dare to sacrifice the Body of Christ."

"I will not consent to that," said the bishop. "You must offer the Holy Sacrifice as you have done hitherto; and do not forget that I am your bishop, and that I carry the weapon of ecclesiastical anathema."

This incident awoke in Eulogius his former ardour. Again, amid the universal cowardice, he was, as Alvaro called him, "the support and panegyrist of the martyrs." He went to meet those who marched to the combat, strengthened their confidence, encouraged them in the hour of despondency, accompanied them to the place of sacrifice and reverently collected the treasure of their relics. Shortly after leaving prison, on January 13, 852, he and some other Christians bore to the church of San Cristobal the bodies of two more martyrs: the priest Gumersindus and the monk Servusdeus. At the same time he was preparing other heroes for martyrdom.

While in prison Eulogius had met a young Cordovan named Aurelius, belonging to one of the first and richest families of the city. Like many others, he was obliged to practise Christianity secretly, since his father was a Moslem. Following the custom of the fashionable young men of the day, he used to listen to the alfaquíes teaching in the mosque, while maintaining close relations with Christian priests. His frankness and good, manly, handsome face, says Eulogius, made him irresistibly attractive.

Aurelius was fortunate in finding a wife who was in the same situation. The daughter of Moslem parents, Natalia, or Sabigotona, as she was called, had been educated in the Mohammedan religion, but after her father's death was placed in the charge of a stepfather who worshipped Christ in his heart and had her baptised. Natalia was rich, aristocratic, and unspeakably beautiful, but her bodily perfections were far surpassed by those of her mind, for, as Eulogius remarked of her, "the glory of the king's daughter is within."

Husband and wife lived for many years without daring to show their faith exteriorly, notwithstanding the remonstrances Natalia often made to Aurelius. But one day, in the market, he saw a man enter, tied on a donkey's back, with his face to the tail. His eyes had been gouged out, his body was bruised, and from his feet hung great iron balls that helped him to keep his balance. Before him walked the town crier, shouting: "This is a Christian who blasphemed Mohammed."

The man was Juan, the shopkeeper, the victim of his rivals' jealousy. His entrance caused an outcry in the market. Jewish surgeons; Castilian slave merchants; men from Barbary, in their white cloaks, crying up their fine chestnut horses to be used for war against the Christians; fanatical fruiterers from the Levantine orchards; Sudanese Negroes waiting in a corner for their purchaser to take them to join the emir's guard; Eastern merchants in white turbans, advertising their tapestries, silks, and jewels from Persia and Egypt, Damascus and Constantinople; the police taking notice, as they passed, of the stalls shaded from the sun by canvas awnings and driving away mischievous and idle persons — all these with one accord broke out into execrations against the poor Christian, piercing him through with looks of wrath and hatred.

This appalling spectacle gave Aurelius a great shock and made him reflect upon his own religion. On returning home, he said to his wife:

"You, my dearest wife, drew me to virtue when I was dead to God and lived only to self. I could not understand what you said then, but now 'the acceptable time, the day of salvation' has come. Let us devote our bodies to chastity and live for prayer. You shall no longer be my wife but my sister; instead of the fruits of the flesh, let us beget those of the spirit, that we may become worthy to die for the Faith."

"O my husband!" exclaimed Natalia, "God has spoken by your lips. This is the sign of our vocation. Yes: we are predestinated for the eternal army. Let us shake off the dust, break the chains and rising up with the desire of that life which never ends, let us hasten to it swiftly!"

From that day Aurelius and Natalia seemed seized with a sacred frenzy. They fasted, prayed, sung together the psalms they knew, visited the monasteries and bestowed large alms on the poor. Their beds were resplendent with rich borders and colours, but it was only to conceal their sudden change from visitors. One of their favourite recreations was visiting those imprisoned for the Faith. Natalia could not tear herself away from the jail in which Flora and María were shut up. She passed days and nights with them to hearten them in their discouragement, enliven their solitude, and give them the advice from Eulogius entrusted by him to her husband.

Meanwhile Aurelius went to the dungeon to which the priests were condemned, and kneeling before them, kissed their chains. But it was Eulogius whom he chiefly sought.

"There I came to know him," said the saint, "there he asked me to teach him, to direct him, and I told him what to do with the two pledges God had given him."

Aurelius had two little girls, whose future was his chief anxiety.[2] Daughters of a father who was a Moslem in the eye of the law, they, too, must be Moslems, without any right to the paternal inheritance which passed to the public treasury whenever the owner abandoned the state religion.

Eulogius' decision may seem pitiless, but it was the only one a priest of Christ could give. "Your souls come first, before your children," he told Aurelius. "God will be their

---

[2] According to the law these two children were destined for certain death if they persisted in following the example of their parents. They seem to have done so. In the year 860, Charles the Bald told a man named Mancius to go to Cordova to collect evidence relating to St. Aurelius and St. George, whose bodies had been taken to Paris. Mancius did so, and on returning to France said that he had witnessed the martyrdom of two young girls of the Cordovan aristocracy. "As the older girl wished the younger to drink, the chalice of the passion first, the latter objected, saying: 'No, sister, I will follow you as my mistress in the coronation as in the combat; never fear that I will forsake you; I will give you the same proofs of love and fidelity in death as I gave in life.' They were beheaded and their souls rose to God carried by the angels." — *De translatione SS. Martyrum Aurelii et Soc., Esp. Sagr.,* X, 541.

Father and Defender. You can put the little ones in some place where they will run no risk for their Faith and insure them an annuity to live on. The rest of your fortune you should give to the poor, in whose hands it will be safe from the rapacity of the state. I know that the public profession of your religion will cost you your life, but a shamefaced Christianity that compounds with infidelity cannot be pleasing to God."

Aurelius and his wife received this advice as coming from heaven, and followed it exactly. Their enthusiasm increased daily, and communicated itself to another married couple closely related to them, named Felix and Liliosa, who sought an occasion to profess their religion publicly in order to still their uneasy consciences. At heart they were Christian, but before the law they were Moslems. In a moment of weakness Felix had pronounced the formula: "God is God, and Mohammed is His prophet." As for Liliosa, her parents were Christians in their home and Moslems outside of it.

One day Natalia said that she had seen the virgins Flora and María, resplendent with light, wearing snow-white garments, with hands full of flowers. They came to tell her that she and Aurelius, Felix and Liliosa, had been predestined for martyrdom since the beginning of the world, and would be joined by a mysterious cenobite whom God was bringing from a distant country.

This news inspired fresh courage in the young athletes. Nothing now could hinder their impetuous generosity. Even Eulogius, astonished at them, exclaimed: "Oh, astounding renunciation of the world! Wonderful divine fervour that gives strength to despise a father's love, to flee from riches, to break the closest bonds, to choose death instead of life, to disdain what is transitory, and to embrace for the sake of eternal happiness dungeons, trials, stripes, torments, as though they were the greatest pleasures in the world."

The two couples, predestined to a glorious martyrdom,

waited impatiently for the great day of their liberation. Meanwhile they fasted, prayed, visited the churches and monasteries, and sought advice from the great Mozarabic teachers.

Eulogius tells of an interview he had with Aurelius shortly before the latter's death. It was in the beginning of the memorable spring of 852.

> I went to the patio of my most serene teacher Alvaro, famous throughout the West for his literary knowledge. I went, as usual, to enlighten my mind by our customary discussions. There I met the soldier of Christ, Aurelius, who had come to consult him about the coming conflict. The illustrious master, the copious fountain of wisdom of our times, explained, with quotations from the Holy Fathers, that he should ascertain his strength and consider the danger he would incur.
>
> "Labour under no illusion," Alvaro said: "your slender throat will encounter the henchman's axe."
>
> "Nothing will terrify me," answered the youth. "Christ is the great Comforter of my life, and all my welfare consists in dying for Him. This world is for me a gloomy chaos; and the sole thought of seeing Him fills me with joy."
>
> As he spoke these words I entered, and he was very glad to meet me. It seemed to us that the Word of God was with us, according to the Gospel promise: "Where there are two or three gathered together in My name, there am I in the midst of them" (Matt. 18:20). After having talked for some time about the deed he was about to perform, he went home full of joy, and greatly comforted, I believe, by our conversation.

The martyrs were ready, but the foreign monk who was to company them had not arrived, and the month of July was passing. At last the longed-for meeting took place in the monastery of Tabanense. There happened to be living there a Syrian cenobite named George, who had come to Spain to collect funds for the five hundred brethren who lived under the direction of the Archimandrite David, in the *laura* of

St. Sabas, eight miles from Jerusalem. The monk was highly respected by the Christians of Cordova for his virtues and knowledge. He spoke Latin, Greek, and Arabic perfectly; performed extraordinary penances; preached long and vehement sermons on austerity; and told the monks of Cordova, that, as an extraordinary mortification, he had never washed his body since he put on the monastic habit. A venerable beard gave character to the austere appearance of this Eastern religious.

Eulogius was captivated by his apostolic zeal and sanctity. George, in his turn, found in the teacher of the Mozarabs a saint and guide. In the monastery of Tabanense the stranger's authority was supreme. One day, when George was preparing to go to the Northern kingdoms, the venerable Abbot Martin and his sister Isabel said to him:

"Come, brother, and receive the blessing of Natalia, the servant of God."

"This is our companion in our combat," said Natalia, when she saw the monk. George did not understand at first, but hardly had he been told of what had happened, when he fell at the feet of Natalia, declaring that he was willing to undergo a thousand martyrdoms.

"But, father," she asked, "how can you condescend to share the company of sinners?"

On that same night Natalia appeared in a dream to the cenobite, leaving him in a cloud of delicious perfumes that recalled the aromatic trees of his country. In a writing by his hand, George further recounts the sequel of this remarkable story. He says:

> Early next morning, we both went down to the city. Entering the house of Aurelius, I prostrated myself before him, begging him to pray for me. At once, in answer to his prayers, a heavenly fire was lit in me, making me at one with them, and henceforth I never left his side. We remained in his home together, thanking God with jubilee.

The blessed Felix and his most holy wife Liliosa were with us. They had sold their property to give it to the poor. I went out to the city to settle some business with all haste, and returned to them, feeling more at peace. They were glad to see me again and thanked God, saying: "We are sure, dearest brother, that God has sent you to us." These words renewed my courage, making me more certain of the divine will.

On July 2, Eulogius heard a knocking at his door before daybreak. He may have thought that Recafredo's emissaries had come to take him prisoner again, but his fears were soon set at rest on recognising his friend's voice. Aurelius had come to take a last farewell.

"We shall be apprehended today," said the martyr.

"Will you have courage when the time comes?"

"God will give it to us, Father. That is why I have come to ask you to pray for us while we suffer. We do not choose to present ourselves before the judge; we prefer that he should seize us. Our sisters will go to church today unveiled; the Moslems will see them and will come for us at once."

Eulogius wept with emotion. He begged Aurelius to offer his sacrifice for the Church and not to forget him when he reached heaven. At the same time Eulogius kissed his hands passionately, saying:

"At last we kiss one another and separate in peace."

Events happened as the martyrs had planned. Moslem women always cover their faces with flowing veils when they go into the streets. On that day, Liliosa and Natalia went to church unveiled, followed by Felix and Aurelius. A policeman recognised them, and approaching their husbands asked:

"What does this mean? Why do you allow your wives to enter the Christian sanctuaries?"

"Because we are Christians," they answered, "and nothing is more natural than that we should venerate our martyrs' relics."

There the matter ended, but a few hours after a picket of soldiers came to the house of Aurelius, shouting:

"Come forth, wretches; come to die, as you are tired of life and love death."

The five predestinated martyrs came out, singing hymns, and, surrounded by the public officers, arrived jubilantly before the judge. Nothing could shake their resolution. They were taken to the prison which became the scene of miracles. The jailors thought it had turned topsy-turvy. There were dazzling lights, mysterious voices, heavenly visions. The fetters fell from the feet of the Christian prisoners. Eulogius went to see his friends to give them his last counsels and the monk of St. Sabas began a short autobiography which he finished in prison.

Five days later the prisoners were taken before the judge in one of the annexes of the fortress. All efforts to intimidate them were as useless as before. Nothing remained but to carry out the law. The intrepid confessors were beheaded on the same day, July 27, 852.

"Lovely and comely in their life are the saints of God," said Eulogius, "they loved one another in life, and in death they would not be separated."

CHAPTER XX

A DRAMATIC *CLIMAX* AND A PANIC

DURING THE first days of August, in the year 852, Eulogius was visited by a young man from Liberia, named Leovigildo, who had taken the habit in a monastery on the mountain near Cordova. He also wished to gain the palm of martyrdom, but thought it right to consult the Mozarabic leader first. Eulogius encouraged him, gave him his priestly blessing, and sent him away strengthened for the combat. At the same time Eulogius' kinsman, Christóbal, was preparing to die. After hearing the master's lectures for some years, he had embraced the monastic profession in the flower of his youth. Leovigildo and Christóbal were martyred on August the first. Their master succeeded in snatching their bodies out of the flames and carrying them to the basilica of San Zoilo.

On September 15, two other youths, Emilia and Jeremias, belonging to the leading families of Cordova, met their death. Both of them spoke Arabic perfectly, and discharged such insults against Mohammed that the Moslems counted the abuse uttered by the other martyrs as nothing, so that their rage knew no limit. They spoke of assassinating all the Christians and rooting out Christianity, but an event took place next day that raised their wrath to the boiling point.

The protagonists were an aged monk, a native of Ilíberis, named Rogellus, and a young Syrian whom love for a life of pilgrimage had brought to the Mogreb. His name was Abdalá, which Saint Eulogius changed for Servusdeus. They both were eunuchs. Resolved to die, they entered the great mosque when large numbers of Moslems filled its numerous naves, and in a loud voice, in the midst of a general stupefaction, began to preach the Gospel and ridicule the doctrine of Mohammed. Recovering from their first surprise, the Moslems fell upon them, with savage cries. "It seemed," said Eulogius, "like the roaring and crackling of a fierce bonfire." The cadí tore the victims from the clutch of the crowd and ordered that they should be beheaded after having their feet and hands cut off.[1]

The Mohammedans had come to the end of their tether, Abderrahmán trembled with rage. His counsellors proposed the most unpractical measures; the fanaticism of the Moslems had reached an unprecedented pitch, and the Christian community was filled with alarm and terror. The emir summoned his viziers to council. The general opinion was that the Christians should all be seized and thrown into prison, to be examined one by one, and those who blasphemed the prophet should be led to the gallows.

A rumour of this terrible project spread through the city and aroused the general panic which is vividly described by Eulogius. Though Eulogius fully includes himself in this we must remember how similar accusations concerning himself are to be interpreted. He here pictures the general scene as he witnessed it.

> We fled, we ran in fear from one place to another, hid ourselves, and cloaked our existence under the friendly silence of the night, shuddering at the sound of a falling leaf. We went from house to house, seeking a safer refuge, agitated and trembling; we feared death by the sword, forgetting, to our disgrace, that we must needs die some day. Perhaps we were not ripe for martyrdom.

Countless Christians had not the courage to endure these days of trial. "They did not wish to flee," said Eulogius, "nor hide, nor suffer with us, and sad to say, abandoned their faith, apostatised, and blasphemed the Crucified."

---

[1] All these martyrdoms are described by St. Eulogius in Vol. II of the *Memorial de los Santos*.

Many who had formerly praised the martyrs and suffered imprisonment on their account, now called them madmen, fanatics, and suicides, adhering to the Archbishop of Seville's party. They were men who had liked Arabian rule, enjoyed its civilisation, and readily adopted its customs. To please the Moslems, they took part in their orgies, shared their abominable vices, kept a harem, frequented the schools of the alfaquíes, read their books with avidity, and even competed with them in writing graceful poems. They here showed more ability than the Arabs themselves in cunningly constructing the final clauses so that they should always end with the same consonant. With his usual exaggeration Alvaro wrote:

> There was not one among us, that did not buy or sell without using the mark of the beast. . . . We delighted in Arabic poems and tales; made no difficulty about serving and obeying the Moslems however wicked they were; passed our life in bodily indulgence and in amassing unlawful riches; were for ever buying for ourselves and our children silks, perfumes, rich and splendid clothing, and all kind of ornaments. For the sake of worldly honours, we falsely accused our brethren before the infidel rulers; handed the sword of information to God's enemies to enable them to behead His people, and went so far as to pay for the privilege of performing such wickedness. And what is this but to trade with the mark of the beast foretold in the Apocalypse?

Alvaro here describes the tendencies of the liberal Christians, the Vitizanos, pertinaciously obstinate in their ancient feuds, living on good terms with the foreign rulers and dazzled by their brilliant civilisation. Naturally they disapproved of the enthusiasm of fervent Christians, which could not but involve them all in the Moslems' enmity. These became the strongest opponents of tradition, the dogged adversaries of the martyrs, the henchmen of the Moors.

Abderrahmán saw this and thought they would be his best

aid in silencing Eulogius. He knew there were not enough prisons in the city to hold all the Christians, and, on the other hand, to do away with them altogether would be a work of much time, as Ahmed the traveller said. It was necessary to stop this monstrous rebellion which embittered his premature old age, and made him fear, Eulogius says, for the security of his sway.

At first he thought Recafredo would free him from anxiety, but finding that the archbishop's authority was limited, he thought of a Council that would side entirely with the moderate faction. What bishop would dare to oppose the sovereign will of the sultan? Abderrahmán sent the bishops of his kingdom an order to appear in Cordova. Their object in meeting was not to deliberate, but to forbid Christians to present themselves for martyrdom.

Abderrahmán knew his bishops, as the Emperor of Constantinople, his ally against Bagdad, knew his. They were not, as a rule, bad men but cowards. A few years later, in 862, they met again, and bribed by smaller taxes, condemned an unfortunate man who was innocent — Abbot Sansón. On returning home, troubled by scruples they sent absolutary letters to the bishop of Cordova, who was the only remaining defender of justice.

This bishop, Saul, was certainly the most worthy among his companions. The Government well knew how stubborn and inflexible he was. Wistremiro of Toledo was probably unable to attend on account of illness; Abderrahmán's counsellors took little interest in him, for, as usual, his presence would only have prolonged the sessions. But two other metropolitans of a more tractable character attended: Ariulfo of Mérida and Recafredo of Seville. It need not be said that Recafredo sided unconditionally with the Moslems.

Two more prelates of the same mind were Samuel of Ilíberis and Hostégesis of Málaga. The latter was to become notorious for his doctrine and scandalous life. Samuel was a tyrant to his clergy and people, ridiculed the doctrine of the Resurrection, lived like a Mohammedan, and was circumcised to make himself popular at court. His position regarding the contention about the martyrs was definite: "He was," said Sansón, "a persecutor of Jesus, imprisoned His ministers and imposed heavy taxes on the altars." He ended by apostatising from the Faith on a Good Friday and having his head completely shaved, in the fashion introduced by Ziryab, the Persian musician.

It is not strange that bishops behaved in this manner, considering that the right of election was in the hands of the infidels. Mitres were given to the highest bidder. Ten years before, Samuel's nephew, Hostégesis, had held the see of Málaga. He had obtained it unlawfully and lived scandalously. All this family seemed designed for the scourge of Christians. Auvarno, the father of Hostégesis, had also tyrannised over Christ's flock. On being brought before the judge to answer for his crimes, he became a Moslem to escape punishment, and was circumcised in spite of his old age.

His son was no better. Being in want of funds to pay those who obtained the mitre for him, he invented a thousand artifices by which to obtain it. The parish priests were charged in each division with filling the bishop's purse, and if they would not undertake this disgraceful office, were subject to the most atrocious reprisals. Many were scourged and beheaded in the public squares by the Moslem soldiers who accompanied the bishop when he made his extortions. The avarice of Hostégesis was insatiable. Needless to say, the third part of the revenues destined by the canons for the restoration of the churches and for the poor were spent by him in orgies and in presents for Moslem magnates.

The employees of the fiscal complained that many Málagan Christians evaded the polltax by hiding themselves. Hostégesis promised them a complete list of the contributors, and kept his word conscientiously. During his pastoral visitation, he asked his diocesans to give him their names and those of their relations and friends, as, he said, he wished to pray for each one of his flock. The Christians fell into the trap, and a complete list of the Christians of Málaga was received in Cordova.

Fortunately for his diocese, Hostégesis made lengthy visits to the capital. Thanks to his well-known prodigality, he could enter at will the court and palaces of the influential Arabs. He often joined the monarch's sons, brothers, and courtiers at splendid banquets which ended in terrible debauches. Abencalamauc, one of his friends, gave accounts of them that scandalised the Christians of Cordova. There sparkled, in spite of Mohammed's prohibition, the most exquisite Andalusian wines. The tablecloths were of Cordovan leather, the vases, according to the latest fashion were crystal, not silver, and rare dishes appeared which had been introduced into Spain by Ziryab.

Among these gluttons was often found a Christian of Cordova who was employed in the Administration. He was the living personification of all that was most vile and repugnant to be found in the decadent Mozarabic Christianity of the time; more perverse than the worst of the Spanish traitors who in the time of Joseph Bonaparte acted as spies for the invader and disgraced their brethren. Eulogius and Alvaro spoke with horror of this catib, this exceptor, this toll gatherer, as they called him, "an iniquitous man, proud, cruel, excelling in vice and riches (*praepotens vitiis et divitiis*), a Christian in name only, who had been from the first the open decrier and enemy of the martyrs." They so hated him that they would not mention his name lest they should deface their writings. We know it, thanks to the Arabian authors, who looked upon him as one of the great personages of the age. He was called Gómez, the son of Antonino, Julian's nephew.

He was an intriguing, heartless man; astute, very ambitious, but with a pliant, penetrating mind, as described by Eulogius, and thus attained to the highest dignities. He wrote and spoke Arabic with elegance, and this, combined with a conscience that accommodated itself unscrupulously to the wishes of those in power, ensured his success. He managed to ingratiate himself first with his chief, Abdalá Ibn-Omeya, then with his sovereign.

He cared nothing for religion, but thoroughly despised those who upheld tradition. No doubt he would have been content to laugh at the enthusiasm that led to decapitation, had he not feared that such madness would lead to the most fatal results. He saw that the Moslems were beginning to treat Christians with a coldness verging on distrust, and he wondered whether they would not end by including the right-minded with the crazy, as he called them, and despoil him of his dignities and riches. This decided his attitude regarding the religious question of the day. "The unhappy man," said Eulogius, "feared lest he might fall from the heights of honour."[2]

This intruder held in his hands the direction of the Council. As the monarch could not assist in person, he sent as his representative this man whose opinions were well known to him. Gómez interpreted the emir's wishes and at the same time defended his own threatened interests. His zeal could not be doubted.

As it happened, Eulogius sat opposite to him, for though only a priest, he was present at the assembly. Even his enemies could not ignore his extraordinary prestige. They also wished to show him how all the authority of a national council declared itself against the cause he defended. Surely this would fill him with confusion and make him change his mind!

However, things did not go as Gómez had expected. He

---

[2] For Gómez, see Eulogius, *Memoriale Sanctorum*, Vol. II, Chap. XV and Vol. III, Chap II, Alvaro, *Indículo Luminoso*, No. 18, and Aljoxaní (translated by Ribera), pp. 139–142.

presented himself among the Fathers in a haughty manner, sure of victory, though bowing and smiling ostentatiously to all parties. He was an artful diplomat. In imitation of the addresses formerly made by the kings in the Councils of Toledo, he spoke to this effect: "My Lords and most blessed Fathers: Our beloved monarch, whom may God preserve for many years, solicitous for the welfare of all his subjects, has called you together today in order that you may restore peace to the Church of God. You know that in this city there have arisen men, mad, fanatical, possessed by the devil, who, weary of life, insult the Moslems, blaspheme their religion, and commit other crimes that the law chastises rigorously. You know, better than I do, most blessed Fathers, that this is suicide, that evil-speaking is forbidden by the Holy Scriptures, and by the whole spirit of our sacred religion.

"But the most deplorable thing is that this frenzy may be prejudicial to the entire Church. We witness now its first effects. Good Christians are suffering for the senseless behaviour of these wretches, and if it continues, Christianity will soon disappear from the whole of Spain.

"Our beloved monarch, wishing to prevent such evils, realises that only your power can find a remedy and trusts to your zeal and great prudence to use it. The only remedy is that you should promulgate a decree, confirmed by the authority of your synod, anathematising as suicides and enemies of public order these fanatics who have sought for death and that you forbid others to defend them, under pain of excommunication."

The declaration of the royal delegate was a conclusive order and was so understood by most of the bishops, who were inclined to submit. The bishop of Cordova alone defended the martyrs. But it was Eulogius who overthrew the plans of the catib. No doubt he repeated the arguments brought forward in the *Memorial de los Mártires* to defend the confessors of the Faith. No doubt he unveiled the hypocrisy contained in the royal representative's speech, showing that the case of the Cordovan martyrs was not new in the Church, and that Holy Scripture had been misrepresented in order to condemn them.

Gómez lost all self-control when confronted with this unexpected opposition. Carried away by passion, he attacked Eulogius, calling him wicked, cruel, the headsman of his brethren, and vomiting forth the most terrible threats. "He vilely insulted me before the Bishops' Council with his viper's tongue," Eulogius said later on, referring to this unpleasant affair.

The bishops were in doubt. They could not ignore the teaching of the Church, but the emir imposed his will with all the fury of a despot. They thought they might escape from this embarrassing position by an obscure and indecisive decree, which they expected would quiet their scruples, content the monarch, and make peace with the dissident party. "Let the past be past," they said. "We do not disapprove of the conduct of those who have sought martyrdom during the last few years; those who wish they had died like them may render them homage if they please; but we forbid Christians to present themselves in future to suffer this holy death."

This is what is called "finding a way out of a difficulty." Gómez was satisfied for the time being; the prelates considered that they had done their duty; Eulogius and his partisans seemed at first to submit. Speaking afterwards of his conduct, the latter said: "Influenced partly by fear and partly by the opinion of the bishops whom the king had ordered to come for the purpose from the different provinces, we deliberated over what would please the ears of the Moslem monarch and people."

They soon realised that this was cowardice, or respect for the cowardice of the high dignitaries of the Church. On examining the terms of the decree, it appeared to contain an obvious want of logical sequence: "By not condemning the martyrs in the past," said Eulogius, "they approved those who might act in the same way in future. What, then, is the meaning of this prohibition? Any intelligent person will see that the Council approves the martyrdoms, but through a timidity not exempt from blame, it does not dare to declare so openly."

This fresh remedy was as useless as the rest. If it had any effect, it was only that of giving new arms to the martyrs' defenders. The persecution became more bloody. Again it became necessary to use disguise, to go from house to house and hide in secret places. Well-known Christians did not dare to appear in the street. A bishop was seized by the police and thrown into a dungeon. Eulogius suffered horribly. Gómez persecuted him with all the rancour of humbled pride. "He was worn out with fears," Alvaro says of his friend, "and was most grossly insulted."

But this was not his chief anxiety; that which troubled him most was to hear the complaints made against him by the weak and cowardly. "May the Lord see and judge between us," they said, as the Israelites did to Moses in ancient times. "You have made us tremble before this tyrant and his servants and put the sword in his hands to kill us. Since those saints entered the combat to speak in the name of Christ before the sultan and preach the Gospel to the judges and viziers, our enemies' taunts have increased and the devil's agents will finally destroy us."

The more valiant trusted that God would deliver them miraculously, perhaps by destroying their persecutor, remembering that the martyrs had prophesied his speedy death. Their hopes were realised suddenly before September was over.

According to Eulogius' account, Abderrahmán went to the terrace of the fortress to enjoy the beautiful prospect. Fishing boats were sailing on the river, on both sides of which stood magnificent country houses, pleasure palaces, and granges. The plain, despoiled of its golden wheat, stretched out grey and flat, scorched by the sun. Here and there were green patches from which rose the songs of the vintagers. Cordova laughed and laboured. The emir reflected on the prodigious improvements of the last few years and looked forward to future progress. Suddenly his glance fell on the gallows from which hung the corpses of the last martyrs. He ordered that they should be burnt at once.

"But, O wonderful power of the Saviour and stupendous might of our Lord Jesus Christ," exclaims Eulogius, "who always helps those who seek Him, opens to those who knock, and hears those who cry to Him! The mouth which ordered that God's saints should be burnt, struck by an angel, was from that moment shut and the tongue could utter no words more. Carried in this state to his bed, he gave forth his spirit that night.

"Before the bodies of the saints were consumed, he was taken to the everlasting furnace of hell."

CHAPTER XXI

A *REIGN* OF GREED AND DESOLATION

ABDERRAHMÁN HAD wished his son Mohammed to succeed him, but the Sultana Tarub had intrigued behind the monarch's back and was on the point of reaping the results of her labours no less than of the gold that she had scattered with lavish hands among the courtiers.

At first no one but two eunuchs, Sadun and Casim, knew of the emir's death, and they were caught in Tarub's nets. At a secret gathering held with their comrades, to whom they communicated the news of the monarch's death, they urged that Abdalá, the son of their dearly loved sultana, be placed as monarch in the royal fortress. No one objected, especially as Mohammed had the name of being so miserly that they could not hope he would bestow on them the splendid gifts to which his father had accustomed them.

Then Abu-l-Mofrih rose. He was a devout eunuch, a fervent Moslem, and had much influence over his fellow courtiers. He eloquently descanted on Mohammed's virtues and Abdalá's vices, on justice, the law, the will of the people and the deceased monarch's wishes. His speech carried the day. Sadun was deputed to announce to Mohammed his nomination.

But Mohammed lived on the other side of the river. It was night, and the doors of the Medina were closed, while a few paces off stood the palace of Abdalá. The household were still awake and feasting as usual. Sadun found no difficulty in having the iron doors of the bridge opened for him and crossing to the other side he reached Mohammed's house.

The prince, who had just risen and was in his bath, came to meet him trembling, for he well knew that Sadun was his enemy. When he saw his father's ring and heard that he had just died, his fears increased. He thought that his brother, already on the throne, had sent the eunuch to kill him. Sadun managed to restore his tranquillity at last by means of protestations and oaths.

They had next to enter the fortress, but the sentinels of Abdalá's palace might stop them. The prefect of the city, Jusuf, son of Basilio, declined to put the civic forces at their disposal. In this difficulty, Mohammed's majordomo thought of a stratagem. Abderrahmán had been exceedingly fond of one of Mohammed's daughters, for whom he often used to send, and it was always the majordomo who accompanied her.

"Dress yourself like a woman," he said to his master, "and pass yourself off as your daughter."

The prince disguised himself and mounting a horse rode in the direction of the fortress. From Abdalá's palace came the sound of voices and music. The guards were jesting and drinking in the doorway, but none the less showed themselves keenly alert regarding passers-by. There was further a slight difficulty about entering the fortress. A porter noticed that Mohammed's daughter was not so tall as this unknown woman and the fictitious princess saw no other course but to raise her veil, show her face, and reveal the mystery. It was the only way in which safe entrance could be obtained.[1]

Finally Mohammed gained the throne, unfortunately for the Christians. Abdalá, a dissolute man, would have been tolerant. He had no religious principles, and it was even whispered that he was indifferent on the subject. Devout

---

[1] We know these interesting facts from the *Historia del Andalus*, written in the tenth century by Aben Alcutia, a Spanish Moor in whose veins ran the royal blood of the Goths. Cf. translation by Julian Ribera, edition of the Real Academia de la Historia, 1926, also Dozy, translated by Castro, Vol. II, pp. 184–192.

Moslems, like the eunuch Abu-l-Mofrih, feared that he cared nothing for the laws of the Koran. Mohammed, on the contrary, was a fanatic, a short-throated, narrow-minded man, with little intelligence but a great deal of cruelty and hatred for Christians.

He liked wine, but less frank than his brother, he found a way of taking it without disobeying the Koran, by drinking the liquor that the Moors called *sabha,* instead of *jamar,* or red wine. The Arabian writers give us a very frank description of his disgusting manners.[2]

Eulogius draws a sorry picture of him. He was cold-hearted and selfish. When he learnt of his father's death, far from feeling any grief at it, he was sincerely glad, and worst of all, was shameless enough to own to this. On one occasion, after a night of orgy in the Rusafa, a beautiful house in the west of the city belonging to the emirs, Haxim, his favourite counsellor, said to him:

"Son of the caliphs, what a fine place the world would be but for death!"

"What nonsense!" exclaimed the emir. "Death is a very good thing. If my father had not died, I should not have reigned."

"This avaricious monarch," said Eulogius, "destroyed his country and lost what his predecessor had gained by his talent and generosity. His pallid face seemed a reflection of his avarice. The eunuchs' forebodings were justified. He began by reducing the pay of the soldiers and courtiers; abolished the monthly gratuities given to the slaves, and reduced the food allowance of the court considerably. He put inexperienced men into office on condition that they should share their salary with him. He exacted accounts with childish minuteness and went so far as to cast in the teeth of his

---

[2] Conde, José Antonio, *Historia de la dominación de los árabes en España,* Madrid, 1874, p. 80.

employees a deficit of five *sueldos*[3] in a sum of a hundred thousand gold pieces."

His avarice made him hated and despised by everyone and disgusted his own family. Report spoke in Cordova of unpleasantness with the women of the harem, which came to Eulogius' ears. The Christians trembled when they heard he had succeeded to the throne. Whenever the question of religion had come to the fore, he had always advocated the most severe measures.

"He was an enemy of the Church of God and a most bitter persecutor of the Christians." His first act was to dismiss all Christians holding office in the court and disband any soldiers who would not pronounce the formula of Islam: "God is God and Mohammed is His prophet." Gómez alone escaped for a time. Mohammed knew of his talent for administration, and liked him for his indifference regarding religion. These measures caused many tepid Christians to apostatise, while the scrupulous withdrew more and more from the court and avoided public charges on account of the dangers incurred by them. The monk Isaac had already done so at an earlier period.

Two years afterwards, however, the court and army were full of Christians again. Mohammed found that he could not continue his policy of exclusion, for the Christians were the most competent administrators. From them he drew the sums he had to pay his coreligionists. As the Moslems were exempt from many taxes, and even the neighbouring districts refused to give to the treasury what they had paid in the time of Abderrahmán, the emir had recourse to filling the public exchequer with the enormous sums that he extorted from these tax-gatherers, exceptors, or publicans, as they were termed. They, in turn, in order to reimburse themselves beforehand, became the oppressors of their coreligionists, so

---

[3] A sueldo seems to have had about the worth of a penny. (Translator.)

that Eulogius overwhelmed them with the most terrible anathemas.

> These exploiters of God's people are rather workers of iniquity than Christians. Envious, unjust, malicious, insatiable; arrogant in behaviour; haughty in speech; ready to promise what they cannot fulfill; they cannot sleep unless they have done wrong, and rise early to start their wicked deeds. Like their master, Judas the traitor, they sell Christ and His members daily for a handful of gold, and — I cannot tell it without my heart being pierced — they force men to deny the Faith whom they ought to protect by their influence. Better that they were thrown into the sea with a millstone around their neck.[4]

Persecution now became more violent than ever. During former reigns the Christians had been able to rebuild, enlarge, and decorate their churches and construct new ones. The emirs overlooked these infractions of the rule of Islam. Mohammed, wishing to apply it with all its rigour, ordered that all churches which had been built since the conquest should be destroyed. The officials, in order to gain his favour, went still farther and Eulogius says that "buildings three hundred years old disappeared." The towers and steeples of the churches were demolished, for "nothing should dominate Islam."

The Christians were intimidated and dispersed. Many abjured the Faith, though only outwardly, "for a large number, cowed outwardly because of their natural frailty, were Christ's soldiers at heart under the white Moslem robes." Eulogius succeeded in bringing many of them to make a public confession of the Faith, in spite of judicial inquiries and punishments. For his own part, he remained hidden, exercising his ministry behind the backs of the persecutors. No tortures had power to make him vacillate. He had a blind faith in his cause and worked for it when he could, and when he could

---
[4] *Memoriale Sanctorum*, Vol. III, Chap. V.

not work, he suffered bravely. "The monarch is making many plans against us," he wrote to the chief authorities of Mohammed's kingdom, "but we place our hope of safety in the Lord, fearing nothing of what man may do to us. We have confidence in Jesus Christ, our Advocate and Lord. He who said 'Behold I am with you all days, even to the consummation of the world' (Matt. 28:20), will save us. So be it."[5]

For a time, no more martyrs presented themselves voluntarily. This increased the insolence of the Moslems, who laughed at the faithful and called them cowards to their face. In the streets, squares, markets, the court, even in the emir's ecclesiastical court, they asked: "Where has the ardour of your soldiers gone? What has become of your rash fearlessness? Why has your flimsy fortitude disappeared, the courage about which you bragged so continually? Let the Christians come, let them run and present themselves before the judge; we shall see whether they are divinely inspired."

Even Eulogius seems to have thought that the era of voluntary martyrs had passed. In those days of anguish he added a few chapters to his *Memorial de los Mártires*, relating the triumphs of the last sufferers. He thought his work was written, not suspecting that he would have to continue it before long.

But Eulogius still owed a debt of friendship to the confessors of the year before. He had asked Alvaro to write the lives of Flora and María, perhaps because he thought he was unworthy to recount such noble deeds, or because he feared that his affection might make him seem partial. Alvaro must have refused and the time had passed until, during March of the year 853, Eulogius met one of the daughters of the martyr Aurelius. She was the youngest, and only six years old, but she knew the priest had been her parents' friend, and was accustomed to be petted by him.

---

[5] *Memoriale Sanctorum*, Vol. II, Chap. XVI.

"Father," the little one said to him, "why do you not write the lives of my father and mother, as you have of the rest of God's saints?"

"Why do you wish me to, little daughter?" Eulogius asked.

"Because if you tell of their conflicts, men will know of God's grace. That is why He made you the teacher of our Church."

"Well, what will you give me if I do?"

"Father, I will win paradise for you."

Eulogius was greatly touched by this affecting scene.

"It is wonderful," he said, "that a child of her age should speak in such a manner, unless she was inspired by Him who from the mouths of babes and sucklings draws perfect praise."

He accepted this as heaven's decree and immediately set to work to finish the second volume of the *Memorial de los Mártires* with the history of the last martyrdoms giving a specially full account of those of Flora and María, the two never-to-be-forgotten virgins, and of those of Aurelius and his generous companions. He felt that to describe their deeds was the most sublime vocation. God did not deem that Eulogius himself was ready as yet for martyrdom, but called him to praise the martyrs, and in this his glory consisted. He prayed:

> O my Lord God, Alpha and Omega, the Beginning and the End, our true Emmanuel, the Origin of my life, the Plenitude of my soul, my perfect Salvation. Behold me spurred on by love for Thy saints, urged by affection for my brethren, compassionating the weakness of those who doubt, incited by hatred of Thine enemies. Wanting as I am in knowledge, weak of intellect and understanding, yet great through trust in Thy bounty and mercy, confiding in Thy goodness, assured of Thy clemency, I shall achieve with Thine aid the work I began, and shall finish it, not as I ought but as I can, or rather, according to the power Thou hast given me. . . . May it obtain for me Thy grace, the blessing of the saints, and peace for Thy Church. May

it be in Thy sight as a mirror of our times, may it bring before Thy throne the memory of the calamities of Thy people, and cause Thee to turn Thy merciful eyes on this refuge in which I write, cancelling the sins that through my weakness the tempter caused me to commit in the past. May this book be the teacher of my life, the glory of my crown, the pledge of my reward. Sanctified by Thee, may it bear the name of *Memorial of the Martyrs* so that one day Thou mayest deign to inscribe me among the memorial of Thine elect, through our Lord, who with the Father and the Holy Ghost is one God, eternal and immortal throughout all ages. Amen.

CHAPTER XXII

MORE *MARTYRS* AND THEIR ENEMIES

EULOGIUS COMPLETED the second volume of his *Memorial of the Martyrs* in the spring of 853. Before summer had begun the Christians again presented themselves in the arena.

The first was a monk named Fandila, a native of Guadix, who had come to Cordova to study in the schools. He also dwelt in the monastery of Tabanense under the fortifying direction of Abbot Martin, the forger of heroes. On June 13, the Moslems beheaded him and the next day took place the execution of Anastasius, a priest of the church of San Acisclo, and of Félix, a monk of Alcalá. Félix was a native of Barbary who, on a journey to Asturias, had become a Christian and a monk.

They had just raised the bodies of the martyrs to the gallows, when a young girl arrived who asked for the judge. It was three o'clock in the afternoon.

"Why did you assassinate my brethren in this way?" the intrepid maiden asked the cadí. "Was it because we adore God and reverence the Blessed Trinity, Father, Son, and Holy Ghost, hating, abusing, and trampling on all that does not conform to this confession?"

On hearing these words, the judge, who must have been in a bad temper, ordered that the girl should be executed immediately. Thus did Digna, a humble nun of the monastery of Tábanos, who never ceased thinking of the crown of martyrdom, realise her longing. She was followed the day after by Benildis, a matron advanced in years, famed for her virtue.

Said ben Soleiman, the judge who ordered these executions, began his office during the last days of Abderrahmán. Mohammed, who on coming to the throne had given the principal offices of the city to those who shared his hatred for Christians, confirmed Said in his position because he was sure of his religious zeal. It was he who sent most of the Christians to execution. No doubt there were occasions when he was more humane and condescending, as, for example, when St. Columba presented herself for martyrdom.

Columba, the impulsive virgin of Tábanos, niece of the founders, was tormented day and night by her one desire of going to Christ. She had a lovely voice and the nuns, her sisters, often heard her sing an antiphon which, "with its touching melody," Eulogius said, "was of Mozarabic origin."

"Open to me, O Lord," sang the enamoured virgin, "the gates of Thy paradise, that I may fly to that country where there is no death and where bliss is enjoyed forever!"[1]

The Mozarabic students have deciphered the ancient melodies composed by the Spanish Fathers who were the glory of the Councils of Toledo. This particular melody may have been written by Eugenius, the saintly bishop, poet, and musician. It feelingly reflects the soul of the virgin, set at rest by the consolations of continual prayer. When we hear such trilling notes, we picture to ourselves Columba's gaze fixed on God, like the lark on high, in a restful, tranquil ecstasy. The bird of melancholy still beat its wings, but gently, peacefully. Hope consoled her heart, her passions were calmed, her flesh trembled, but trembled as though with joy on remembering that kingdom where there is no death but joy is ever-

---

[1] The Mozarabs sang this melody at the Offices of the Dead and of Martyrs. We owe to P. Germán Prado, whose fame as a Mozarabist is well established, the transcription of the original neums. These, together with a few other examples, are all that is left to us of the immense musical treasury of this liturgy.

lasting. The last modulations of the ancient antiphon, so profound, so inspired, are a jubilant expression, an interior, calm jubilee, of a deep longing soon to be realised.

This longing increased in Columba's soul without depriving her of her holy serenity, won at the cost of so many struggles. The triumph of Digna, her companion, increased it, as did the chant of the clergy of San Cypriano, for Columba was living with her sisters in a house near the church, since the emir had destroyed her convent — "the nest of peace" as she called it, "the nest of fanaticism" as it was termed by the martyr's enemies. The forest that had been enlivened by the humming of the monastic hive, was now mute and solitary. A few years later, and it would be awakened by the clamor of other ascetics, the Moslem *sufíes*. At the end of the century, Abenmassara, the philosopher, took refuge among the ruins to escape from the fanaticism of the alfaquíes; the youths of Cordova, attracted by his eloquence, flocked in crowds to hear him. To the teaching of Eulogius and of Abbot Martin succeeded the audacious doctrine of the Moslem, who, by devout practices and mystical allegories, knew how to mask his materialistic pantheism in the style of Empedocles.

Though Columba had gone to live near the church of San Cypriano, she still longed for her heavenly mansion. One day, summoned by supernatural voices, she went out into the street, though she did not know the neighbourhood. Moslems passed by wearing brilliantly coloured cloaks, women wrapped in ample veils, workmen hurrying to their tasks. It was an autumn morning, bustling and alert. Columba, unaccustomed to such a crowd, lost her way. She did not know where death — or rather victory — was to be found. It is always more difficult to meet with victory than with death.

At last she stopped one of the passers-by and asked the way. The roads were long, narrow, and tortuous, but by diligent inquiries, the young girl found what she sought: the judge's house and the judge himself. Said bade her come in. She entered calmly and began to speak very gently, discreetly, and quietly.

She sought for nothing less than to convert the judge, but the judge, captivated by her gentle speech and beauty, did not listen. It really is not easy to convert a Moslem, still less an alfaquí whom the anti-Christian policy of Mohammed had entrusted with acting on his bias for persecution. Said did not dare to condemn the girl. It seemed better to leave the solution in the hands of the viziers. Probably the vizier was either in Seville or on the south coast, where the leading Omeyas usually spent part of the autumn.

On being taken into the palace, Columba acted in the same manner, with great firmness. Her audience was increased — a reason for preaching with fresh courage.

"Do not imagine," she said, "that Christ's bride is so easy to seduce. You promise me great riches, but who is more rich than He? You promise me an earthly marriage, but is anyone more handsome than the most beautiful among the sons of men? Where is there any church or religion more holy than the true Faith of the Gospel, which, preached to the whole world by the Apostles, makes us certain that all prophecy opposed to it is a fraud. Then, renounce what is vain, and seek the safe guidance of the Gospel. Be not called abortions of death, begotten in darkness, but sons of light. For our Lord said to us: 'He that followeth Me walketh not in darkness. . . . And everyone that liveth, and believeth in Me, shall not die for ever'" (John, 12:46; 11:26).

This was St. Columba's sermon, but the viziers, who were not in the humour for sermons, though preached by the gentlest and most prudent of lips, condemned her to death, returning hatred for love. An executioner led the virgin to the river banks. Columba was so delighted that she did not know how to repay the headsman for such kindness. She gave him a generous reward, perhaps a gold necklace she used to wear. Then she bent her slender throat; the axe fell; and her head rolled to the ground.

A few days after, some monks found her body in the river and took it to Eulogius, who ordered that it should be buried outside the city, in the church of Santa Eulalia.

The remembrance of Columba was graven in his heart beside that of Flora. The virgin of Tábanos is one of the characters he paints most lovingly. At the end of her touching history he could but appeal to her with the confidence of one who had been her intimate friend:

> Finally, O most holy virgin, do thou, who while living, didst adorn the Church with the example of thy life, and when dead dost defend it with the protection of thy merits, forget not me, thy devout client, save me from the deceptions of the world, snatch me from the tempests of this life, and after death, obtain for me the rest of paradise!

Columba died on September 17, 853, and on the eighteenth took place the martyrdom of her friend Pomposa, a nun of Peñamelaria, daughter of the founders of that monastery, which still flourished. Pomposa had long wished for martyrdom, but her parents, knowing this, carefully locked all the doors of the abbey, until, on the night between the seventeenth and eighteenth of September, one of her brothers took it into his head to lay hold of the key and open the principal door. The young girl, who was watching him secretly, drew back the bolt, followed him, and disappeared in the darkness. At daybreak she entered the city, and the nuns of Peñamelaria received the news of her death almost before they had discovered her flight.

The partisans of Eulogius rejoiced at these martyrdoms, but they furnished a fresh incentive to the hate and tyranny of the Moslems. The emir had fits of rage and stupor bearing all the signs of madness. "Inflamed by intense anger," Eulogius said, "and as though beside himself with wrath, he was aghast at the triumphant daring which defied his regal majesty." In the first impetus of this savage anger he gave forth a terrible edict: all Christians who did not apostatise were to be killed and their wives sold as slaves publicly. Most of the councillors disapproved of these extreme measures which the sultan himself found were excessive. Persecution went on, but the decree was withdrawn.

It was not pity that influenced this ferocious man: the extinction of the Christians was merely deferred. He had first to subdue the regions that his avarice and intolerance had driven to rebellion. Eulogius and his cause had many sympathisers in Toledo, and Toledo had thrown off the yoke since the beginning of Mohammed's reign. The leader of the rebellion was a Christian named Sindola. The Toledans took possession of Calatrava, marched as far as Andújar, and threatened the capital of the emirs itself.

Muza, the governor of the northern frontier, also declared for independence, forming a kingdom that had for its centre Saragossa. Certain chiefs were already agitating in Estremadura, having thrown off the mask. Ordoño, king of León, took part with the rebels and sent them his troops. The Cordovan army was twice routed. In the spring of 854, the allies suffered a considerable loss near Toledo, which was not decisive as the city remained independent.

A year later there arose in the east another danger which would cause great trouble to Mohammed. It was instigated by Ibn-Meruan, captain of the emir's own guard, a renegade Spaniard of the region of Mérida. While he had acted as conspirator in former risings, he was now peacefully serving his sovereign when, one day, the Minister Haxim, who looked upon him with no favour, said to him before the viziers: "You are more worthless than a dog."

Thirsting for vengeance, the captain left the court, called his friends together, and returning to his own country with them called to arms all the renegades and malcontents of the districts of Mérida and Badajoz. He preached a new religion that was halfway between Christianity and Islamism, and having joined Alphonso III, from whom everyone received help who rebelled against the sultan, became for twenty years a dangerous and implacable enemy of his former sovereign.

Hence it was fear that, in a measure at least, made the emir prudent. But even though he did not have the ferocious decrees carried out which he had first planned, yet his intolerance gave the Christians no truce. The persecution was so fierce and malevolent that, if we may believe the statements of Eulogius and Alvaro, few had courage to withstand it. The number of apostates was enormous. Many only feigned to apostatise, saying in defence that in such a struggle, dissimulation was lawful. Some were shamefully cowardly. "Those who seemed the pillars of the Church, its foundation, its elect, presented themselves uncalled before the judge and in the presence of cynics and epicureans, anathematised God's martyrs. Christ's pastors, the doctors of the Church, bishops, abbots, priests, grandees, and influential men, cried out in public that the martyrs were heretics and fully deserved death."[2]

Gómez was one of the apostates. Mohammed's proselytism had brought this about. At first, when he drove all Christians from the palace, Gómez retained his post, and his influence over the emir grew daily. He was given charge of the chancery on account of the illness of the Chancellor Abdalá Ibn-Omeya, and Mohammed is even related to have said: "If Gómez were of our religion, I should gladly name him chancellor."

However, during September, 853, Gómez received an order to deliver up all his papers. This was a blow which his faith, already feeble, could not support. Knowing the intentions of the emir, he abjured Christianity and became a Moslem — a most devout and edifying Moslem. "He who formerly rarely entered a church," said St. Eulogius, "now hardly ever left

---
[2] *Indículo Luminoso*, No. 14.

the temple of impiety." The Moslems called him "the dove of the mosque," so pious did he seem and so strictly did he keep the precepts of his new religion. Mohammed, having succeeded in his plan, recalled Gómez and delivered to him the seal of the chancery and with it all his former confidence.

Henceforth Gómez behaved like a true renegade, ceaselessly interfering in all matters relating to the Christians, in consequence of having renounced his faith. One would have thought he was bishop of Cordova. He caused priests who venerated the martyrs to be removed from the churches, putting others who were in his confidence into their place; he had daily read in the assemblies of the faithful letters of anathema against the confessors and their defenders; he summoned the monks and the most zealous among the Christians and made them swear on the cross and the Gospel that they would not present themselves spontaneously for martyrdom, threatening them with the most atrocious tortures unless they submitted to his orders.

Gómez had now a new colleague, a bad Christian and one entirely devoted to him — none other than the leader of the Christians, Servando. Mohammed knew his men well and had given Servando supreme authority over those of his own race. Sansón, his contemporary, gives a companion picture of him corresponding to that of Gómez by St. Eulogius. The moral delineation of these two notorious rascals were so alike that an historian could easily mistake one for the other.

According to the distinguished Abbot of Peñamelaria, Servando was stupid, insolent, vain, arrogant, miserly, cruel, rash, stubborn, and haughty. Son of a servant of the Church, he had recoiled from no kind of baseness that would gain the monarch's favour. He met Hostégesis at court and was at one with him, and Hostégesis married him to his niece. "Solomon's words were fulfilled," said the good abbot: "birds of a kind flock together, and the wicked man found one worse than himself to join him."

The Christians hated Servando with all their heart as well they might. Knowing that the best way to increase his power was to fill the public treasury (he had learned this from Gómez), he now overwhelmed his fellow believers with exactions until he drove them to apostasy. Not content with killing the living, he did not even respect the dead, for to increase the Moslems' hatred for Christians, he exhumed the bodies of the martyrs resting in their coffins in the churches and delivered them to the sultan's ministers, complaining of the audacity of the fanatics who had dared to give honourable sepulture to those who suffered by the law of the monarch. He was one of the worst enemies of the martyrs and of their protectors, for whom he set traps with fiendish dexterity. He tried to get rid of Sansón, whom he disliked to see in the palace. When his relative Hostégesis, who had a mania for philosophising, made public the new theological opinions that had fermented within his brain while he drank at his orgies, Servando was the most enthusiastic partisan of his heresy. In the meantime, Sansón, persecuted by him, was obliged to flee from Cordova, and had to content himself with loading his enemy with all the most opprobrious names of his embittered pen.[3] But Bishop Saul still remained indomitable and scrupulously avoided all communication with his adversaries.

Confronted with these "mad dogs," as Alvaro called them, Eulogius continued to encourage the defenders of the truth. Alvaro was still at his side and at this date, 854, decided on writing his *Indículo Luminoso,* a violent diatribe against the Arabianists and a fervent defence of the confessors of the Faith. His arguments are the same as those of Eulogius, but his style is more powerful, precipitate, and obscure. He speaks with incredible crudity of Mohammed's luxury, yet declares

---
[3] See the *"Apologético de Sansón,"* Prologue of Vol. II, No. 6, *Esp Sagr.,* XI, 380–381.

that he leaves much to say in another book, which he never wrote. Even the first has reached us in an unfinished state, and was probably never completed. It shows that his hatred for Mohammed and Islamism increased as he grew older.

Eulogius, too, had taken up his pen again. Persecuted by the rage of Gómez, he was obliged to change his abode constantly and live in a state of continual anxiety. His school had been dissolved and he hardly dared to appear from time to time in his church of San Zoilo. In the midst of all these dangers, he found time to write. Monks and people looked upon him as the historian of these hazardous times, and he promised them that, so long as he lived, his pen would be at the service of the martyrs. For a time he thought that his task was done:

> I never expected that after so many tribulations, such terrible, intolerable anguish, any one would present himself in the arena. But however my work may extend, never will I be silent or give up what I have begun, but will continue to the end as I promised my brethren.

This was written in the third volume of the *Memorial de los Santos*, which gives the history of the four first years of Mohammed's reign. St. Eulogius was as enthusiastic as ever, though he speaks of weariness and depression, comparing himself to a tired traveller who never comes to the end of his journey.[4]

> I am like a traveller who, with strength exhausted, sometimes thinks that he is near the end of his journey, and feels all the more weary for halting frequently. Sometimes he believes that the end has been reached and his heart is full of joy, but the road is still longer than he believed and the deception torments him cruelly. I thought this book was finished and rejoiced that my little bark had crossed a

---

[4] This third volume, which Eulogius thought would finish his work, the *Memorial de los Santos*, was written before the year 857 and after that of 855.

stormy sea and safely reached the quiet, longed-for haven; but now I must weigh anchor and set forth again. The wind is contrary and I fear the heavy swell of the high seas. I have no sails of eloquence and learning, my mind is filled with thought of dangers from my persecutors, who threaten and surround me. Yet I trust that I shall be delivered with gain to myself, by the bountiful aid of Him who made me worthy of the society and friendship of the saints to console me with the triumph of those whose loving converse was my greatest joy.

This trust did not fail: the holy martyrs watched over their eulogist and friend. A short way to go, a brief struggle, and he who sang their praises would rejoin those he praised. His crown gleamed now in the distance.

CHAPTER XXIII

A LULL IN THE DEADLY *STORM*

AFTER 854 the persecution became less rigorous. During the two following years there were only nine martyrdoms, caused for the most part by Moslem fanaticism. For instance, the priest Abundius did not seem by nature heroic, yet when brought before the judge by his enemies, he confessed his faith manfully. But Ludovicus, a relative of Eulogius, presented himself in the court of justice, abused Mohammed, and was beheaded. Argimirus and Aurea, victims of the people's bigotry, were the last two martyrs of the year 856.

Aurea belonged to an influential family connected with the cadí of Cordova: Argimirus had been a Christian judge. Both were elderly, and expected to end their life in a monastery, but the Mohammedan inquisition did not allow them.

Though the *chusma* sought for blood and vengeance, the leaders of the persecution seemed to have forgotten their original intention. Mohammed realised that he had other and more dangerous enemies than the martyrs and devoted himself to crushing the rebels. His troops marched against Toledo every year, but with little result. In 855 they reached Burgos, a fort recently built by the kings of León; next year the army was directed to Barcelona, and for a time subjected the Beni Lope of Saragossa.

Meanwhile Hostégesis was feasting and amusing himself; feasts and fasts were all the same to him. As for Gómez, he had more serious matters to think about. In spite of all his honours and riches he was very unhappy. He could not sleep in peace, enter the palace without fears, or walk along the streets in safety.

The dread of Haxim, the sultan's favourite, everywhere pursued him. Haxim ben Abdelaziz, the nephew of renegades, viewed unfavourably the eminence of this other renegade, more dexterous than himself in winning popularity with the Moslems by his feigned piety. Before the apostasy of Gómez, Haxim had performed all the duties of the caliphate, and the direction of all affairs was completely in his hands. Suddenly, Aljoxaní says, the talents of Gómez ben Antonián became known, showing his capacity for undertaking the most delicate negotiations. Henceforth the minister began to concern himself about his new rival and to plan his ruin. The chancellor was absurdly frightened of him; no one whom he himself persecuted was so timorous. Haxim's hatred would not let the object of his persecution sleep in peace even after his death. He spread a report that Gómez had died a Christian, and persuaded the most influential men in Cordova, nobles, alfaquíes, and courtiers, to present themselves before the judge to testify to the Christianity of Gómez in order that his property might pass to the fiscal. The emir finally ordered it to be divided among the sons of Gómez.

If the persecutors were now more tolerant, the Christians also moderated their zeal. Recafredo might feel satisfied. The bishops were on his side, the upper classes favoured him openly, and in sympathy with them was all the Christian community of the capital. Alvaro himself had ceded to the present more moderate demands, and probably Eulogius as well. They had not been asked for a full retractation of their opinion, only for a promise not to offer themselves spontaneously for martyrdom or to incite others to present themselves before the cadí. They were allowed to venerate the martyrs who had suffered during the preceding years. Out of love for peace, the two friends accepted this condition, which in no way violated their conscience.

Saul alone remained intractable, and refused to communicate with his opponents. The bishops had launched a decree of anathema against him, so that men called him "the accursed," but from his hiding place he avenged himself by anathematising his enemies. Most of the Cordovan Christians were excommunicated. In his attitude the bishop was swayed by a monk with a long beard and wornout habit, whom Alvaro described in his *Indiculo Luminoso* (No. 19) as a crafty hypocrite.

Alvaro had some dealings with both the bishop and his secretary. When, namely, the bonds of his long friendship with Bishop Saul were broken, Alvaro had a severe illness that brought him to death's door. As was the custom of the time in such cases, Alvaro asked for the penance whereby he bound himself, if he recovered his health, to perform all the practices imposed by the discipline of the early Church on penitents. One of them was to abstain from Holy Communion until absolution had been received from the bishop.

He asked for a priest of Recafredo's diocese (he may have been Eulogius), to perform the ceremony. The priest in question cut Alvaro's hair, gave him Holy Communion, traced on him a cross with ashes, recited the *Miserere*, and after saying other prayers addressed the penitent in the following words:

> I have given you the penance for which you asked. Study henceforth to live chastely, honestly, soberly, and devoutly. Avoid all impure words and actions; take no part in worldly affairs; nor be ambitious of what is temporal. Be as though dead to the world.

Alvaro recovered from his illness and religiously fulfilled these counsels, but found it very hard to be deprived of the Holy Eucharist. If he presented himself in church, the priest gave him blessed bread. This was the law for penitents. This distressed him deeply. At last he decided to ask for absolution and wrote to Bishop Saul whom he begged to send a priest to absolve him, offering to perform any other work of supererogation imposed upon him. "I am ready to obey any order," were his words, "if I am not deprived of the remedy of Holy Communion, for it grieves me greatly to be kept away from the feast of the Marriage of the Lamb. I hope to learn your decision this week; if not, I shall be obliged to apply to your brethren the bishops, for I cannot remain so long deprived of the Body and Blood of my God."

The bishop's reply could not have been more ungracious. His anger at Alvaro's defection and his desire to bring him back to his party, made him contradict himself in the strangest manner. "Seek absolution from him who gave you the penance," he began. He then showed a disposition to grant it himself under the condition that Alvaro came to receive it in person, and ended by excusing the severity of his answer under the pretext that he had not recognised the handwriting of the sender.

"But now," he added, "having recognised your writing, I wish to write to you affectionately for the remedy of your soul, that you may seek what is holy and avoid the company of the wicked. . . . Think well over what I have said, so that you may receive the Sacrament of Reconciliation. . . . And if you will not listen to me, do as you think best or as prudence dictates."

Alvaro read between the lines the influence of the bearded monk, the bishop's counsellor, "of that despicable, wretched man," as he called him, "that disturber of his country, that busy sower of heresies." As for Bishop Saul, Alvaro told him, "That venom cannot have come from your head but from a stomach filled with wine."

The poor monk emerged from his angry description with a very blemished character, nor did the bishop fare better. "As for the rest," Alvaro ended, "your behaviour matters nothing to me. The Lord of all things is the Judge of my conscience who can cure the sick without waiting to be asked.

Though the priest and the levite leave lying by the wayside the man who was illtreated by thieves, the merciful Samaritan will come later, take him to the inn, pour oil into his wounds, and pay the innkeeper."

Saul, deserted by all, saw that he must give in. Already, in his correspondence with Alvaro, he showed a disposition to submit if a large majority of bishops in the Council required it. The Council was held in 857, and henceforth the Church of Cordova was able to breathe afresh. Saul retracted, was absolved by the bishops, and himself absolved those he had excommunicated. From that time, he appeared again in his churches. A letter from him to a metropolitan, probably Wistremiro of Toledo, gives an account of the matter:

> I own to you, my most holy lord, that on hearing the vast amount of texts quoted by the holy Fathers, filled by compassion for the people, I was overcome, and revoked my former standpoint in the presence of the whole assembly.

Later on, Saul refuted an error of his former partisans that was no doubt renewed by his astute confidant, the ancient propagator of heresies, of whom Alvaro tells us. Proud of their virtue and the firmness they had shown before their persecutors, these extremists affirmed that the sacraments were invalid unless administered by holy priests. Saul spoke of these heretics as coldhearted in regard to the Lord, disdainfully rigorous, wanting in knowledge, and filled with the wind of vainglory. He would not, however, weigh them down with his anathema, for after all they had borne witness to the truth, though their present puritanism endangered their own faith.

We see, therefore, the new attitude of Eulogius, Alvaro, and the bishop. Far from hating the martyrs, they venerated them and considered them the greatest honour to their country, yet in order to avoid fresh dangers for the Church, they submitted to some of the impositions of the emir and his representatives. In opposition to the detractors of the martyrs, who inevitably went to swell the ranks of the Moslems, and of the extremists, who ended in becoming heretics, there stood again, as in the past, Alvaro, Saul, and Eulogius, surrounded by the more fervent Christians.

This condescension of the chief Mozarabs did not diminish by a jot their enthusiasm for the confessors of the Faith, for we still meet them at their side, consoling and venerating them. Nor did their conscience allow them to repulse those who in a moment of weakness had pronounced the formula of Islam, but had returned to the Faith.

In the year 857 two martyrdoms of this kind occurred of which the story will be told in the following chapter. Their touching history is a fresh revelation of Moslem fanaticism.

CHAPTER XXIV

A TRIUMPHANT *MARTYRDOM*. THE APOLOGÉTICO

IN THE province of Cabra lived three brothers, one of whom was a Mohammedan, another a Christian, and the third, Rodrigo, was not only a Christian but a priest as well. One night, while disputing about religion, the Christian and the Moslem became angry and fought with each other. But when Rodrigo sought to make peace and threw himself between them the two brothers turned their wrath on him until finally he lay unconscious and half dead on the ground. The Moslem, a fanatic and proselytiser, then laid the wounded man on a bed and had him carried on the shoulders of some of the neighbours through all the towns of the district, meanwhile crying aloud in the streets: "Here is my brother the priest, who, enlightened by God, has embraced our religion, and wishes to make it known before he dies."

When Rodrigo recovered he became aware of what had happened. Refusing to ratify the trick his brother had played, which under the law now bound him to Mohammedanism, he fled to the mountains around Cordova — "as if," wrote Eulogius, "he could avoid the martyrdom that had been prepared for him from the creation of the world, and by hiding from the impious persecutor could escape from the gaze of the loving Redeemer who followed him in order to raise him to His kingdom. This happened during the first fury of the persecution, when in Cordova, the ancient national city and now the flourishing capital of Arabic rule, all the towers of the basilicas were demolished and the cupolas of the churches destroyed, together with the spires containing the bells that daily called Christians to unite in prayer. The gloomy, malevolent man who sat upon the throne had thoroughly understood his father's intention."

Five years later, in the beginning of 857, Rodrigo left his hiding place and entered the market of Cordova with the clerical tonsure and dress. He was walking fearlessly past the vendors' stalls when someone near by launched at him a torrent of insults, and at the same time a furious hand gripped his throat. It was his Moslem brother who had recognised him and who dragged him angrily before the cadí.

The cadí did his utmost to convert the priest. He promised him riches and honours and threatened him with death. All the cadís used every effort to prevent martyrdoms. Not that they cared much whether they shed a Christian's blood, but zealous, faithful Moslems saw in the courage of the martyrs a veritable defeat of their own faith. Later on, when Oriental philosophy had undermined Mohammedan beliefs and sown rationalism in the upper classes of the royal city, judges saw the matter under a different aspect. But the judge before whom Rodrigo appeared was a faithful apostle of the prophet, who sought to win him over. Yet Rodrigo, too, knew how to preach:

"You may propose these things to those who believe in your religion," he said, "as for me, to whom to live is Christ and to die is gain, I can only repeat what the holy doorkeeper of heaven said: 'Lord, to whom shall we go? Thou hast the words of eternal life' (John 6:69). Why should I cease drinking from the fount of life in order to draw water from a pool fouled with the mud of falsehood and fetid with vices?"

Rodrigo was imprisoned in a dungeon where he met another Christian, named Salomon, who after having denied Christ repented of his apostasy. Cheered by one another's company, the prison seemed to them like paradise. The judge had them separated, and blamed the jailors severely. But this had no effect. He addressed them two or three times in vain, and at last decided to condemn them to death. Before going to execution, the confessors threw themselves at the feet of all present, whom they begged to help them in their last combat. Then, giving one another the kiss of peace, and rudely pushed on by the soldiers, they went to the place of execution. There the judge appeared once more, making them all kinds of promises.

"It is useless for you to trouble yourself," said Rodrigo, "we are very sorry to see you sunk in the gulf into which you want to cast us. In fact, we feel such an immense contempt for Islamism that we would not let our dogs profess it."

Irritated by this reply, the judge gave a signal to the headsmen, and the martyrs, signing themselves with the cross, bravely awaited the stroke of the axe. Rodrigo's head rolled on the ground; Salomon's remained joined to his trunk. The bodies were hung on separate gallows.

At this moment a man strode through the crowd of spectators, without a glance at the Mohammedan authorities, and amid the general stupefaction passed to where the martyrs hung. It was Eulogius. He tells us:

> Meanwhile I, Eulogius the sinner, who had resolved to write of the deeds of these saints of God, when the rumour of their martyrdom spread throughout the city, inspired by a divine daring, hastened, after having offered the Sacrifice of the Mass, to see their sacred remains, fearing no more to approach them than if I had been one of the bystanders. These mutilated corpses were so beautiful and lifelike that if anyone had asked them a question, he might have thought they were about to speak. That I am not telling a falsehood, my gentle Redeemer will bear witness, who will be the Judge of what I am writing.

Eulogius could see some of the Moslems picking up pebbles stained with the blood of the martyrs, washing them carefully, and throwing them into the river, lest the Christians should venerate them as relics. A short time afterwards the bodies of the saints were cast into the water, and the judge ordered that a notice should be given imposing most severe penalties on anyone who entered the river to seek for them.

Nevertheless, soon afterward everybody in Cordova knew that a priest of the southern suburbs had the sacred relics in his house. On learning this, a vast multitude left the city to do honour to the heroes' relics. Eulogius was with them, as on the day of the execution, and has left us a vivid description of the nocturnal festival, for it was held during a night in the springtime. No moon shone, but the stars stood out in the sky like the golden letters on the blue friezes of the grand mosque, wherewith Mohammed had adorned it. And all the place was bright as day with the countless lights that were burning there.

The crowd wept for joy. Their mourning had been changed into a universal rejoicing. All signs of sadness had disappeared. The bishop arrived, escorted by his priests. Removing the hood that covered his head, he began by kissing the venerable remains. A delicious perfume came from the sacred relics and penetrated the crowd. After twenty days, the bodies were still as fresh as when Eulogius had seen them where he stood at the foot of the scaffold. The procession of priests and monks reached from the house where the remains were reverently laid, to the neighbouring church. The faithful filled the air with the murmur of their melodies. The temple resounded with the sacred echoes of psalmody, and thousands of lamps lighted its vaults. One might have said that the King of heaven himself had descended, with all the splendour of His army of the blessed, to witness this wonderful spectacle.

Perhaps, here and there, some tolerant Moslem, slightly addicted to the new philosophy, may have mixed with the crowd and watched the scene with feelings not untouched by admiration of what he saw.

A short time after, in fact, written by the hand of Abu Amir ben Xohaid, appeared the description of a nocturnal festival held by the Christians. Abu Amir had seen no objection himself to joining the uncircumcised and taking part in their ceremonies. Favoured by the darkness he entered a church and was kind enough to tell what he saw, even though not without a lamentable admixture of his own prejudices. Perhaps his words may give us a better impression of what now took place:

> The pavement was carpeted with bunches of myrtle, and the whole building was adorned with signs of rejoicing. The chimes of the bells delighted the ears, and the eyes of the worshippers shone with fervour.
> The priest entered, accompanied by the worshippers of Christ, wearing beautiful ornaments, and the songs and rejoicings ceased. They did not take water from vases, but collected it from the stoups in the palm of their hands. The priest stood in the midst of his brethren, kindling their fervour and sipping from his chalices which delighted him with their fragrant aroma whenever he raised them to his lips in sweetest libation.
> When the ceremony was over, he retired with his nocturnal companions. How many times did I inhale in that temple of perfume — of the wine of youth, together with the old wine of the priest! There were beautiful youths, enraptured with joy, who bowed humbly and modestly before the priest. The priest, as though to prolong my stay, entoned his psalms repeatedly near me.
> Boys, whose cheeks glowed with the rose of modesty, offered me wine. They were like the gentle doe, shy at its lord's gaze.
> These tender boys received Communion from the priest, who gave them red wine to drink and pork to eat."[1]

The function ended at dawn, and Abu Amir returned home, intoxicated with the perfume of the old wine and the

---

[1] J. Simonet, *Historia de los Mozárabes de España*, Appendix IX, p. 820.

rosy cheeks of the young clerics. It seems to have been that very nocturnal festival which Eulogius described: "The lights went out, the hymns ceased, and the Christians, separately or in small groups, walked home through the narrow streets."

Eulogius went in silence, his soul filled with profound joy. He meditated on the triumph of that day, on the great manifestation of faith, on the outburst of enthusiasm for the cause of the martyrs which he had now been defending with all his strength for ten years. The depth of his emotion is reflected in the last page of the *Apologético*. For the deep impression made by that glorious night had not entirely disappeared; and it may have been the sunrise of the following day that found him writing this beautiful prayer — the last that came from his pen:

> I have gone forth to meet your enemies, I have sung your sacred victories, my patrons, ye illustrious witnesses of Christ, valiant warriors, splendid conquerors, defenders of the Christian people. I have sung your victories that I may expiate my sins, and aid those on the way to the Kingdom. No, you cannot look unkindly upon him who spoke the truth about you. I feel sure that I am pleasing both to you and to Christ. Therefore, I beg you — I, the sinner Eulogius, poor in merits, paltry in sanctity, and great in sin — to help me by your intercession among the fearful scandals of the world and to deliver me from the torments of hell that I have deserved by my faults.

So ends his last book: the *Apologético*.

This volume contains more than the life of the two last martyrs: it is a new defence of martyrdom. Such of the faithful as already were half Mohammedans continued still to deny that the name "martyrs" could be applied to those who had been executed during the last few years. They no longer urged as their objective the spontaneity of the martyrdoms, since this difficulty had been brilliantly refuted by Eulogius in his *Memorial*. They now based their arguments on other grounds, differing but slightly from the former, yet presented in a comparatively new manner which required a fresh refutation.

They dwelt chiefly on the difference between the pagans of the first persecutions and the Arabs. The pagans were men sunk in every kind of vice and error; they employed every kind of torture: scourging, burning, hooks, wild beasts — whatever cruelties the human imagination could invent. But the persecutors of the present time are devout men, adoring one God only, and acknowledging a divine revelation from heaven. They did not torture their victims for the pleasure of it, but with a single blow, which hardly hurt them, sent them into the next world. It therefore sufficed — so this argument concluded — that by this easy death the martyrs should obtain the remission of their sins, without people also lavishing in their honour illuminations, canticles, and praise.

Thus argued the tepid Christians. St. Eulogius answered:

> What does the kind of death matter by which these saints died? . . . Is it not the selfsame motive, zeal for God and love for His kingdom, that crowns him who dies amid the most atrocious tortures and him who placidly bows his head on the block to the headsman? Do they not both fulfill Christ's precepts equally by despising the allurement of pleasure, renouncing love for parents, children, wives, and all the delights of this life? And what suffering is more terrible than death? What more terrifying than to see the axe above our head, ready to fall and cut short our existence? The crown is not promised to him who resists for a long time, but to the victor. It is not the more or less rapid death that makes martyrs, but the cause for which they die — that they die for the Faith, that they lose their life for Christ who bestows the crowns.

With this vigourous reasoning, this fervent and persuasive eloquence, Eulogius opposed all his adversaries' objections, but his speech gained fresh ardour when he spoke of the boasted piety of the Mohammedans:

No, we ought not to call these men worshippers of God, but followers of vanity; for not only do they not revere the vital precepts of the Gospel, that have spread over the whole world, but they fiercely persecute those who confess that Christ is true God and true man. They continually assail God's inheritance with their ridicule, prevent the divine rites of holy religion, and abuse those who practise it, while placing their faith in the incantations of a possessed and pestiferous man.

The Koran was for Eulogius a series of ridiculous legends; the Mohammedan religion a consecration of all the vices; its worship, a school of hypocrites and wicked men. He was irritated, above all, by the *almuédans,* who "like asses, with distended jaws, opening their impure lips preposterously, and stopping their ears with both hands, give forth their monstrous prayer with so horrible and savage a cry that even the prophet himself could not have endured it."

He, like Alvaro, saw in the prophet a miserable deceiver, an anti-Christ impersonated, with no more intelligence than the camel on whose back he rode. Mohammed's life was involved in legends, both for Christians and Moslems. Eulogius knew the sources of both, but naturally gave more credit to the accounts of Christian origin. While looking over the books in the library of Leyre, he found in a codex of the Councils, a brief biography of the prophet which he copied most carefully. This curious narrative he reproduces in the *Apologético.* It is filled with extravagant fables.

That a Christian writer of the ninth century should have given credit to such legends may perhaps surprise the modern reader. And yet underlying the grotesque imaginations were substantial truths which they symbolised. These stories were found reproduced in various monastic writings and were copied by Vigila, in Albelda; by Sarracino, in San Millán de la Colgolla; and by other scribes in Silos and Cardeña. As for accurate historic data, it must be admitted that even in these times we know little of Mohammed. Eulogius knew what the Moslems told about him, but naturally, all they recounted seemed to him but idle tales and nothing more.

His judgments on Mohammedanism, it may nevertheless be affirmed, are substantially correct. What Eulogius said about its morality, its doctrine concerning Jesus, its teaching about the future life and other points of Islamic belief, coincides with what we know now of this theology. He speaks vehemently, with an excusable vehemence, in some of his descriptions. The voice of the *almuédan* was for him an iniquitous command. Many a time had he seen the Moslems stop to listen to it, turn their face to Mecca, raise one hand to their right ear to catch the inspirations of the good angel, tap the other ear with the left hand to repel the evil inspirations of the bad spirit, and finally, recite the prayer called for by the exhortation of the *almuédan*.

Eulogius could not put any faith in these exterior formalities. He was displeased with Moslem morality, which manifested itself to him day by day in the vices most horrifying to a Christian. Having been educated in the most austere asceticism, polygamy was repugnant to him, authorised and freely practised as it was by Islam; but Mohammed's ideas of the heavenly paradise, with its lovely houris, its splendid banquets, and its promise of every imaginable pleasure of the senses, made him shudder.

For Eulogius and Alvaro, Mohammed was anti-Christ, the antithesis of Christ personified. This enemy of our Saviour, they said, consecrated to gluttony and luxury the sixth day of the week, which because of our Saviour's Passion should be a day of fasting and sadness. Christ preached chastity to his disciples; Mohammed taught his followers coarse delights, filthy pleasures, incest. Christ preached marriage, the prophet taught divorce. Christ commanded sobriety and fasting; he preached feasts and the pleasures of the table.

All that we know of the corruption reigning in the

city of Cordova confirms these diatribes of the leaders of the Mozarabs. Eulogius was in the right in condemning the Moslems and bad Christians. To find fault with Eulogius and his followers in this sanguinary drama is to misunderstand the true position of the Christian community in the centre of the caliphate, and fail to appreciate one of the finest manifestations ever made of the soul of Spain.

In this struggle, a struggle both of race and religion, the Spanish and Christian spirit was on the point of disappearing, overwhelmed by the intolerance of the invaders. The servitude of the Church had become intolerable; the Arabs, sure of their dominion, had broken every treaty. Christians were reduced to misery. The Ulemas, the incarnation of fanaticism in that age, ceaselessly excited against them the hatred of the people and the aversion of the sultans; the laws were such that many Christians found themselves obliged to renounce their religion or take the consequences, and once admitted into Islamism, they were by no possibility ever permitted to leave it. Half the martyrdoms were caused by this prohibition. The remaining half protested in the only way they could.

For a sincere Christian, Mohammedanism was scandalous in countless ways: family life was destroyed, justice was warped, slavery allowed, polygamy practised to an incredible extent, despotism enthroned, and the most shameful passions were honoured. The Church could not keep silence before such a spectacle; her silence would have been equivalent to approbation. She protested by the lips of Eulogius and his followers. No one could speak better in her name than he whose whole life had been a defence of Spanish tradition, threatened by the mentality imported from the East. He spoke courageously in condemning this false religious and moral attitude that came to destroy his own; he bore witness against it when the sword glittered above his head, and in this consists his greatness as well as that of his upholders.

CHAPTER XXV

THE TWOFOLD VINDICATION OF *EULOGIUS*

"FROM HIS youth," says the biography, "Eulogius walked sadly in this world's ways. His longing to mount to heaven grew daily, and his body was for him a mortal burden."

He held that true wisdom was that of the martyrs who hastened to exchange this life for a better. Each martyrdom drew from him cries of rejoicing. "We ought to leap for joy at the combats of these confessors, and celebrate with happy minds, liberty of heart, and hymns on our lips, the rapid ending of their glorious career. . . . They so longed to see God and to enjoy the company of the blessed, that they generously despised all the gains of this fleeting life, rightly thinking that it was better to suffer for a moment, in return for which they would rise straight to heaven, than to endure with terrible anxiety the artifices of the evil one during a long and dangerous period."

Eulogius had often taught this doctrine in the churches and monasteries, but had not yet personally brought it into act. When persecution grew fiercer, he fled, disguised himself, and avoided by every means the sword of the persecutor, while at the same time fulfilling his mission, studying, or else encouraging the timid under protection of the night. His teaching conformed with his life. No one ought to present himself before the persecutors unless clearly and evidently called by God. Martyrdom was an eternal predestination that God made known to the heart of the martyr by exterior or interior signs. Eulogius would have wished for this predestination, but his humble self-contempt made him judge himself unworthy of such glory. Soon, however, he would receive the call, clear and definite. Then he would respond to it unhesitatingly, and like a hero render up his life.

At present, martyrdom seemed less likely than before. Eulogius was to be met again in his church of San Zoilo; perhaps he once more reassembled his disciples, who had been spared by the sickle of persecution, and began his lectures to them as of old. Meanwhile, Mohammed's thoughts were bent on the laurel crown of military victory. No doubt he had realised that the Christians of Cordova were less dangerous than the rebels of Toledo and the mountains of León and Navarra.

In 858, for the first time in ten years, there was no single martyrdom. Religious life began to reorganise itself among the Christians. The martyrs' courage had been beneficial in every way. The Moslems showed greater understanding and tolerance, and a short time afterward such notices as the following were sent from the royal palace to the cadí:

> The chancellor salutes you, and declares that the Spaniards who speak the Romance tongue must not be treated with contempt. You know perfectly well what should be done to carry out our pact with them.[1]

Two events happened to the Christians of Cordova that year in which Eulogius must have seen divine approbation of his work.

During March, two French monks from the monastery of St. Germain des Prés, Paris, came to the capital. One was Usuardo, author of the famous martyrology. His abbot, Hilduin, had sent them to Valencia to seek for the body of St. Vincent; but before they reached the Pyrenees, they learnt that St. Vincent's remains were now in Benevento. They came to Barcelona, seriously disappointed at the news, but not inclined to return with empty hands. But their host, Suni-

---
[1] Aljoxaní, *Jueces de Córdoba* (Ribera's translation), p. 228.

fredo, one of the most influential citizens of Barcelona, assured them to their great delight that there were enough martyrs in Spain to fill all the monasteries of France. He referred to the recent victims of the Cordovan persecution. Above all he spoke to them of Aurelius, the generous friend of St. Eulogius, and of George, the Eastern monk. The French visitors were touched by these stories and determined to undertake the journey to Cordova.

"I do not think that you can reach Cordova," the merchant said, "but if you do, I promise that you will come back rich. However, I do not advise you to make the journey; you would incur certain death."

As nothing could frighten the Parisian monks, Sunifredo was obliged to let them go, securing for them important letters of recommendation. They finally reached the emir's capital; their desire, however, to secure the sacred relics of the SS. George and Aurelius could not be so easily satisfied, for the monks of Peñamelaria firmly refused to part with the venerated bodies. However, the French religious did not give up all hope. They were resolute, and after several discussions, the community consented, although unwillingly. Bishop Saul himself had to go to the monastery to aid in bringing this about.

At last the two strangers were able to return, after having passed about two months in Cordova. They set out on the Vigil of the Assumption, "a day clothed in rose colour" as the medieval hagiography naïvely remarks, "on which the sun rises brilliantly after having newly washed his chariot."

With them they carried an enormous piece of luggage fastened securely and marked with the seal of the bishop. It was directed to Charles the Bald, so that the Moslems might believe it contained nothing more than presents for the king of France. The bodies were wrapped in choice woven stuffs, magnificent gifts from the nun Bábila, Leovigildo's sister. A crowd of Christians assembled to take leave of the French monks, weeping all the while over the loss of their martyrs.[2] No doubt Eulogius came forward to give a farewell kiss to the bodies of his friends.

A few years afterward another scene of the same kind would be re-enacted when his own body would, in turn, be reverently taken away to foreign lands.

Though this translation grieved Eulogius deeply, at the same time it was a great consolation. The Christians of Cordova could see that by foreign monks, impartial judges of the case, their martyrs were regarded with the same honour as those of the early Church.

Before long, Eulogius received fresh tidings that produced in him a quite different feeling. They concerned the death of his friend, the aged Wistremiro, and his own elevation to the dignity of Archbishop of Toledo, Primate of Spain. The bishops of the diocese had had their eyes on him, and the Toledan citizens, with whom he was very popular, received with enthusiasm the news of his election. This was plainly a challenge to the emir of Cordova.

Mohammed had ended his expedition to Toledo satisfactorily, so affording the French monks the opportunity of returning to their country, but his own success had been only moderate. After ordering his engineers to mine a bridge, he drew his enemies to it. When finally the bridge gave way, many Toledans found their grave in the Tagus. The court poets told the tale in pompous dithyrambs; but Toledo remained independent and — what must have annoyed the emir deeply — a short time after acclaimed as head of the Spanish Church his mortal enemy.

No doubt Mohammed could in many ways impede Eulogius in taking possession of his see and did not neglect to

---

[2] The interesting history of this translation of the sacred relics, written by Aimon, a monk, the companion of Usuardo, in the monastery of St. Germain des Prés, can be read in the *Latin Patrol*, Vol. cxv, 939-948.

use them, but the citizens of Toledo declared that while Eulogius lived, they wished for no other archbishop. Eulogius himself never left Cordova to take possession of his new dignity. "God," said Alvaro, "made no delay in placing on his head the mitre of the heavenly bishopric; for if it is true that not all bishops are saints," he added maliciously, remembering Hostégesis and Samuel, "it can be said that every saint is a bishop."

Mohammed deprived his rival of a mitre on earth, but gave him a crown in heaven.

CHAPTER XXVI

LUCRETIA. *EULOGIUS* RECEIVES HIS CROWN

AT THE time of our present narrative there lived at Cordova a young girl, rich and of noble birth, in whom all the grace and courage of Flora seemed revived. "She flourished," said Alvaro, "amid wolves. That is, her parents were Moslems. She herself was a rose whose sweet perfume scented all the churches."

Leocritia, or Lucretia, as she was called, had found a good catechist in a religious related to her who instructed her in the Gospel and baptised her. The maiden embraced her new religion with such fervour that she ended by practising it publicly. Such audacity inevitably brought about her death. In vain did her parents try to bring her back to Islamism. Lucretia resisted caresses as bravely as she did threats and punishments. Not a day passed without her being cruelly ill-treated.

She thought of flight, as Flora had before, but her home was more carefully guarded; besides, she did not know where to go. In this difficulty, she had recourse to St. Eulogius, sending him word of her situation by some servants. The saint ordered her to leave the house immediately, for her life and faith were threatened. It was not easy to escape, but Lucretia found out how to vanquish the difficulties by craft. She began to seem more yielding to her parents, to practise the ablutions of Islamism devoutly and say its customary prayers; she feigned abhorrence for the austere practices taught her by the Christians, asked for fine clothes, perfumes, Arabian books, and even for risky amusements. Her parents gave her all she wanted, satisfied with having rooted out the accursed ideas of the Christian religion.

Meanwhile, the wedding day of one of her relatives arrived. Lucretia, dressed in her best, wearing her most precious jewels, with two red carnations in her hair, such as the women of Cordova wear now, left the house, saying that she was going to the marriage. Her parents, who felt sure of her, calmly let her go, but in vain did they wait all day for her return. When they learnt that their daughter had not been at the wedding, they knew they had been tricked, and full of indignation, with the aid of the police ransacked every corner of Cordova. Many persons who were suspected were arrested, scourged, and tortured.

In the meantime, Lucretia constantly changed her dwelling to escape from her persecutors. From the first she found refuge and kindness in the home of Eulogius, who now lived alone near the church of San Zoilo, with his sister Anulona, the virgin consecrated to God. His brothers' occupations had dispersed them in different directions, and his mother may have been dead. Lucretia found a father in Eulogius and a sister in Anulona. The two women were soon the closest of friends.

Unfortunately, the house of the great friend of the martyrs was the place the Moslem police suspected most. Eulogius realised this, and "disturbed by the idea that the ewe lamb might fall into the power of the wolves," sought day by day in his friends' houses for some corner where he could hide her. From time to time he went to see, instruct, and inspire her with courage for the future. He advised her to prepare for divine grace with fasts and vigils, and meanwhile he passed the nights in prayer prostrate on the ground in the basilica of San Zoilo. No doubt he remembered the interior conflict he had undergone while teaching his beloved Flora the road to death.

One night Lucretia knocked at his door. She wanted to talk to Anulona, whom she had not seen for some time, and to consult her teacher on an extraordinary phenomenon that occupied her thoughts. While at prayer, her mouth was filled with a delicious taste that gave her great enjoyment.

"It is the sweetness of the heavenly kingdom that is drawing near you," Eulogius told her.

All three spent the night in prayer. They could not sleep, since Lucretia had to return to her usual hiding place before daybreak. They waited some time for the companion who was to fetch her, but who did not come. At last she arrived, but it was too late. The young girl could not safely pass through the streets by daylight, so it was agreed that she should remain where she was until the following night. She stayed, but shortly afterwards a small body of foot soldiers surrounded Eulogius' house. It was the Saturday before Passion Sunday, "Lazarus' Sunday," as the Mozarabic liturgy called it. Eulogius had finished saying Tierce and his heart was full of anxiety and trouble. He trembled for the little ewe lamb who trembled near him. He also dreaded the incertitude of his own future, and in the midst of his gloom and disquietude, surrounded by an atmosphere of infamous espionage, the formulas of that Hour of the Liturgy seemed to bear for him a meaning they had never had before. The sacred liturgy embraced him in its arms like a mother, caressed, consoled, and nourished him with holy words that seemed to have been written for that special time.

First came words of intrepid defiance to the guards that drew near: the words were those of Isaias:

"Who will contend with me? . . . Who is my adversary? Let him come near to me. Behold the Lord God is my helper: who is he that shall condemn me? Lo, they shall all be destroyed as a garment, the moth shall eat them up" (Isa. 50:8, 9). Eulogius recited these words while thinking of his enemies. He felt complete confidence in what our Lord said and knew that God would keep his promises. Then there came a verse that was more intimate, which the Apostle St.

John seemed to address to him in that supreme hour. "Fear not," he appeared to say, "fear not the bitter draught of death."

"We are now the sons of God; and it hath not yet appeared what we shall be. We know that when He shall appear, we shall be like to Him: because we shall see Him as He is" (1 John 3).

Finally came Christ's infallible words: "Now I go to Him that sent Me" (John 16:5). . . . "On the last and great day of the festivity, Jesus stood and cried, saying: If any man thirst, let him come to Me and drink. He that believeth in Me, . . . out of his belly shall flow rivers of living water" (*Ibid.*, 7:37, 38).[1]

This cry filled Eulogius' soul with courage. He had thirsted intensely for the waters of life; from his earliest years he had walked painfully the ways of this world. At last his desires were to be realised. The soldiers entered and ransacked the entire house. Lucretia was the first to fall into their hands. Then they seized her master, who there received the first blows, and shed the first blood of his martyrdom.

He was next brought before the judge, whose face was convulsed with anger. This cadí was not the simple, devout Said ben Soleiman who had sent so many Christians to their death. The latter had died some time before, and Mohammed had replaced him by a man who enjoyed his complete confidence: Ahmed ben Zaid. Eulogius said of him that the devil had armed him with an instinct of ferocity and his cruelty held the city of Cordova in terror. This agrees with the testimony of Aljoxaní, who calls him a holy man, but the most severe of holy men, with a very harsh temper. Those who assisted at the court of justice dreaded his sentences; it sufficed that anyone spoke to him with the slightest want of civility to incur imprisonment.

---

[1] *Liber Canonicus.* Edition of Dom Morin, Maredsous, p. 116.

When Eulogius reached his presence, Ahmed was suffering from one of his frequent attacks of temper. He knew more than enough of the history of this Christian priest, in whom a devout Moslem was bound to see the chief enemy of his religion and race, and a formidable conspirator against the throne of the Omeyas. Eulogius enjoyed such prestige that for ten years he had preached the Christian Faith and Spanish nationalism, together with hatred of the foreign religion and resistence to the emir's impious orders, without any of his enemies having dared to arrest him. But now that he was brought before the judge, they held him in their power in an unhoped for, unforeseen manner. Hardly anyone knew that he had been seized.

"What business had you with the young girl, that you should hide her in your house?" thundered forth Ahmed, with fury in his eyes.

Eulogius replied with perfect calm and patience, showing, as Alvaro said, the sweetness and sincerity that characterised his speech:

"Judge, I hold a sacred office that obliges me to give the light of the Faith to those who ask for it. I can deny it to no men if they truly seek the righteous way of life. It is the mission of the priest, a duty of true religion, the command of my Lord Jesus Christ. This young girl came to be instructed in the Faith, and I could not send her away, for Christ has given me the office of a teacher. I tell you frankly that I taught her our law, as I would most willingly teach it to you if you asked me."

While the accused was speaking, Ahmed fidgeted nervously in his seat. He could find no way of punishing Eulogius for this audacious statement. Near him was seated an insignificant, dwarfish man, with small bright eyes and impassible face. He was Amer ben Abdalá, his secretary, who had attained great influence over him, and who finally supplanted him as judge. The client of one of Abderrahmán's daughters, he was the first man of Spanish descent to occupy the chief magistracy of the kingdom.

The people of Cordova, always jocose, called him "the crested lark." His manners were gentle, he spoke with exquisite politeness to everyone, and could not but be disgusted with the ridiculous scenes caused by his chief's irritability in the court of justice, much to the amusement of listeners and idlers. He spoke with an amiable smile, but almost without movement of the lips. The words seemed to come from the interior of a rock. When Eulogius appeared, he seemed to take no notice of who stood before him. He calmly took up his pen and prepared to write, as usual. He rapidly took down the judge's words and the answer of the accused, and then remained motionless, awaiting the judge's decision.

Ahmed looked round, made a signal to the executioners, and told them to bring the rods.

"Why did you send for them?" asked Eulogius when he saw them.

"To take your soul away from your body," answered the cadí.

"No," replied the priest courageously. "Do not imagine that you destroy my body with scourging. If you seek to return my soul to God who gave it, you had better sharpen your sword. I am a Christian as I always have been. I confess that Christ, the Son of Mary, is the true Son of God, and your prophet is an impostor, an adulterer, and a demoniac, who leads you by the way of perdition and prevents your seeing the holy paths of life."

Eulogius had at once resolved upon his course — the course of dying, to seal with his blood the principles he had defended all his life. His proselytism did not suffice to incur capital punishment. The judge had only meant to inflict an ignominious penalty; but for Eulogius, the last Hispano-Roman of Andalusia, the illustrious descendant of one of the noblest families of the patrician city, death was preferable. And now he was guilty of death for having blasphemed Mohammed. He reminds us of St. Paul when he declared to the proconsul that he was a Roman citizen. Ahmed ben Zaid did not dare to take such a responsibility as that of condemning the guilty man to death. Eulogius was elected Primate of Spain; he was the most highly respected priest in Christian Cordova, and his execution might cause complications in that city, in Toledo, and even in the northern parts of Spain.

Ahmed commanded that he should be taken to the royal palace, where a tribunal was improvised at once, composed of the highest officials in the government: viziers, eunuchs, secretaries, and officers of the royal guard. One of them, a friend of Eulogius, was touched with compassion at seeing him and spoke to him affectionately:

"I understand," he said, "simple or crazy persons bowing their heads uselessly before the headsman, but you, respected by all the world for your goodness and learning — is it possible that you have decided to imitate them? What madness has made you hate life in such a way? Listen to me, I beseech you, submit but for one moment to inevitable necessity; pronounce but one word, and then follow whatever religion you like best. My colleagues and I promise that we will never seek you out or molest you."

These were the words of a loyal friend who overlooked an explicit law of his religion to follow the sacred law of friendship. We do not know who he was. The emir had beside him Haxim ben Abdelaziz, who managed to keep his position until Mohammed died; Abdelruf ben Abdelsalem, whom the sultan favoured for his military valour; Gómez the apostate, who still had great influence; Mohammed ben Muza, who grew in power with his sovereign until at last he became prime minister; and the eunuchs Abenguéchih, Chodar, and Fatín, who were distinguished for their love of literature. Eulogius realised that all Moslems could not be involved in the same anathema. He rewarded his faithful friend's compassion by a smile of gratitude; his answer was gentle and affectionate, but firm.

"Oh, if you only knew what awaits us who adore Christ! If I could infuse in your breast what I feel in mine! Then you would not speak thus to me, but would hasten to despise worldly honours." Therewith he continued speaking of the Gospel promises, the peace of God's servants, the spiritual joys of the heavenly kingdom, and the vanity of earthly things.

"O princes," he said, "despise the joys of an impious, unruly life; believe in Christ, the true King of heaven and earth; deny the wicked prophet who has cast so many nations into the fire of hell."

These words angered the viziers, and Eulogius was condemned to death. On leaving the council chamber, a eunuch dealt him a blow, and the martyr, remembering the words of the Gospel, turned the other cheek to him, saying: "Strike this cheek too."

The eunuch did not need to be asked twice, and Eulogius was awaiting the second blow when a patrol of soldiers appeared and took him to the place of sacrifice.

He walked there serenely, his eyes calmly fixed on the distance. Light from above inundated all his being and enwrapped his transfigured form. He knelt before the block, raised his hands to heaven, said a short prayer in a low voice, and making the sign of the cross, bent his head tranquilly; "thus, despising the world, he found life." While his body fell, a bleeding trunk, his soul rose radiant, and disappeared in the wondrous abyss of the glory of God.

"This," says Alvaro, "was the noble combat of the teacher Eulogius; this was his glorious end, his marvellous transit. It took place at three o'clock on Saturday afternoon, March 11, 859."

CHAPTER XXVII

EPILOGUE: THE AFTERMATH

NEWS OF the execution of the chief of the Mozarabs spread rapidly throughout Spain. The chronicles of the northern peninsula, which hardly mention occurrences in Cordova, give a most exact account of the day of his martyrdom. Toledo, which must have cherished great hopes of its future prelate, surrendered soon after his death to the sultan's troops, and Mohammed chose for it an archbishop after his own heart. Numerous miracles were reported in Cordova which increased the fame of the glorious Cordovan martyr.

A large number of the citizens witnessed on the day of the execution a strange occurrence in which Alvaro saw an evident miracle. As usual, the executioners threw the martyr's body into the river, down which it began to float slowly, on the surface of the water. Suddenly, with a rushing sound, something darted through the air above the crowd and reached the body, over which it hovered. It was a dove of marvellous whiteness.

"A miracle, a miracle!" cried the Christians, while the Moslems picked up pebbles from the river banks to throw at the white messenger from heaven.

A flood of stones fell on the mutilated body of the martyr, but the bird evaded them skilfully, flying in circles and cooing tenderly. Some more daring among the infidels got into the boats and tried to catch the mysterious dove, but she rose in the air and sat on a tower of the neighbouring city wall, never taking her eyes off the sacred relics.

The Christians looked upon this event as a sign that heaven

approved of the action of the Mozarabic chief, but no one dared to recover his body, for fear of the Moslem police. It was not until two days later that they could take it to the church of San Zoilo, where his head already rested. As the Cordovan Christians filed past it his face wore a heavenly expression of peace and grace, but those "most beautiful eyes," that had been a beacon light to the souls of so many during their days of suffering, no longer beamed. In the meantime St. Lucretia slept her last sleep in the church of San Ginés; she had died courageously for the Faith four days after her teacher.

Holy Week was just over. The faithful of Cordova commemorated our Lord's Passion without forgetting that of his martyred doctor of theology, and while the Paschal *alleluias* resounded, great preparations were being made in the church of San Zoilo. Its community were proud of their martyr; it was there that he had been consecrated to God, that he had chanted the Canonical Hours, that his doctrine, his zeal, and his sanctity had shone forth. They asked that the body of the invincible hero, the kindly teacher, the loving brother, should be placed in the most honourable part of the building, the principal apse, near the ashes of the titular saint of the church, the ancient athlete of Roman times.

After the Feast of Pentecost, came the great day — the first of June. The Christians of Cordova filled the church of San Zoilo, which was splendidly adorned. Bishop Saul entered, surrounded by his clergy; Alvaro came, bearing on his face the traces of a premature old age that soon after bore him to his grave; then came the martyr's friends of his early days, his grateful students, the monks who had listened to his words of encouragement that now were cut short by the headsman's axe; the crowd of the faithful who remembered the gentle and patient, strong and devout words of the preacher who had now gone from them — words such as perhaps they would never hear again.

A new tomb had been erected in the apse; it was surrounded by coronas, tapestries, flowers, candles. Perhaps it may have been decorated with fine sculpture in the Oriental style: the Good Shepherd, bringing back the lost sheep to the fold and giving His life for it. Some skilfully written script was seen on the recently carved stone: it was the epitaph composed by Alvaro in honour of his friend:

> Here lies the kindly martyr and learned doctor of the Church, Eulogius; a light that will not go out, a name beloved throughout the ages.

The censers rose and fell, rose and fell again, filling the church with perfume. Clergy and people, thousands of voices in unison, sang the hymn written for the feast by the same friend, the most faithful of any we hear of at that time.

> This is the solemnity of our Eulogius, the great martyr: let us pay to the Lord the homage of our chant and faith.
> This day commemorates great deeds: the day on which we sing sweet canticles, the balsam of the weary traveller.
> Christ's wrestler, powerful in speech, famous for his doctrine and glorious death, has been crowned with glory, and his name will flourish for ever on earth and in heaven.
> He will obtain for us that the Ruler of all things will destroy the barbarous power that caused his death. May he trample with all his might on impious teaching and cause the Faith again to flourish, that it may raise us to the shining heights of heaven.[1]

While the numberless multitude of the faithful sang this melody, Saul, throwing back his episcopal vestment, approached the sacred relics enveloped in precious wrappings, kissed them devoutly, and with the help of his clergy bore them to the new tomb near the high altar.

Then, during a religious silence, the voice of the reader

---

[1] This hymn, the epitaph and the memorial of the first translation of the martyr's relics, is to be found at the end of the saint's life. See *Esp. Sagr.*, X, pp. 161–163.

echoed among the arches of the church as he read the history of the martyr's passion, the last homage offered by Alvaro's touching friendship. It was a history of what many had witnessed, a history of what all knew, but to which everyone listened with deep emotion. They seemed to see before them the saint of the peaceful smile, the beautiful eyes, the quiet voice, the polished manners, the candid, charming, gracious man, whose hands, gentle yet energetic, had moulded his own destiny. Of the multitude present there, one had been directed by him into the path of learning, another had been taught to love the quiet of the monastery; one had felt the force of his words in the hour of dejection, another, seduced into error and evil had been brought back by him to truth and virtue.

All knew him as their father, and the guide of their Church. When over his body, hardly as yet grown cold, the bishop raised the Sacred Host, they wept for gratitude and joy, and all hearts were touched at the remembrance of the past.

No one profited so much as Alvaro by his friend's death. He was often seen kneeling near the new sepulchre, his head bowed or touching the ground. He felt happy, yet wearied by the weight of sorrow. He was now old; his hair had slowly turned white; he was drawing near to the grave, to eternity; the time of his friendship with Eulogius faded into the distance. He had felt so sad, so lonely during the first eight days, the days of Holy Week, but in the month of the joys of Resurrection the alleluias had a new sound for him. The first year passed, and a year away from Eulogius seemed a century.

His life was also embittered by poverty. The religious conflicts, exorbitant taxes, the robberies of the slaves who were defended by the sultan, his own generous alms to the monasteries and indigent — all this combined to make him poor who had been rich in youth. He did not venture now to speak to the great men who had been his playmates as a child. He was even forced to seek the help of Count Servando to be saved from some unprincipled men who tried to despoil him of the land remaining to him.[2]

He was further troubled by the thought of his wickedness, his pride, his insolence, as he called it. His life seemed to him void of good works, right living, and truth. He forgot his conflicts with heretics, the persecutions he had undergone from the infidels, and the enthusiasm with which he had preserved his faith amid general apostasy. He was anxious even about his own faith, and it was that which moved him to compose his swan song, his *Confession* — a passionate, mournful little work, that sometimes reminds us of St. Augustine's *Confessions*, and at others of the *Lamento de la Penitencia* of St. Isidore. It gives a minute account of his beliefs, and a detailed, exaggerated list of his sins.

But in his hours of sadness, of anguish and grief, the remembrance of Eulogius enlightened his troubled soul and sustained his body, wearied with struggles. He, Alvaro, had not deserved martyrdom, but his friend's blood sufficed to purify even him. He remembered the words Eulogius had whispered in his ear while alive; he took down from the wall of his room the reminiscences of their friendship; he turned to the bookshelf where lay the parchment, letters, illuminations, that had been sanctified by his friend's touch. All these things seemed to him the mysterious transmitters of purifying grace, and made him imagine that Eulogius was still beside him.

> "Now," he wrote at the end of his biography of the saint,
> I must address my words to him, to remind him of our long friendship, for there is no doubt that he hears me and attends to my prayers. Yes, O sublime martyr of God, Eulogius, name sweet to my ears! Listen to thine Alvaro, who invokes thee, and is united to thee by the bond of charity. In the world thou didst call me friend; now that

---

[2] Cf. "*Epistola Alvari Romano medico directa,*" *Esp. Sagr.*, XI, p. 151.

thou art in heaven; help me by thine intercession. May the portals of my soul open to receive the kingdom of the most high God; may my proud head bow to receive the most sweet yoke of Christ! I long for eternal life and thirst for the rest of the heavenly kingdom; but thou must cleanse me, my beloved, with the fire of thy love, now that thou dost enjoy eternal bliss near the fount of life.

Death that had separated the two friends, could not destroy their friendship. Eulogius interceded for Alvaro in heaven, and helped him visibly to bear the trials of old age; Alvaro kept Eulogius' memory green on earth, told of his heroic actions, wrote his life, encouraged devotion to him and enriched the altar of his tomb. He tells us of it himself in a simple, almost childish, yet touching way:

I, my sweet Eulogius, have glorified the memory of thy name as best I could. I have told of thy generous deeds, explained thy teaching, and sung of thy sublime combat, that thy name may ever be illustrious in heaven and on earth. I have built to thy memory a monument more durable than bronze, that neither tempests nor fire can destroy. I have erected a statue of pure gold and precious stones that the envy of tyrants can never overthrow. I have founded the fabric of thy greatness and erected on high the tower of thy dwelling, that thou mayest be as a lighthouse for travellers in this life. I have adorned thy name with jewels, where the gold of the topaz shines beside the whiteness of snow, that the confines of the earth may behold thy light. I have scattered on thy sacred ashes white flowers that the summer heat cannot wither. I have anointed thy precious body with the aromatic nard of the Gospel, that the sweet perfume of thy sanctity may last through the ages. I have performed the offices of friendship so that as thy life makes thee shine in heaven, thou mayest be illustrious on the lips of men.

How can it be doubted that Eulogius repaid from heaven the loving obsequies of his friend? We know nothing of Alvaro's last days. Historians tell us, without authority, that

EPILOGUE: THE AFTERMATH

he died two years after Eulogius. A century after, the church of Cordova celebrated his feast on November 7.[3]

We know nothing of the end of this restless but lovable character. He is like the sudden violent swell that the winds raise on the sea and that disappears. So Alvaro's life slipped by, agitated by an endless restlessness that drew him to eternity. We see him driven on by his strong, passionate temperament until, one day, he is hidden from our sight. Yet we descry him in the far distance, for an instant more; one last longing still disquiets him: the longing for eternal peace. "Thou knowest that I long for the rest of the heavenly kingdom."

Though the two champions of the traditional Spanish nationalism were dead, their spirit animated the Cordovan Mozarabs for a long time. Abbot Sansón, the worthy sucessor of St. Eulogius in the school of San Zoilo, inherited his affection for the restoration of the language for which he had done so much. From time to time, the Christians presented themselves before the cadí, abused Mohammed, and ensanguined the waters of the Guadalquivir. The monks kept the laws and customs given them by St. Eulogius. In the middle of the tenth century there still existed to the south of Cordova the monastery of Santa Eulalia, which proudly venerated the relics of St. Columba, the holy virgin of Tabanense. It was ruled by an abbess named like the last queen of the Goths, Iquilio, or Egilona, who is commemorated in an epitaph dated 936. At the same time the monastery of Armilatense, famous for its delicious fish and the well-known seedbed of martyrs, had for abbot the priest Daniel, a humble monk and good soldier, as his funeral oration declared, quoting St. Eulogius.

Nevertheless the Mozarabs tended daily to Islamism. It was necessary to translate not only the Bible but the Visigothic

---

[3] The calendar of Recemundo gives: *In ipso est festum Albari, in Córduba.*

laws and canons into Arabic. In the time of Abderrahmán III, Bishop Recemundo wrote an ecclesiastical calendar in Arabic. St. Eulogius' work was a strong reaction against Moslem influence, but it could not stem the evolution toward Mohammedanism noticeable in every class of society. Sooner or later, the ideal that had possessed him all his life must be realised: the destruction of *the ferocious, tyrannical dominion* of the Omeyas must be brought about, and its place taken by an empire that would restore the former religion and laws of the country.

It was for this that Alvaro prayed in the hymn he composed for his friend's feast, and God would bring it about. But centuries of suffering and humiliation must first be undergone. In the sight of God, says the Psalmist, a thousand years are as a day. In the meanwhile the enslaved Christians would have to take the bells of Santiago to the mosque of Cordova; after that, the Moslem slaves would bear on their shoulders the Cordovan lamps to the cathedral of Santiago.

For a time it seemed as though deliverance might soon be at hand. During St. Eulogius' life there dwelt in the province of Rayya (Malaga) a knight named Hafsún, of illustrious Visigothian lineage. One of his ancestors had been known shortly before the invasion by the name of Alfonso. Hafsún had a son, Omar, a rough, arrogant, daring, turbulent man. His frequent quarrels obliged him to retire to Africa, where he engaged himself as apprentice in a tailor's shop. One day an old Andalusian entered the place with a piece of cloth for a garment; he looked steadfastly at the young assistant and asked who he was.

"He is an Andalusian from Regio," said the tailor, "who is learning the tailoring business."

"Do you know the mountain of Bobastro?" the old man asked Omar.

"I know it well," answered the youth, "I lived at its foot."

"Is a rebellion taking place there? It is impossible."

"If there is not one now, there soon will be." The visitor was silent for a moment and then continued: "Do you know Omar, the son of Hafsún, who lives there?"

On hearing his name, the youth grew pale and lowered his eyes. The old man looked attentively at him and noticed that he had a broken front tooth. This convinced him that he was Omar himself. Like many others, the elder firmly believed in the restoration of his race and wishing to direct the youth's indomitable energy toward a worthy purpose, exclaimed:

"Do you expect, unhappy boy, to escape from misery by plying the needle? Go back to your country and take up your sword. You will become a terrible foe of the Omeyas and the king of a great nation."

Omar had found his purpose in life; he returned to Spain, settled at Bubastro, assembled the *muladies* of the region, any Arabs that were discontented, and the Christians who still dwelt in the country. He then waged a heroic war against the sultans, ruled over the districts of Rayya, Seville, Archidona, Ecija, and Jaen, proclaimed himself king of southern Spain, and reached in his forays the very walls of Cordova.

The alfaquíes ran through the streets of the capital, crying; "Shame on thee, vile courtesan, sewer of impurity and profligacy, the dwelling place of anguish; shame on thee who hast neither friends nor allies. When the leader with the great nose and sinister face reaches thy doors, thy fatal destiny shall be fulfilled!"

On this occasion Cordova was saved. The restoration of Spain was not to be accomplished by Moslems nor by men contaminated by long association with the invaders. The enterprise must be more radical. Omar was a great leader, but a large part of his army was composed of Moslems. He himself was a Mohammedan, and though later on he returned to the religion of his forefathers, neither he nor his partisans could blot out the stain of two centuries of Mohammedanism.

Omar was abandoned by his army at the critical moment when he felt sure of entering the capital. The battle of Poley (891) was a literal desertion of his troops. Their leader was obliged to take refuge among the rocks of Bubastro, whence he continued molesting the sultans until his death. Five thousand prisoners were taken by the conqueror. Forced to make their choice between apostasy and death, they gave their lives with heroic courage. Only one soldier failed when the headsman approached him.

Servando, too, had died a martyr for his country. Servando, the mortal enemy of Christ's martyrs. In former times, his hatred for Christianity had surpassed that of the sultan. But twenty years had not passed in vain; such a period means much for a man of his temperament. The national party grew stronger by degrees; the sultan became more impoverished, older, more unpopular and feeble. Servando, who was extremely foresighted, began to pay court to those he had persecuted, succeeded in forming a large Christian party of men weary of Moslem despotism, and with its help conspired against the sultan in the very court itself. His intrigues were discovered and his brother fell into the hands of the police; but Servando managed to leave Cordova with some of his accomplices, and entering into an alliance with Omar ben Hafsún, began to attack the Moslem garrison in the castle of Poley. He left his refuge at night and returned at daybreak, leaving terrible traces of his track in the country round Cordova: ruined houses, unburied corpses, villages burnt to the ground, tears, and blood. No one knew the land better than he, and Mohammedan historians call him a brave soldier. But one night it was his lot to lose, and his corpse lay stretched on the ground.[4]

---

[4] Ibn Hayan gives an account of Servando's death. See Dozy, II, 323.

Deliverance could not come from the south. Its inhabitants were thoroughly infected by the influence of the new civilisation. During his lifetime, St. Eulogius had looked for help from the independent kingdoms of the north, and soon after his death, he sought there a safe place in which to take his last sleep. The translation of his body was symbolic. By its means, he entrusted the realisation of his chief desire to the strong, indomitable mountains that had preserved Spanish tradition in all its purity.

APPENDIX

THE MANUSCRIPT LIBRARY OF *EULOGIUS*

THE FOLLOWING is a partial and tentative reconstruction of the list of books in the manuscript library collected by Eulogius. We may at all events be confident that these books were familiar to him, while the list enables us to form a really excellent and accurate conception of his library.

Chief of all was the Bible, which was then called "a library." Next came the liturgical books: the *Manuale*, with the Masses for the whole year; the *Liber Ordinum*, a kind of ritual; the *Euchologium*, a collection of prayers for every day; the *Liber Comicus*, containing the Gospels and Epistles of the Mass; the *Psalterium* with the *Hymnarium;* the book of sermons and homilies; and the *Passionarium*, containing the legends of the martyrs.

Spanish writings of the seventh century formed a large part of the library, for Eulogius wished to restore the Visigoth tradition: Isidore — *Beatus et lumen, noster Isidorus* — with his *Etymologies* and other moral, historical, scientific, and liturgical books; St. Julian, the *Doctor Egregius,* famous doctor of theology, with his *Prognosticum* and *Antikeimenon;* St. Eugenius with his poems, and St. Ildephonsus with his treatise on Our Lady's virginity. There was also the collection of the letters of St. Braulius of Saragossa, being copied by the scribe who was finishing Samuel's manuscripts, together with the letters of other famous Spaniards.

Alvaro possessed a large volume, with red titles and capital letters, that included the twenty books of the *Etymologies,* the letters of St. Jerome, a short account of the death of St.

Isidore, the treatise by Licianus of Carthage on the immortality of the soul, one by Evancius of Toledo against those who believe in the purity of animals' blood, and various letters from Licinianus, Fructuosus of Dunio, the Gothic magnate Bulgarano, King Sisebuto, and Caesarius, governor of Cartagena. Alvaro did not agree with Evancio's teaching and wrote notes in Arabic on the margin of his work. Elsewhere his annotations were in Latin, signed Albarus, with a most elegant flourish.[1]

Eulogius also had works not only of the Spanish Fathers but of the Fathers of the Church as well: St. Clement, Origen (whom Juan of Seville called the "illustrious doctor," and Alvaro entitled the "abominable heretic"), Saints Cyprian, Basil, Ephraem, Anastasius, Hilary, Ambrose, Caesarius, Junilius, Fulgentius of Ruspe, Lactantius, St. Lucherius of Lyons, and St. Gregory the Great, one of the most illustrious teachers of medieval Spain. There were also the writings of Claudian, Arnobius, and Boethius.

St. Augustine took a prominent place with his works the *Trinity*, the *City of God*, the *Enchiridion*, the *Questions;* next came St. Jerome with his large collection of letters and Biblical commentaries, an abyss and boundless ocean of knowledge, as Alvaro called him. There were also the writings of Aquila and Theodotian, a Latin glossary, a chronicle of the times, a large manuscript of lives of the Fathers of the desert, another of the councils and papal decrees, a *Forum Judicum*, the laws of the Visigoths, and a *Codex Regularum*, a collection of monastic rules including those of St. Pacomius, St. Basil, and other Eastern Fathers, also those of SS. Fructuosus, Isidore, Leander, and Benedict. The latter may have been added after the journey through the Christian regions of Spain.

---

[1] Guillermo Antolin, *Catalogo de los códices latinos del Escorial*, II, 364 The codex mentioned is signed: &, I, 14.

Eulogius had also a small number of Mozarabic books that he cherished with special affection; among them were the works of his master Esperaindeo; letters and writings of Alvaro; treatises by Vincencio and Basilisco, two teachers of the truth whom he had known when a child. Among the works of heretics that he had read, Alvaro says, were Migecius and Elipandus; as their antidote he possessed the able refutation of Beato of Liébana, with his commentaries on the Apocalypse, adorned with strange miniatures. Two books indispensable for every medieval library were Cassian's *Conferences* and *Institutions*.

The historical works were those by Hegesippus, Josephus, and Orosius; grammar was represented by Aelius Donatus, and an anonymous book on the rules of grammatical art; geometry by a volume on that subject. As for Baquiario, "our Baquiario," as Juan of Seville called him, and Apringio of Beja, another Spaniard of the sixth century, no doubt Eulogius knew them also.

He was proud of his collection of the classics and poets: the *Satires* of Horace, and perhaps his *Odes;* the *Aeneid,* the *Eclogues* and *Georgics* of Virgil; Juvenal's *Satires;* fragments of Ovid; some treatises by Porphyry and Cicero; the epigrams of Persius, which Eulogius quotes, together with those of Martial; a book containing sentences of the philosophers, and finally the distiches attributed to Marcus Cato, known in all the schools of that time.

Beside these were ranged the writings of Christian poets: Avienus, Juvencus, Sedulius, Dracontius, Prudentius, Alcimus, Corippus, Venantius Fortunatus, St. Aldhelm (an Anglo-Saxon bishop, time of Venerable Bede) and St. Eugenius, the most accessible Spanish poet during the Middle Ages.

If we add to these works a few more, such as a treatise on calculation, panegyrics of the Byzantine emperors, a comic volume entitled *Solomon's Supper,* written by a Spaniard signing himself St. Cyprian, and perhaps a poem by Lucan, we can form an idea of the literary atmosphere in which St. Eulogius dwelt. Perhaps he did not succeed in collecting all these volumes, but he certainly knew them. They formed a glorious residue of Isidorean culture.

www.ingramcontent.com/pod-product-compliance
Lightning Source LLC
Chambersburg PA
CBHW030137170426
43199CB00008B/107